Emily Murphy's biography reflects the vividly entertaining life of a compelling personality—one of Canada's most distinguished daughters. Always a crusader, she accumulated what is probably the longest "Who's Who" of any Canadian man or woman, and was known personally to thousands.

A woman of tremendous power, driving enthusiasms, and infectious humour, she was born the year after Confederation, and her life-story spanned its first tumultuous sixty years. As Janey Canuck, a writer of rich and enchanting prose, she was known to many thousands throughout the world. As the first stipendiary magistrate to be appointed in the British Empire, hers was an engrossing woman's-eye view of crime, insanity and drug-addiction. As the originator and leader of the famed Appeal to the Privy Council, by the five women of Alberta, hers was the privilege of having women declared "persons" and thus eligible to the Senate.

Thousands who did not know her personally will respond to her controversial ideas and challenging demands on men and women as citizens of a great country. Because her life was so packed with interest, and because she lived it so valiantly, her story is an absorbing and important addition to Canadian biography.

Here is the record of a stimulating adventure in living: colourful stories of the strange and famous men and women Mrs. Murphy knew; poignant vignettes of life in a Woman's Court; the human hope of salvaging young girls from an outcast's world; the uncovering of the drug menace and her dramatic struggle to thwart it. It is the record of a frank and gallant woman—truly, a Crusader.

EMILY MURPHY—CRUSADER

EMILY FERGUSON MURPHY

EMILY MURPHY
CRUSADER
("JANEY CANUCK")

By

BYRNE HOPE SANDERS

TORONTO
THE MACMILLAN COMPANY
OF CANADA LIMITED
1945

PRINTED IN CANADA
T. H. BEST PRINTING CO., LIMITED, TORONTO

To

MY MOTHER AND SISTER,

AND TO

EMILY MURPHY'S DAUGHTERS

PREFACE

Emily Murphy wrote this book herself.

She herself kept a record for history, in her careful habit of filing important letters; her diary-like continuity of writing; her dramatization of high moments throughout her life, in words—published, or unpublished.

I have tried whenever possible to retain her own phrases, so that moods of the woman might speak in them, and reveal that vital humanity which was her most impressive characteristic in life. Other books will be written about Emily Murphy, for many aspects of her life will demand a more detailed and comprehensive development than appeared essential to this portrait. But it is my hope that the everyday people of Canada, whom Emily knew so well, will find in these pages a reflection of her richness of heart and mind.

In yet another way, Emily Murphy has written this book. Without her spirit as part of my consciousness during the five years of my struggling authorship—it would never have been completed.

We met but two or three times. My association with her was almost entirely within my editorial work. However, a year or so after her death in 1933, when I knew a biography was contemplated, my mind leaped to the possibilities. Later when the opportunity came to me, I was more than eager to begin it.

That was in 1938. For the next three years, I studied and analyzed the thousands of letters and documents she had amassed. Half the manuscript was completed.

Then came a call to Ottawa on a wartime assignment, when the rigorous schedules of evening work I had set myself at home, seemed impossible. But as the tenth year since Emily's death approached, and my honourable pledge to complete the biography remained unfulfilled, I knew that time must be found, somehow. Since half my time was spent travelling in Canada, I began to salvage hours on trains, on planes, to study; even on boat journeys from Digby to St. John, and Vancouver to Victoria. With determined regularity at home I picked time up around midnight; hoarded week-ends. Gradually, I felt again the driving power of her work; so mine gathered momentum.

Always—Emily was there. No matter how weary I have been physically, nor how spent mentally, whenever I have forced myself to the typewriter, and begun again to read, to search, to build—I have felt the invigoration of her spirit.

As I worked, the magic of her mind would be upon me. Sheer delight, perhaps in the discovery of some new fragment of her adventure in living; spirit enriched with an unusual point of view; laughter welling at some unexpected humour. Within half an hour, I would be stimulated, often actually excited.

Emily Murphy, bless her, was there, captured in her own words, to help me, with the same lusty generosity of spirit she would have shown had she been with me in actuality.

Perhaps others may glimpse an echo of her spirit, to re-invigorate their own crusading against the dark powers of life. May it be, then, that her sisterhood of thinking women will see afresh the dream she dreamed for them, and work to bring it nearer completion. May it be that boys and girls, sensing what she made of her life, will carry on the measure of her hope and forward-looking mind, into the world of tomorrow.

My deep appreciation goes to Emily Murphy's daughters, Evelyn Murphy and Kathleen Kenwood of Edmonton, for their devoted work in checking the manuscript; also to her husband, Rev. Arthur Murphy, and to her sister, Mrs. Ferguson-Burke of Toronto. My gratitude to my sister, Dora Sanders Carney of Victoria, for her help in editing and revision; and to my own family for their patience with the author under the almost fanatical impetus which held me to the task of finishing the biography—often at the expense of my home-making conscience. "Mummie," says my ten-year-old David, wistfully, "I'm afraid my teacher will have to write you a note about these holes in my stockings."

My thanks to the editors of *MacLean's Magazine*, *Canadian Home Journal, Chatelaine, National Home Monthly* and *Saturday Night*, for permission to quote from articles in their pages. My acknowledgment to the publishers of Janey Canuck's books, for permission to use extracts from them; to Cassell and Company, publishers of *Janey Canuck in the West* and *Open Trails*. To Hodder and Stoughton, publishers of *Seeds of Pine*; and to Thomas Allen, publisher of *The Black Candle*.

BYRNE HOPE SANDERS.

Ottawa, April 23rd, 1945.

CONTENTS

ILLUSTRATIONS

INTRODUCTION

By

NELLIE L. McCLUNG

People who knew Mrs. Murphy only slightly did not know her at all. Those who saw her in court, passing sentence on evil-doers, with all the dignity of her position, may have sometimes thought her hard. Certainly there was nothing maudlin or weak about her ruling, but there was always a kindness in her sternness. She hated wrong-doing, but was always sympathetic to the wrong-doer and anxious to win her to a better way of living.

No one will ever know how many wayward girls were set on the straight path by her kindly ministrations. Many a time I have been asked by her to come out into the kitchen to speak to some young girl she had brought home with her, to give her a chance to forget the past and begin life again.

"Circumstances were just too strong for her," she would say. "What chance had she with the curse of that pretty face? Life is a conspiracy against a girl like that, but she's going to be all right now. She has had a hard lesson and we'll get her a position out of the city. I just could not let her go to jail."

Mrs. Murphy was a firm believer that the heart of youth is incorruptible and undefiled. "There is a core of sweetness in the heart long after the body has been polluted and the mind darkened by sin and some day I will write a book about that; a book which may do something to help these poor little wayfarers."

I know she had this book draughted and the opening chapters written, but alas! the night fell too soon for its completion.

Mrs. Murphy's mind was like a great encyclopedia. Many a time I rang her up to be put straight on a quotation. It was fitting that the last thing recorded of her was that she had gone to the library, seeking information. She was a woman of many gifts, but one of the greatest of these was her ability to collect and coordinate knowledge; her clarity of vision in making a valuation of it, and a gift of expression which, at its best, was not surpassed by anyone in her generation. Her books can be read again and again with increasing delight. I love to read her swelling phrases, her chiming sentences. I often wish that she had retired from her active work years ago and given herself to literature. I believe she wanted to do this but something held her to her work in the Police Court. I think it was a burning love of justice; a maternal desire to protect the weak and to bring to naught the designs of evil persons, for Mrs. Murphy loved a fight, and so far as I know, never turned her back on one.

There was in her too a childlike love of fun and nonsense, a James M. Barrie streak of whimsical make-believe. She loved parodies and limericks and pageants; she loved the dramatic in life and saw it with an artist's eye.

There was not a trace of jealousy in her, she wanted to see everyone do well, and was ever ready to speak the encouraging word. To young writers she was particularly encouraging, and was never too busy to advise the many people who took their problems to her.

Although the shock of her sudden death came like a crushing blow to all of us who loved her, it was the way she would have chosen, and in this connection one of her devoted admirers, Miss Helen Weir, who for years conducted a women's employment bureau in Edmonton, a great-hearted Scotswoman, rose to heights of eloquence when I saw her here at the Coast soon after Mrs. Murphy's death. This is what she said to me:

"You and I have lost our friend, and the sad and sorrowful have lost a sure defender, but wasn't it glorious the way she went? In life and death she proved she was a person. All her life she fought for the finer things of life, not for herself for she already had them, but for the other people; and she died like a person, in full possession of her faculties until the last. There was no withering of beauty or brain, no falling of the leaves, no winter of decay, no cry for help, just a quiet passage from the light of earth to the glory of heaven. She was never old. She lived like a person and died like a person."

Her reference here was, of course, to the famous petition presented to the Privy Council in 1929 by the five Alberta women, which forever settled the question of whether or not women are persons. To Emily Murphy belongs the full honour of this momentous undertaking, the story of which is told in the pages of this book.

I have never ceased to miss her, and this feeling is common to all of the old circle who are left. What good talk we often had around her hospitable table and what pleasant evenings when she read to us bits of Hakluyt's *Voyages*, the Autobiography of Benvenuto

Cellini or beautiful prose of Walter Pater and Jeremy Taylor! She had a way of bringing all things to life. These words of Sir Charles G. D. Roberts* might have been written by her:

"For I have fared far and confronted the calm and
      strife;
I have fared wide and bit deep of the apple of life.
It is sweet at the rind, but oh, sweeter still at the core,
And whatever be gained, yet the reach of the morrow
      is more."

NELLIE L. McCLUNG.

Lantern Lane, Victoria, B.C.

---

*From "On the Road", *Selected Poems*, The Ryerson Press (Toronto), by permission of the publishers.

EMILY MURPHY—CRUSADER

PART I

CHAPTER I

Foundations

"The great lesson of modern science is that nothing really "happens". There is no such thing as chance, for every act in your life has a causative force. Everything is pushed from behind."

JANEY CANUCK.

I

HER LIFE began in a home which was a prototype of many others in early Canada.

Just around a corner on the road from Cookstown to Barrie, Ontario, stood the Ferguson place. Set well back behind its grouping of trees, it emanated a sense of protective family comfort. The windows watched the four vistas of the world, over well-tended fields and pastures that swept away in rhythmic curves. Maple woods cut the sky-line with sharp precision. Snake fences stitched feathered lines between the properties and over the horizons.

Beyond the fences and beyond the hills lay the newly created Canada.

For it was on an evening early in March, 1868—one year after Confederation—that Dr. Buchanan's nurse laid a baby girl in the curve of a mother's arm. Isaac

Ferguson, sitting beside his wife, studied her and the baby, proudly. "She's not in it with her mother for good looks," he said, "but the little one has a strong face."

"Strong!" scoffed his wife. "And her only a few hours old! It's a sweet face she has. And she's for my comfort. You've the lads to attend to."

"She'll be Emily, too, then."

"She'll be my darling always," whispered Emily, and set her cheek against the soft fuzzy head of the baby in that first caress all mothers know.

There was a tap on the door. It opened to the nurse again.

"The boys, madam. For a moment?"

Two lads, both with the Ferguson brow and heavy-lidded eyes, tip-toed in bashfully. Their boots clacked on the wooden floor in spite of their care, until they reached the bed, and stood, frightened at the air of solemnity in the room.

"Here's a wee sister for you," smiled their mother. "You must love her very much, and look after her all your life."

"Where did you get her?" asked Tom, who was four, and beginning to look about him for explanations.

Emily gently smoothed back his hair. "Your father bought her in Barrie," she said serenely. "He thought she was a doll. Luckily we've got plenty of baby clothing in the house for her. So we'll be all right!"

II

It was to a rich and noble life the Ferguson babies were successively welcomed. Perhaps its very beauty, in after years, made Emily Murphy the passionate defender of all whose lives were weighted with too much misery.

Her childhood was spent in the comfort and hilarity of family life in a small village. There was plenty of room; plenty of money; plenty of love.

The countryside knew them as the "young Ferguson divils" and hearts were warmed by their healthy mischief and fun. As the years went by, six children grew up in the house, bursting from the doors in their eager pursuits, exploring the woods round about, doing their chores in the garden, or running in the endless games of childhood in the pasture field beside the house.

There were six of them: Thomas Roberts, Gowan, Emily Jemima, William Nasssau, Annie Jessamine and Harcourt.

The pattern of their days lay about the small village, whose only contact with the outside world, in their childhood, was by stage-coach over corduroy roads. Lights gleamed at night from only two hundred homes; but against the simplicity of the life about them, that of the Ferguson family was highlighted with the dramatics of those who had lived before them.

Four Irish grandparents they had; and what stories their mother knew of them! It might be the saga of Ogle Robert Gowan who, the children felt, was a very great man indeed. He had become an Orangeman when he was only seventeen. As a youth in Ireland he saw the cruel work of the Rebels, when, on "Bloody Friday" they burned the family home, Mount Nebo, to the ground. Years later, he sailed with his household of nine for Canada, and bought an estate of four hundred acres, Escott Park, near Brockville.

It was in Brockville, in '37, that his wife, Frances Gowan, who was Frances Colclough-Turner, a member of the family of Sir Thomas Colclough, Knight of Tintern Abbey, designed the flag bearing the inscription "Down with Elgin and his rebel-paying Ministry". It was hoisted on the lake-front during the visit of Lord Elgin, and has ever since been called "Mrs. Gowan's Petticoat". There had been high feeling about the Rebellion Losses Bill, which gave compensation for losses suffered as a result of the Mackenzie Rebellion in 1837. The Orangemen did not see why some of the rebels should, as they felt, actually benefit from their treachery.

A grand tale, this, that set young Emily's mind to dreaming of how she would have waved that flag, high, high over the people's heads. The children played the story often, with Tom as Lord Elgin, Gowan and Will and Annie as the populace, and Emily as their grandmother.

"How about *cutting off their heads, mother?*"

No, not tonight. Or not before church. There's no time for it. Emily the mother felt the story was too wild to repeat often.

But her small daughter, the first night she was old enough to consider it, grabbed Will's arm on the way upstairs to bed. "What's it about, Willie?"

"It's terrific! Grandfather's father—that's the Gowan one—put his horse over a five-barred gate, and cut off the head of an outlaw with one sweep of his sword on the way over . . ."

They played that one often too, jumping over a pasture rail, with the heavy-blossomed weeds as outlaws.

Grandfather Gowan had founded the Orange Order in Canada. He became known as the "Father of the House", because he had been in parliament for twenty-seven years. Some named him also, "Father of the Press", because of the way he had worked with newspapers to fight for the unity of Canada and for its allegiance to the British Empire.

The story of Grandfather Ferguson was a sad one. He had died at sea, when he sailed with his family from Ireland. But his young wife and six children had followed his plans for them, and settled in Simcoe county.

"Father was the youngest of all the Fergusons!"

"And mother was the youngest of all the Gowans!"

The children knew every detail of the story by which, in the best fairy-tale tradition, these two had been wed.

Isaac Ferguson was in comfortable circumstances as a landowner, able to send all his children to private schools in Toronto, and to graduate his sons from University. His children learned a comfortable hospitality in a home which was the centre for many activities. Their parents were very much a part of the early political life of the province, not only through their close association with Ogle R. Gowan, but through his cousin, Sir James Gowan, who was a noted Supreme Court Judge, and later, a Senator.

Uncle Thomas Roberts Ferguson, too, who had married their mother's eldest sister, Frances, was, to the children, a double sort of relative, and one of the most colourful figures of the period. He was a member for Simcoe and Cardwell for many years and, in the early days, had many adventures in the stormy "open ballot" meetings. He was a huge man, known as "Fighting

Tom" Ferguson to everyone. The family took violent partisan sides with him, and the stories he told, as one of a Tory family in a Tory county, gave the children a rich and rare understanding of the political battle-field.

Although so generally known as "Fighting Tom Ferguson" he was really a man of peace. On one occasion, in those days of open balloting, a fight seemed imminent at a campaign meeting. Now Mr. Ferguson had an unconscious habit, in rising to speak, of drawing up his coat sleeves, exposing his cuffs. In the heat of debate, his followers read this as a sign to clear the house of the trouble-makers. As they leaped to their feet, at this particular meeting, Mr. Ferguson's voice was heard above the uproar, saying, "Quiet, my lambs!" From that day, the Simcoe County Conservatives have always been known as "The Lambs".

"My Uncle Thomas had, indirectly, a great influence on my life," Emily wrote later, "for through him I acquired a number of hatreds that were wholly illogical but which have explained to me the psychology of family vendettas, and other devices of the unforgiving which make for the retarding of the human race. It happened that my father and his several brothers kept strict tally of all the prominent opponents of Thomas at the hustings. As a child, I cherished these black hatreds in my heart, and looked upon the opponents with their families as dogs and infidels beneath the dignity of human reproach. Indeed, it was not many years ago that I received something in the nature of a shock when I learned that my mother had sold a piece of the family estate to one of the Tuckers. A Tucker! Why, My God, it was this Tucker's grandfather who once wrote an insulting verse about Thomas, which became an election ditty and caused the utmost mortification in the breasts of all my family."

Mr. Justice Thomas Ferguson, too, was a favourite cousin. Many a time when he came to Cookstown, he would tell of his most interesting cases. Enthralled listeners in the background on these occasions, were three of the Ferguson boys who were later to become noted King's Counsels at the Ontario and Manitoba Bar; and one, who, in his turn, was to be a Supreme Court Judge. Listening, as eagerly as her brothers, was a little girl with dark hair and serious eyes, who was to be appointed the first woman magistrate in the British Empire.

On one occasion when Sir John A. Macdonald, Sir Charles Tupper and Mr. D'Alton McCarthy were attending an important political meeting in nearby Barrie they were welcomed as guests about the massive old Ferguson table. Also at dinner that evening were "Fighting Tom" and his handsome wife Frances, the bachelor uncles Andrew and 'Miah, with other members of the fine old families of Simcoe county. Tom and Gowan in their new velveteen suits, and the ten-year-old Emily in her new silk, sat with the younger children very quietly on the stairs while dinner was in progress, waiting patiently for the exciting summons to the dining-room that would come with the coffee and liqueurs. They had all shared the bustle of preparation for so great a man as Sir John, and knew all about his friendship with their grandfather Ogle R. Gowan. Grandfather had recognized Sir John as a coming man, and persuaded him to enter public life. He supported him staunchly in his newspapers and on the floor of the

House—though, on occasion, he had opposed his ideas, too, just as staunchly.

As they were ushered in to the august company, Sir John beamed on the handsome little quintette and asked if anyone could recite for him. Oh yes! Emily could. The boys were too shy and Annie too small. But Emily had just learned a new piece in school. Smiling at her eagerness, Sir John lifted her to a chair. With a sweeping bow, and her feet in the third position for dancing, she announced her title, "The Burial of Sir John Moore".

The pride which had been shining in the boys' eyes vanished. With horror they listened to her solemn rendering of the awesome lines,

"his corpse to the ramparts we hurried" . . .

Mercifully, at last, it was over. The boys, scarlet-faced and scolding, surrounded Emily in the hall. How could she? Didn't she have any sense at all—to stand up there and blather about the funeral of one Sir John with another their honoured guest? But Emily, flushed with triumph, would not be downcast. Didn't she have a quarter to show how much Sir John had liked it?

III

"Those were wonderful times," Emily wrote years later, "when I wore copper-toed boots, and had only the rudiments of a soul—those carefree days when my hair was done in fierce little pigtails, and I was not so much as halfway wise. But, for that matter, who was wholly wise? Even my father wasn't wise. Mother was sure of this, for it was he who taught me how to ride, play cricket, hoe the garden and carve. It was wholly natural that Mother should object, for she herself was ever dainty in her ways, as anyone must be, who wears hoops and dances the mazurka."

Young Emily's father was a man of very definite opinions. For one thing, he believed in the equal sharing of responsibilities by the boys and the girls of his family. This point of view was to affect his daughter Emily all her life, and may have been responsible for her great achievement, the declaration by the Privy Council in England that women were as much "persons" as men. Her father insisted that in chores about the house, boys and girls must share and share alike. They must weed the garden and help to care for the lawns and shrubberies, pile the wood, or help on occasion with the work inside the house. Each must ride well and learn to care for his own mount. Each must cherish the principles of sportsmanship in whatever was undertaken.

In everything, they were trained alike—with one disciplinary exception. It was the boys only who were whipped in the little room off the dining-room, when their mischief had gone too far. Emily and Annie would stand outside the door and cry, too. "It is entirely thinkable that, in spite of their tremendous outcries and loud promises of amendment, I was, on more than one occasion, the greatest sufferer," Emily wrote. "They were frauds, those brothers. My father never punished my sister or me, though he often threatened us, albeit with a twinkle in his eye. After the flight and blight of the years, as I muse on my father, this kindly whimsical twinkle of his is more concrete to me, and more individual, than the memory of his face or figure. He was a man of strong positive qualities. God's hand did not tremble when he made this father of mine."

He insisted that his children learn to write properly, and so, every Saturday, brought a teacher the sixteen miles from Barrie to teach them penmanship. His directions were firm and clear. "I don't want any of those inane flourishes they teach in the public schools, and I don't want any of the angular, cramped or backhand styles either. Teach them to hold the pen properly. To move their muscles with the least exertion, and to write clearly with a stub pen, after the manner of the British folk."

As a result, Emily was able, throughout her life, to write for hours at a time, without weariness. She never used a typewriter, and found the effortless penmanship her father had insisted upon, one of her greatest assets in the prolific writing she was to do.

A sense of mutual devotion and service was a strong *motif* in the family life of those days. There was so much fun at home when families were large. So many minds suggested amusement, so much stimulation existed among themselves that the young Fergusons developed a fund of common experience and founded a life-long camaraderie.

Emily's association with her mother was a particularly happy one. The child liked to watch the older woman as she went about her duties, admiring the wide-spaced, large eyes, and the hair, parted in the middle and worn coronet-shaped about her head. She was enchanted by the flower-patterned frocks her mother wore, and her soft-flowing grace. She liked the faint fragrance of violets that lingered about her.

If Emily were very good, she was allowed to sit on

a low chair in the parlour on the afternoons that ladies came to call from neighbouring country homes. Mousey-still, she watched them sip their cherry cordial and handle their tea-cups, as they chattered.

Many hours were spent with her mother looking over the scrap-book. It was full of beautiful steel engravings, clipped poetry, news about the activities of the large family's relations and about the Orange Order. They kept the scrap-book with care and devotion and the girl spent so much time enjoying it, that, in later life, collecting similar material became one of her most characteristic hobbies.

It was from her mother, too, that Emily learned the Collects, the Rubrics and prayers, and even the Thirty-Nine articles, from the Anglican *Book of Prayer*. No Sunday was complete without a recitation of the special Collect for the day, repeated with due reverence, perhaps subconscious, for the dignified and beautiful prose that so influenced much of her own writing.

The Fergusons were both members of the Church of England, but, in those early days, there was no Anglican church in Cookstown. So it was to the Methodist church that the Fergusons went every Sunday for many years. But it was in St. John's Anglican church, family legend has it, that a very young Emily, in vast pride at her new sunshade and matching silk frock, sat for some time with the sunshade up, before she was noticed by her devout family. Why, she protested, should so much beauty be folded away beneath the pew?

With the twinkle in his eye more pronounced than ever, Mr. Ferguson sat through many a sermon by the Methodist preacher on the evils of card-playing. As daughter Emily was one day to describe it, "The card-table in our parlour was the scandal of the neighbourhood, for it was a Methodist circuit and only the few Anglicans played whist. Although this was the only card-table in our vicinity, numerous were the sermons preached concerning the perniciousness of the game. This was a sore point with my little mother, but, so far as I am aware, it nowise interfered with her cross-ruff and finesse."

When the Anglican Church of St. John's was built in Cookstown, Isaac Ferguson sent his children to the Rector to learn Latin. He himself had been a student at the old Victoria College established in Cobourg, and he knew the pleasures to be found in the classics. He always remained faithful to the Methodist congregation which had served in pioneer days and which he had helped to establish, but his children were confirmed in the Anglican church and became members of it. Isaac also deeded as a cemetery to St. John's, the pasture-land near his house, over which the children had romped for so many years, reserving in it a family plot for them and their children in perpetuity. Subsequently, the family never spoke of dying, but of "going back to Cookstown".

In writing of this one-time playground for their family which has become their last resting place, Emily Murphy says: "They were not always pleasant and lovely in their lives, these kinspeople of mine, for they often quarrelled, as Irish families are wont to do; but in death they are not divided. In whatever part of the world they die, they are brought back here to sleep. Their histories might fill a book—a book of tragedy; a story of young men cut off in the heyday of their suc-

FRANCES COLCLOUGH-TURNER   OGLE R. GOWAN

ISAAC FERGUSON   EMILY JEMIMA GOWAN

cess, of perplexed meanings and frustrated ambitions."

IV

Each July, on the eve of the "Annyual", as Mother
Gibson, the housekeeper, always called it, the fluting
of pipes and the roll of drums, sounded from the open
windows of the Orange Hall. Presently with a growing
medley of lusty voices, and the bedlam of boys and
their delighted dogs, a little procession marched up
the road to the wild and shrilling music of the Orange
band.

Up the road, round the corner, and into the Ferguson
garden they trooped, to circle the lawns in honour of
Ogle R. Gowan's daughter. The heavy ornaments that
were set, as a rule, on the pedestals by the gates, had
been removed, and jars of Orange lilies flamed in the
dusk. Lights from the house streamed across the wide
verandahs and onto the lawns, to reveal the Ferguson
family waiting to welcome their neighbours. There,
like a figurine from Godey's *Lady's Book*, stood Emily,
daughter of Ogle R. Gowan, hand on her husband's
arm. Beside her, stood Ogle Gowan's grand-daughter,
another Emily, loving every minute of it.

The Cookstown Orange band serenaded Emily
Gowan Ferguson every year. It must have been a fine
thing for the child to remember the affection of all
these friends, to whom her mother meant so much, because of the traditions behind her. It must have been
an impressive realization, when she understood that
they were honoured so, not only because of what they
were—but because of what their forebears had been.

Ogle's grand-daughter would feel emotion choking

in her throat, and find it a relief to turn where the village children were climbing on the fences and crowding on the croquet lawn, shouting, "Look at Willie! Look at Gowan! Annie's got a new dress. Proudie! Proudie!"

When the pipers had shrilled to the last their traditional salute, they, and most of the villagers, trooped into the welcoming old house. Ready for them were rows of cups and saucers, stacks of sandwiches, and cauldrons of coffee, simmering on the great kitchen stove.

Those were unforgettable evenings, but ah! the Glorious Twelfth itself! Up early, everybody joined in preparation for "The Walk". For days the women had been "redding up" and airing the regalia. Formal coats had hung in the summer breeze after being sponged and pressed. Decorations were re-furbished, hats were brushed; boots shined. Nothing was neglected.

In those days Orangeism was a very active force. The Order had been founded in Ireland in the difficult days of adjustment following the Battle of the Boyne. It was introduced into Canada in 1830, with Ogle Robert Gowan its first Grand Master. Two years later he was appointed Deputy Grand Master of all the provinces then united under the British North America Act.

They were turbulent times, engendering fierce partisanships and burning loyalties. There was the Rebellion of 1837, the struggles over the Clergy Reserves, and the Rebellion Losses Bill. For some time the Party Procession Act was in force, and to march on the historic Twelfth was to commit a statutory offence. Then came the Fenian Raids, when Irishmen from across the border for a time threatened the stability of Canada.

The Orangemen rallied whole-heartedly and many who marched in Emily's childhood had fought ardently with their fathers and grandfathers in defence of their country and their Queen.

To support the principles of the Christian religion; to maintain the laws and constitution of the country; to afford assistance to distressed members; to promote laudable and benevolent purposes as lead to the due ordering of religion, Christian charity, law, order and freedom; these were the objects of the Order as laid down in its Constitution. Forty years after its establishment in Canada, no other secret society or public association of English-speaking Canadians approached in any respect the strength in numbers and influence of the Orange Order.

So the Orangemen of Cookstown and the surrounding district marched every Twelfth with a consciousness of their power and a conviction of their right. They had fought with unflagging zeal for their principles. They knew, too, that in every county on the same day, and at the same time, their fellow Orangemen were staging similar demonstrations.

The "Walks" were held in such towns as were centres for the hamlets round about. So, through Cookstown, Alliston and Beeton marched the men from Clover Hill, Robinson and Bradford. The Fergusons travelled in the "chariot", which Isaac had given to his bride. It was the only one of its type in the district, and would hold all the family comfortably. It had, they said, two peculiarities. There was always room for one more, and it seldom took anyone's dust; never, if one of the boys were driving!

To young Emily, the dramatics of the day were immeasurably satisfactory. She loved the general air of celebration, and the inter-family good nature so evident everywhere. People in their best bib and tucker came on foot, in buggies, on horseback, by train, in carriages —all with an air of adventure about them.

The Parade itself was surely the essence of Romance. "King William," of course, came first, his banner triumphant. It was the Marshal of the Lodge, in each community, who rode the white horse; and very handsome he looked in the costume which, traditionally, the Prince of Orange had worn when crossing the Boyne. Head high, in a scarlet coat with bands of blue and purple and yellow, across its flowing sleeves, he was a proud symbol of a noble tradition. Behind him marched the band, brilliant in streamers and be-ribboned cockades, playing the stirring music that meant ever "No Surrender", whatever the words might be. Then, behind the symbols and banners of the Order, came the brethren, walking solemnly to re-affirm their definite and active faith. There were tricorn hats with ostrich plumes, white helmets, and a variety of peaked, military caps with pompoms or cockades. Some wore the ordinary stove-pipe hats, but all had rosettes and ribbons, sashes and brilliantly decorated jackets.

Fortified with her knowledge of what it all represented, Emily saw them marching as the knights of old, the plumes in their helmets quite as fine and gay. The designs on the devoutly wrought banners were each a wondrous tale in themselves, for she was versed in their meaning as were few grown-ups. She recognized over and over again the Seal of Solomon, the Ark of the Covenant, the open hand and the clenched fist, the key, the lamb with banner, and the round face of the sun with its rays of life-giving light. She had learned to quote the inscriptions before she could read them: "The glorious, pious and immortal memory", "The Protestant Religion I will Maintain".

The men of home marched by. There was Cousin Ogle, and many a Ferguson and Gowan relative. There was Father, with his special twinkle for them. There were the men of Cookstown, homely neighbours, who, remembering the struggles of the past, marched as though they listened to music heard afar off.

Watching and absorbing with precocious sympathy this re-pledging of loyal support for old principles, stood young Emily, thrilled and eager. Some day she was to join battle in provinces not yet a part of Canada, for problems still unstated; for freedom not yet glimpsed. Destiny was preparing her even then for its purposes in the West.

CHAPTER II

Eager Feet

Ever since the days of Mother Eve, a woman's lot has been made for her by the love she accepts.

JANEY CANUCK.

I

IN ITS PROSPECTUS, the Council of The Bishop Strachan School of Toronto, to which Emily was sent in 1882, stated:

> "It is the desire of the Lady Principal that the pupils should, before leaving home, or during the vacation, be provided, as far as possible, with all the necessary wearing apparel, as it is inconvenient that their time and thoughts should be occupied with such matters, while at school."

True enough, Emily agreed. But there was another side to the question. It was definitely inconvenient that so much of her time during the summer should be occupied in endless fittings with the seamstress, Miss Sally Lee. It had always, in fact, been inconvenient. The Ferguson children, Emily wrote later, avoided a fitting as they would a whipping, and, when fairly caught, balked and fidgeted like young colts.

However, Miss Sally was used to them. She had been coming to the Fergusons for years. She had "shortened" Emily, made her school frocks, her Sunday bests, her confirmation veil. She was to make Emily's wedding veil, and the christening robe for her children; but, at the moment, it was a green alpaca for a Toronto boarding-school. She knelt before Emily's well-knit figure, and adjusted the green alpaca; smooth over the young breasts and slender waist; billowing in folds over the bustle; fluffed with white at the throat.

Sally Lee leaned back, her head cocked in study, a little smile of triumph showing, in spite of her mouthful of pins.

"Just a minute, Miss Sally! Please. I want to see it."

Skirts held high, the girl raced down the stairs into the parlour to stop before an enormous mirror, set on a marble base. Emily came to it as to a friend, for she had pulled herself up to stare into its incredible depths as a very little girl. All her recitations, with gestures, had been rehearsed before it. In it all her new frocks were studied critically.

Now, at fourteen, with her childhood passing and the old life at an end, she came before it again, intent on this new problem of fashions for a city. The frock was very becoming, and she noted with satisfaction how its colour shadowed her hazel eyes.

Small, dark and laughing, was how the people of Cookstown described Emily, and nicknamed her "Sunshine". She was only a couple of inches over five foot tall, and weighed, to her chagrin, one hundred and fifteen pounds. About her was the fresh vigour that comes with much riding along country roads, and she moved with the lissomeness developed in the running pursuits of childhood, so lately left behind.

She must stand on a chair to see how the deep hem of her frock swept the tops of her high-laced boots. She must turn her back and try to see how she would look to anyone walking behind. She must curtsey . . . so. And shake hands . . . so.

Miss Sally called insistently. The frock must be pressed and folded in tissue against the girl's departure for school.

II

On first consideration, it seems strange that Emily, in her writing, never referred to her life at Bishop Strachan's, except as a contrast to her life without its walls. One of her schoolmates, writing after her death, said that she seemed to make little impression on the girls, and showed none of the dynamic personality which was to come.

In studying her life more closely, one realizes that in fitting so quietly into the school routine she was, in fact, showing character traits which were to dominate her life.

Emily was always at home, in whatever situation she found herself. As we shall see, many situations were strange, frightening, and utterly at variance with what she might have chosen. To them all she brought an acute, antennae-like awareness, not only of the situation itself, but of those most concerned with it. She was always learning, and always conscious of what was going on around her. Nothing daunted her, because she was never afraid to assess honestly what was demanded of her, in relation to what she wanted to gain.

She found here, in classes with daughters of bankers, the clergy, and professional men, more opportunities to increase her understanding and love of words. Her school books, meticulously cared for, show how through her innate appreciation she went far beyond the customary routine of the classes. Look at her volume of Browning's Poems, and see how every page is underscored with notes—not in the fashion of those who want quick information for class recital, but with a devotional sense. Every nuance of meaning, every unusual phrase is interpreted carefully. Even the indices and addenda have been combed for the exceptional word. She developed, too, her love for collecting material. In all her books, she has gathered pictures and pasted them lovingly into place. Her Browning has every bare space filled with cuttings that show him at all ages. Among them are pictures of his tomb in Westminster Abbey; of his body lying in state in the Palazzo Renicco.

There is ample evidence that she was an excellent student, and went with ease to the top of her class. Her reports pasted in her scrap-books show nothing but highly approving adjectives, and the re-iterated statement that the girl "works admirably".

A photograph taken when she was seventeen shows a proud tilt to her chin, and a calm confidence in her candid eyes. About her throat is the Alexander Manning Medal for general proficiency — a beautiful jewel, set on a silver dog-collar and presented by the mayor of Toronto.

She was more of a self-educated woman than one who was inclined to be academic in her scholarship. Her mind was too agile to be restricted by any for-

mula. Previous to her years at Bishop Strachan's she
had known only the haphazard teaching of the village school. Yet her mind developed impressive proportions through her own avidity for knowledge and understanding.

Throughout her 'teens the girl learned much that
was invaluable. One can visualize her during lessons,
intent and devout; intent because of her eagerness to
learn, devout because of her appreciation of what she
read. Outside the classroom she was still the high-
spirited Emily of Cookstown days. With her fat pig-
tail swinging down her back, her long black skirts about
her ankles, she played tennis or croquet, explored the
ravine paths with her classes in botany, or walked in
the school "crocodile" to the Cathedral of St. James,
down by the lake.

That she was popular goes without saying, for she
was already showing that warm-hearted interest in
other people which, all her life, made her so many true
friends. The world at Bishop Strachan's with one exception was much to her liking, and in it she grew in
grace and understanding, and a love of her fellows.

The exception, as Emily recounted it in after years,
was the fact that in boarding-schools of that period,
the girls went hungry to bed. After the evening meal
of apple-sauce, bread and butter, would come a study
period or piano practice till bed-time. She wrote of
how she and another girl stole downstairs late one night
to eat the remains of the sandwiches upon which the
Lady Principal supped before retiring. Just as Emily
was putting her hand on the contents of the plate,
there was a sound in the darkness. She screamed. It
was Miss Grier's dog—but the alarm had been given.

At her graduation, when the girls piped shrilly in the school song a verse written about Emily, she probably sang as cheerfully as they, with her father's twinkle in her eye.

"Monitress, medalist, good as can be,
Will very soon mount to the top of the tree."

III

The pull of home was as strong as ever, and holidays were full of its remembered delights. That first Christmas, there was excitement almost too much to bear, for a new baby awaited their arrival. Harcourt Ferguson, who became one of Canada's most distinguished King's Counsel, and best of friends to his "Big Sis", was born in time to be the central figure for the Christmas rejoicing. At his christening, the streamers of the Orange Order were pinned to his robe; and, said the boys later, the colours of Upper Canada College as well. A few months after, on the eve of his mother's serenade before the Glorious Twelfth, he was placed very carefully on a cushion, and marched behind the fifes and drums to the Orange Hall, to be presented to the members.

It must have been in these Christmas holidays that Emily went for a week-end visit with her schoolmate, Georgina Nesbitt, in the nearby village of Sutton. She tells us herself that she was about fifteen when she first met Arthur Murphy.

It was on a bright Sunday afternoon when, dressed in her green alpaca, she raised bright eyes to acknowledge the introduction to a blond young giant. Arthur

Murphy, with his six foot and more, towered over the small Emily. His eyes were as blue as gentians, and full of laughter. At twenty-six he seems to have recognized her very definitely, for it was not long after that he was suggesting she hurry in her growing-up, so that he might marry her.

Emily seems to have been just as certain, for, she wrote, "I fell in love many times in my 'teens, but there was never anyone, really, but Arthur."

Musing on this, she notes: "A woman's lot is made for her by the love she accepts."

It was her good fortune to find love in a personality that complemented her own outlook on living. For while Emily was always vigorously active and absorbed in people and their lives, she found in Arthur the mind of a mystic and a dreamer. In him, too, was the spirit of the true pioneer. He tired quickly of a work that was completed. His spirit searched ever for new worlds. It was Arthur who was to lead her on and on into new situations, which she must meet with a vision that fulfilled his own. He was to be known to the world through her books as "The Padre", that gentle soul with a compelling sense of humour. Yet, while succumbing completely to her charm as a human being, Arthur maintained the dominating position in their partnership. In letter after letter, written throughout the years, one finds the repeated contrast of the plea, "Ask Father to do nothing till I come" set against the equally repeated cry, "Father will never listen to me!"

When Emily met him first, he was studying for Holy Orders at Wycliffe College in Toronto, and lived in Rosemont, only sixteen miles from Cookstown. He was as fond of driving as the Fergusons, and the distance became just a pleasant drive on a holiday morning. Thereafter, he became a part of the young people's adventuring, and went with them frequently to the third concession line, perhaps to pull a sack of green butternuts, which were placed in the attic to dry against the home-coming in December. Or, in the Easter holidays, they drove to a certain farmer to buy five gallons of maple molasses—seductive amber stuff "the like of which," writes Emily, "I have never since tasted."

There were afternoons when, while the boys yarned around the fire, Emily put on a pink apron and went to the kitchen to bake cookies. She was never fond of cooking, but knew well what a decorative picture she made, emerging from the kitchen, cheeks flushed and hair loosened, with her plate of fragrant delicacies. The boys greeted her with shouts of approval. Their delight and admiration were flattering. Arthur, his long legs stretched to the warmth, teasingly dubbed her "Cookie".

"Cookie!" The name stuck and she answered to it the rest of her life. Many, many times, in the years when she was almost overwhelmed with her eternal struggle against injustice, she wrote home and signed her letters "Cookie". It was a talisman in her mind, which brought with it memories of those dear days when they were all young, and the pattern of the years still unfolded.

Then . . . but let her tell you of her romance herself!

"I had many pictures taken," she reminisced in one of her books, "in groups, or alone, and one that was taken with my sweetheart. Ah yes! I was always interested in someone or other, and often felt woefully naughty when my mother reprimanded me—but not inconsolably so, just as if I had eaten all the jam tarts . . . There was this sweetheart with whom I had my picture taken, the very tall one with the fair hair, who said he was going to marry me when I grew up. He was a student at the University when I was fifteen or thereabouts.

"On Saturday afternoons, one of my brothers, who were then at Upper Canada College, would call and take me out, promptly transferring me to the custody of this young divinity student, whom I shamelessly mulcted for teas, chocolate eclairs, rides on ice-boats, sail-boats, or any kind of a boat. He brought me Valentines too, and books of poetry, in which he wrote things in Latin or Hebrew, so that my schoolmates might not read them, but which he translated accurately for me.

"Did I marry him when I grew up?

"Of course I did.

"Since then I have lived so much, and have been so happy, that possibilities for a future life have never disturbed my days. It would be asking too much of the Deity to expect another period like it. Truly it would!"

IV

And so they were married.

Arthur, as a student priest, had been inducted into the parish of Forest, a village two hundred miles away from Cookstown, down in western Ontario. Throughout the summer he wrote to Emily, describing how, from nothing at all, he was building a church and gathering a congregation so that he would have an established "living" for his bride.

Every week Emily wrote to him, letters full of the family, and details of the wedding. It was to be in the Anglican church of St. John's, where she had been confirmed, and her friends in the village were planning to decorate it for her, themselves. Harry Webb, the caterer in Toronto, was sending waiters and food for the reception all the way by train, for it was planned to have a hundred guests sit down to the wedding breakfast under a giant marquee on the croquet lawn. She was to be in white satin, with her five bridesmaids in rainbow tints. The boys, of course, would be ushers, with Arthur's brother. It was all going to be very, very beautiful, and she was certainly the happiest girl in the world. She slipped a blossom into every letter, and fifty years after, "The Padre" remembered the perfume that always lingered about her letters.

Emily and her mother whirled through the weeks in the excitement of bridal parties, for both the Fergusons and the Murphys were well known throughout Simcoe county. So it came to the night before the wedding, August 23rd, 1887. She had been persuaded to stay quietly at home. Her parents were visiting neighbours, and the boys, who had come home for the wedding from their studies in law and medicine, were partying somewhere.

Emily was undressing in her room, lingering, as all girls do, over details of toiletry on this her last night at home. Her wedding dress, swathed in protective sheeting, hung in the cupboard. Her veil was folded in a long cardboard box across the room.

Her dress! How would she look? How would she stand? Was it really perfect?

She could not resist her characteristic urge to practise. Swiftly she unwrapped the covering from the creamy satin; tenderly she slipped it over her head. So. And the veil . . . so!

Down the stairs she went on cautious tip-toes, round the corner and over to the friendly mirror in the parlour. The old house was quiet, its rooms clear and ready, tables and cabinets were perfumed with their polishing, cleared for the flowers to be brought in on the morrow.

Into the dusky shadows of the mirror came Emily, as she had come so often. Her veil, embroidered with crystal beads and tiny imitation pearls (Miss Sally Lee's work) was set about her head with orange blossoms. She tilted her chin to try its most effective angle for the wedding march.

It was difficult to see, for the oil lamp was on the centre table and threw dark shadows about her. Carefully she carried it, set it on a stool beside the mirror.

There . . . that was better. Now she could really see.

"I, Emily, take thee, Arthur . . ."

Outside the woods darkened under the stars. In the Ferguson home, one light burned that night—an oil lamp set close, very close, to an old mirror, and before it, a nineteen-year-old, on her wedding eve.

"In sickness and in sorrow" . . .

With the sound of a shot, the mirror splintered.

Emily screamed, and seized the lamp. Too late! Its heat had cracked the glass in a fan of curving lines.

V

Her mother comforted her, somehow, and together they planned how they would disguise the accident. For the mirror could not possibly be moved, set as it was into the wall.

Lace curtains, said her mother. Draped across the sides—and draped, mark you, with Irish pride and serenity.

After the ceremony on that long-ago high noon in the little church, to the cadences of the prayers which have pledged the marriage vows of so many generations, the guests crowded the rooms of the old house. It had been an exquisite wedding, they said. The bride was at her prettiest; and the groom a fine-looking man of God. The whole affair was one for congratulations; and there's nothing so merry as a wedding party.

"But," recalled Emily, in after years, "some of the women saw the cracked mirror behind the lace curtain, and they watched me with curious and frightened eyes."

CHAPTER III

Rector's Wife

Perhaps if we only love enough, we may be
successes in living.

JANEY CANUCK.

I

EMILY fitted into her new life with grace. As the
wife of the popular young rector, she automatical-
ly became the focal point of village interest; as the
daughter of Isaac Ferguson she was well used to that.
She soon found that while the individual make-up of
her audience was different, the general effect was the
same. These people of Forest were as friendly and
homelike as those she had left in Cookstown.

But try as she would, the girl did not find her new
dignity always easy to maintain. As a woman of sixty,
Emily Murphy described it for the first time, when she
set down a few notes for "My Career as a Parson's
Wife".

The chronicle was never finished, but lay in her desk
for years. There are sixteen scraps of paper, held with
a rusted pin—scraps caught from the pot-pourri of
material which flowed across her desk. They are torn
from mimeographed notices, British income-tax reports,
Press Club notices, old cash ledgers, legal bills, and
out-dated correspondence. It was a method she loved
to follow.

It is interesting to realize that in all her writing, most of it autobiographical, she never referred to this period of her life. The article was only in the preliminary stage; but, fragment that it is, still conjures vividly the 'teen-age bride.

"I found that, as a bride of nineteen, I had to take Bible classes, be president of the Missionary Society, play the organ, speak at meetings, organize the entertainments and bazaars. I was, however, acquiring a stability that fitted me for half a dozen other duties. Every duty in life fits you for another duty.

"I don't know that I was a model parson's wife. (How could I be at nineteen?) But I'll say I loved every soul in the parish, and I'm kind of thinking they loved me too.

"I knew it after the day I got 'the worse for liquor' because they patted me on the back and put their arms around me and said 'dear child' and things like that.

"You see, I had been used to drinking cider at home. We used to have a barrel of it, but it was kept sweet. I was calling on an English couple, the very salt of the earth. Tom was an old miner and he wanted to treat the 'parson's missus' well. So he produced his hardest cider from the cellar, and the parson's missus loved it, and innocently drank more than a glass. It was a hot day, and when the missus got to the rectory gate she found there was a latch on the gate but it refused to open.

"When the parson and some friends came out of an afternoon meeting, and found her standing here, crying, there was the very dickens to pay. The Padre, who is a champion boxer, and six feet, was going to 'smash' old Tom and Mrs. King. The dear things—just as if they knew I couldn't 'carry' cider. How could they know?

"And there was the time I was a bad example in church. You see, it all came about by their giving me the front seat of the side aisle, right at the front of the church, where everyone could see me and notice if I joined in the creed, psalms and general confession. It always made me nervous and I hated it.

"Then old Dr. Nache sat right behind me, and nothing ever escaped his humorous, and often wicked, eye. One Sunday morning, while waiting for the service to begin, in that dead silence when everyone, looking eminently proper, glances around the church, passing inward comment on everyone else, I suddenly broke this sacred silence, by laughing aloud with great distinctness.

"I placed my hand over my frightfully offending mouth. It was too late. For the whole church was laughing with me.

"It is true they did not know just what the elderly imp had said to me, but they knew it was something about Mrs. M—, the leader of the choir, who minces with smartness up the aisle with a peculiarly abrupt and abbreviated tread, of about two inches to every step.

"Now this remarkable gait of hers had always puzzled and fascinated me, but I never could figure out upon what she had modelled it—just how she came to walk like that. What the doctor had snorted out— just as if he could bite her—was 'hen on a hot griddle! Hen on a hot griddle!'

"The Padre was terribly ashamed of me, and I was

so ashamed of myself that I went home to my father for three whole weeks. It seemed as if I could never dare to sit in that dreadful seat again, with Dr. Nache behind me, and all the congregation watching me. But I did. I just arrived back without a word, opened the door of the Padre's room with a sudden bang, and said 'Boo!' as loudly as I could. He forgot himself too, just as I did in church—forgot that he was shaving, and got lather all over my face. Then we both laughed aloud.

"So ended one of my failures in my career as a parson's wife . . . Well, not quite. For I found the women of the parish had put enough preserves, and pickles in my cellar to last a year; had baked a huge Easter cake for me, and some puddings. Oh yes! Come here till I tell you. There was a large, large parcel for me in my room. My name was on it, but you could never guess what was in it. The women of the parish had had several sewing 'bees' while I was away, and this was my first baby's layette—all there, every stitch, from bandage to bonnet.

"Tut, tut, who says they hadn't forgiven me for betraying myself into a laugh that Sunday in church? And that they didn't like mothering the parson's wife, instead of having her mother them in the usually accepted style?"

II

Emily spent about ten years as a minister's wife in towns and villages throughout Western Ontario. They were years which saw the transition from high-spirited girlhood into equally high-spirited maturity; years in which her eager mind developed new capabilities for understanding; in which she knew the ecstacy of motherhood, and its bitter grief. In them she and Arthur founded an enduring friendship; learned to think, and to laugh together.

In the early days she accompanied her husband in much of his parish visiting. Tucked into the buggy or cutter beside him, she found a continual enjoyment in their association, as she questioned him on his work; argued vigorously; chattered a lot; listened often. They had opportunities for a companionship in his work which is the good fortune of few marriages. They spent many hours together, driving, not only about the village and its countryside, but to and from the mission station of Thedford, twelve miles from Forest. Every Sunday afternoon, following morning service in Forest, Emily and Arthur drove this twenty-four miles together and began the comradeship they were to know in drives over thousands of miles together in the old world, and the new frontiers of the Canadian West.

These two young people, however, built their friendship not only in the parochial work but in their hours of reading together. Emily, fresh from her studies at Bishop Strachan's school, developed her remarkable memory still further by indexing all of Arthur's books and memorizing his quotations. It became one of their amusements to have her pick the volume and the page for some reference Arthur needed.

They began to fill immense leather-bound ledgers with quotations and references for the sermons which were bringing Arthur local fame. One of these ledgers is before me now, marked "D". Those marked A.B.C. were completed in the first year or so of marriage, but this one, "D", covers many years. In it there are over four hundred pages filled with material, most of it as effective and compelling today, as it was before the turn of the century.

Night after night, the young wife sat with one of these immense books propped up before her on the round table under the centre hanging-lamp. Her wide skirts lay about her high-buttoned boots. Her thick hair coiled in dignity around her head, loose tendrils softly framing her intent face.

In the "D" ledger, at Arthur's suggestion, she noted similes for salvation, colourful, dramatic, vividly interesting; stories to illustrate her husband's sermons, based on Napoleon's throne, on lepers in the Sandwich Islands, on the Johnstown flood, the Sultan of Turkey. Here she entered quotations from famous preachers of the day, from Ruskin, Carlyle, and the classics. All of them are written with force and devotion, for Emily loved the full invectives, the sonorous phrases.

III

While Emily entered with her usual energy into her life as a Rector's wife, she brought to her worship no blind, unthinking acceptance.

She divided her religious life, in after years, into four aspects:

> The youthful and fervid
> The academic and doubting
> The maternal and social
> The older and peaceful

As a young girl she had been extremely conscious of the sinfulness of sin, and would fairly groan in earnestness when she tried to answer the questions in the little book she was given for self-examination at her confirmation. She had known what she described as a kind of seraphic uplift, a fervour for contemplation that might properly be described as an aptitude for God. Shortly after her confirmation, her faith became unsettled so that she found herself deeply involved in anti-theological thinking.

This was, she said, undoubtedly, the loneliest place on the curve of her religious life. In this period of scepticism, she could not pray at all. "How absurd it seemed," she wrote in retrospect, "that I, the fly on the wall, should strive to guide the machinery! Indeed, I had gone further and believed with the old German mystic, Angelus Sibelius, that the will of God, by its very nature, was immune to petitions. To me, sin was no longer statutory—something to be penalized or wiped out by assent to a series of doctrines. Wicked people were only good material that was badly managed—a heterodoxy from which I have never entirely recovered. This period led me, for years, into a study of comparative religions, and of the Gods of Egypt with all their symbolism and strange enticement. I learned many things therefrom."

As the years passed, she repeated the Apostle's Creed, for instance, abrogating to herself the right to interpret the terms in wider or narrower significances. She believed, with Dean Inge, that we do not make religions for others, and should not permit others to make them for us.

But agreeing with him—she promptly began to ask

questions. Do not many of us, she wondered, make religions, if only by our pen or tongues, by our actions and examples, which others, in the home or office, follow, although we may be wholly unaware?

IV

With the birth of her first baby, Kathleen, in Forest, eleven months after her marriage, Emily found a new understanding for the symbolism of her faith. "This was how my soul became conscious, as never before, that the Word was made flesh, and dwelt among us, and that he was wrapped about with swaddling clothes. To me, the mother and child became the central part of Christianity and I believed, as even until now, that their symbol was an eternal one—the symbol of life itself."

Knowing motherhood when she was barely twenty, Emily gave a devotion to her children which enriched all her life. She dedicated to them her young strength, and an intelligence that knew, even in their childhood, the basis of justice and the laws of retribution. In many articles later she jeered at those who spoke of the tears and sacrifices of a mother, believing that the recompense was a full hundred-fold, "and that, really, is quite a good rate of interest."

When Kathleen was a few months old, tragic news came from Cookstown, for Isaac, after months of suffering, had finally been persuaded to go to Toronto to see a specialist. There he received his death sentence—cancer. Emily was so distracted with grief, that Arthur suggested she take the baby and visit her home for a few weeks.

But she found the old house in a sad commotion. Her father was in agonies, and her mother frantic with the worry and strain of nursing him. The house seemed full of people—all of whom were concentrated on Isaac's tragedy. Realizing that she was only adding to the general confusion, Emily came home again, and returned to Cookstown thereafter only for the family funerals. Isaac died the next year, in 1889, and, soon after, his wife sold the Cookstown property and moved to Toronto where two of the boys were at Osgoode Hall studying law, with Gowan in medicine and Annie at Bishop Strachan's. A few months later, a fire swept the southern half of Cookstown, and the Ferguson house was obliterated. When Emily returned in middle life to visit two small graves in the family plot, the only remnant of her old home left was the pear tree under which she sat to muse; a tree which she and her father had planted on a spring afternoon.

The Murphys were about three years in Forest, years during which Arthur began to build a reputation not only for the picturesque force of his preaching, but for his business acumen. His was not the type of mind to find satisfaction in sermonizing alone, although the pulpit was always the focal point of his work. He believed in keeping closely in touch with the families in his congregation, and in working with his vestry in the financial set-up of the church. So effective was he, that throughout his ministry he received many calls a year to other parishes.

For ten months the Murphys were in Watford, another small village, and then came a call which he could not resist. The nearby city of Chatham sent him an appeal for help. Wouldn't he come and lead them out of their troubles? The church was $20,000 in debt; the congregation dwindling. In spite of the storm of disapproval from Watford, he accepted, explaining that he felt a more imperative work awaited him. His was the crusading spirit, and he was very definitely one of the adventurous churchmen of the period. The uncompleted task, the challenge, the unsolved, called to him irresistibly.

Chatham had been one of the "underground railway" stations for the escape of slaves from the nearby American border, and fully one-third of the population was negro. It was known fifty years ago as the city of the three M.s—mud, mulatto and malaria. The Murphys, like many others, had to take quinine regularly to keep clear of the fever. In spite of this precaution, Emily was stricken and faced months of poor health with a rebellious spirit. It was difficult for a girl, used all her life to glowing health, to find herself ailing and "poorly", as the parishioners termed it.

Emily's second daughter, Evelyn, was born in Chatham. The young wife began to find less time for parochial visiting with her husband, but her social popularity more than offset any lack of this kind. Her intense personal interest in those she met, and her impulsive little gestures of friendship accumulated so much credit for her among the congregation that she missed many of the pitfalls usually lying in wait for a minister's wife.

A small private income meant that the Murphys could keep a maid and a nursemaid, but Emily was far from idle. In addition to her own home duties she learned shorthand to make her note-taking for Arthur more affective. She had begun to study oil painting in

Watford, and spent many hours on it in Chatham. She had a natural talent and finished a number of canvases which hang today in her daughters' homes. Critics say that if she had had the opportunity for advanced training, she might have won as much fame as an artist, as she did as a writer and a human being.

The Murphys knew their first grief as a family in Chatham. With the after-effect of the malaria fever, the tragedy effected Emily's health for several years. One evening, just before her third child was born, she was walking down the stairs with an oil lamp in her hand. She stumbled in her long dressing-gown, and fell. The lamp exploded, and her gown caught fire.

Arthur was there in a second, the fire put out, and Emily carried to bed, but all their care could not prevent a premature birth and a very delicate baby. Emily was almost fanatical in the devoted care she gave the child Madeleine; but in spite of it, the little girl died at nine months. Emily blamed herself bitterly for the loss of her baby, and with her lowered resistance, could not throw off her endless soul-searching. If only she had been more careful on those stairs; if only she had tied her gown more tightly about her waist; if only she had gone more slowly, she might not have lost her little one. Madeleine haunted her, day and night, for many months. Together she and Arthur attended the little white coffin to Cookstown where it was laid under the sod of the cemetery which, as pasture field, had been Emily's playground. On the sole of the baby shoe Madeleine had worn, although she had never walked, Emily wrote, "The dove found no rest for the sole of her foot, and she returned unto Him into the ark". The shoe was tucked into a box and kept in her bureau drawer. Years later it was passed on to her daughter Evelyn for safe keeping.

On a Sunday four years after their arrival in Chatham, Holy Trinity church was crammed, to celebrate the almost unbelievable achievement of the congregation and its minister. The church was debt-free. The $20,000 was paid in full, and a fine pipe organ installed, and paid for.

Here was success, and complete satisfaction—but not for Arthur. His mind yearned for the struggle of uncompleted work; for the battle which may be lost if every ounce of energy is not constantly in use. He felt, with Emily, that if the struggle ends, half the fun of living is gone.

When, a few months later, the town of Ingersoll asked him to come and help in the up-building of St. James, why, Arthur asked, should he linger in a work which someone else could carry on? So, with Emily in poor health, and still grieving for her lost child, they sold some of their furniture and moved to Ingersoll.

Sold, by mistake, was the baby's cradle, in a job lot of household items. The error was not discovered until the family was settled in Ingersoll. Emily wanted the cradle badly, and Arthur got it for her. He went back to Chatham, found the auctioneer, tracked down the farmer who had bought the cradle, practically lifted the farmer's baby out, and paid him a good price for it. In time, the cradle moved out West with the Murphys and rocked many babies in the new province— among them the grand-children of the Lieutenant-Governor. Emily herself was to see her grand-daughter standing, for the first time, on wobbly legs, hanging on to this very cradle.

V

The three years in Ingersoll proved among the happiest in Emily's whole life. The present was sweetened with comfort and contentment; the future promised well.

The Rectory was the most comfortable home they had known. It was spacious and dignified. The garden was large and decorative, and full of fruits and flowers. Arthur's income was sufficient for them to live at ease. Ingersoll is one of the prettiest of Ontario towns, and the young wife found her life blossoming into a new tranquillity.

On a May morning in 1892, Emily's last child was born—a dainty little girl. A wit in the congregation had asked whether with a "Kathleen, Eveleen, and Madeleine" in the family, the new baby would be called Vaseline. But the child was named Doris Baldwin, after the Right Rev. Maurice Baldwin, D.D., Bishop of Huron Diocese, who had become a close friend of Arthur's. From the moment the baby's pansy blue eyes gazed on her mother, Emily lived in an ecstacy of adoration for the little girl.

There is a photograph of the family taken about this time which carries with it, across the years, the aura of their radiant home life. Arthur the visionary looks far into the horizons. The young mother's head is bent in an unconscious caress towards her three little daughters: Kathleen, the dark and imaginative; Evelyn, the fair and laughter-loving; Doris, the fairy-like enchantress.

Happiness and health flowed back for Emily and she knew a period, ideal in any woman's life—that of

established and all-promising motherhood and wife-
hood. Her high spirits bloomed again as of old, and she
lived with the full enjoyment of every pleasure.

There were friends a-plenty, and the Ingersoll Rectory was always full of guests. On Sunday evenings,
after church, the little girls hung over the bannisters
watching the friendly gaiety that centred in the hospitable rooms below. Emily played hostess with the
same lavish delight that her mother had known, and
ordered her household groceries as her father had
done—in large quantities.

So another Emily sat on summer evenings telling
the family stories to her children. The Irish grandparents, of course, and the Orange parades, and the
old horse, Rodney, that would allow all five young
Fergusons to climb on his back at once, until he was
tired of them—when he would shake his skin so vigorously that they all fell off.

The little girls clamoured for more. "The heads-off,
mother!"

This Emily told the tale with gusto, and a full-swing-
ing arm. Still the picture of that other Emily haunted
the tale, and she added, "My mother did not think that
a suitable story for little girls!"

The children loved best of all the tales of their own
parents' adventures. Arthur told of the day he brought
friends home, to find his young bride standing on the
gate-post—checking to see if the train of her gown
would reach the ground from that height. Or the other
occasion when friends were startled to find their minister's wife jumping from the apple tree beside them,
to greet them with laughter and the prize apple she
had reached. Emily crinkled her face in chuckles again,

protesting, "But I was so young, Arthur! And a childhood with brothers! I couldn't *always* remember!"

Her own favourite was the story of Arthur and the old negro who came to mend the cistern in Chatham. Arthur was insistent that the price be quoted for the job before it was started. The negro was equally insistent that he could give no estimate. When he was down the cistern, still refusing to quote a price, Arthur pulled up the ladder, and suggested that he would keep it up until a figure was named. "I tell you, missus," the negro said to Emily later, "I done saw somepin today dat the Lord Jesus never met up with! I met my equal, I did—and dat's more 'n He ever did!"

So the years flowed by, and the end of a century approached. Emily's world was the small Ontario town; her mind was concentrated fully on her husband's work and success, and on the development of her three children. Outside the home lay the friendly world of the parish and district. To be young and popular; to have work to do, and hopes to dream upon; to be needed—and fulfil that need with serene confidence— could any young woman ask more of life?

She went, always, to Evensong, to sit alone in her front-left pew, and listen to the age-old chants of the Anglican music. With the majestic words of the prayers sounding in her heart and mind, she would close her eyes, to be swept back again to the years in Cookstown with her brothers beside her, and her old home awaiting them after the service. Now the lights of the church flowed out over the lawns, to her own nearby home and its children, asleep in the nursery. Her husband was reading the prayers and she knew the sermon he was to preach. He was an undoubted success,

THE MURPHY FAMILY, 1901, LONDON, ONTARIO

EMILY, IN EDMONTON, 1926

ARTHUR MURPHY, TAKEN IN ENGLAND, 1899

EMILY WITH KATHLEEN AND EVELYN AT INGERSOLL, 1894

with an ever-increasing fame. The Bishop, his friend,
predicted a noble future for him. Emily Murphy, Rector's wife, bowed her head upon her capable hands,
her whole being flooded with gratitude.

Then came the final prayer, muffled, hung on the
thread of Arthur's voice. "May the blessing of God
the Father, God the Son, and God the Holy Ghost, be
with you now, and for evermore".

The dim chanted "Amen" followed, and the sound
of people moving out towards their own lives again.
Emily liked to linger on her knees, and then to mingle
with the congregation, smiling, nodding, whispering.
She could feel the love and devotion of the people
flowing about her.

She crossed the lawn to the garden bench by the
church, to wait for her husband. The Bishop had been
down today for confirmation, and she was eager to
hear from Arthur the news he had brought, the opinions he held about certain developments in the parochial work.

Presently the vestry door was open and in the yellow light her husband stood, silhouetted. Then he came
to the bench where he knew he would find her.

He was troubled in spirit, and filled with an agony
of indecision. Bishop Baldwin had spent some hours
with him that afternoon, full of new plans for Arthur.
He wanted the young cleric to leave the solidarity and
security of his church work, to become a missionary,
not in far distant lands but right here in Ontario. There
was a vital need, Arthur explained, for men who could
preach salvation effectively, to travel on missions about
the province.

Emily listened, bewildered, as he explained the details. There would be no set income, only the collections they might receive at the missionary services; no definite home, but a constant travelling through the towns and villages of Ontario. The family life must be broken for a while.

How could he ask Emily to give up all this serene and happy life and come with him on what might be a desperate adventure? Suppose he could not win souls in the allotted few days' mission in each community? Suppose he failed in his mission work? Once out of the accepted group of successful ministers with prosperous parishes, could he ever get back again? They were safe now. They were successful. And yet the call was so urgent. It was so hard for the church to find competent preachers for this Missioner's life.

Emily, keeping the consternation out of her voice asked,

"What do you want to do, Arthur?"

He who was so forceful in the pulpit was halting now, groping to find the right answer. He knew only this: the need was very real. He had the qualifications —and the Church had called on him. He did not feel happy in living too easily, when there were so many who needed his help for their soul's salvation.

Emily listened, and considered intently, what he was saying. She watched his earnest face, his eyes shadowed with his inner turmoil. "How can I refuse help to those who need it? . . . And yet how can I ask you to give up all this? But—oh, Emily, will you?"

CHAPTER IV

Missioner's Wife

It would seem that she whose heart is wisely
blithe has an enduring holiday.

JANEY CANUCK IN *Open Trails.*

I

A S MISSION PREACHER for Huron Diocese, Arthur's life was not changed in its fundamentals of
work and service. In the various parishes, congregations sat before him, identical in their spiritual needs
and responses. The only difference was that to him
they were strangers, rather than families whose personal history he knew well. The tenor of his sermons
and their preparation was the same except that they
were keyed to a greater intensity by reason of the time
limitations. Now he had only two weeks to arouse an
inner determination towards salvation in those who
listened to him, instead of the more leisurely years of a
parish ministry. His work was what it had been with
the tempo quickened and intensified.

But for Emily his wife the change meant a complete readjustment of her physical and mental outlook.

Gone was the home life in which she had known a
traditional serenity and security. She and Arthur lived,
for two years, in a succession of small hotels through-

47

out Ontario, or stayed with church members in the various parishes. The comfortable, steady income had disappeared; they were dependent upon the special mission offerings at the services.

She who had always loved her own possessions and who gathered about her many treasures that were symbolic of her interest in all she saw and learned, moved from lodging to lodging. About her had been the sound of children's laughter; her neighbour's companionship; the community's approval. Now, the little family, with the children's nurse who travelled with them, moved always among strangers. Emily had been the focal point of interest for all the parish activities. Now, she was always the stranger, just the wife of the visiting Missioner, to be asked to dinner with full "company" dignity by the church's leading members, or talked to, shyly, at afternoon teas.

She saw much less of Arthur, too, for he was working at fever pitch. The life of a Missioner entailed, as a rule, two weeks in each parish, with three Sundays for services. There were three sermons every Sunday, and one for every evening of the week. There were afternoon meetings, and interviews with scores of men and women who had some personal trouble to discuss with the preacher. There were always details of the next Mission to plan, and he must spend some time with the local rector and church officials. With all this, he must read as much as ever.

There was little time, then, for the leisurely comradeship Emily and Arthur had known in the early years of their marriage.

She awoke to days of unbelievable freedom from household responsibilities. She attended Arthur's services, and read more avidly than ever, but, compared to the overflowing home life she had known for the past ten years, there were many empty hours in each day that challenged her with their possibilities.

Released from so many restrictions, Emily's interests began to broaden. Hitherto, the people she had known were considered directly in relation to her own environment and routine, whether of the Fergusons in Cookstown, or the rector's home in Chatham or Ingersoll.

Now, the men and women she met had little to do with her own existence. They merged, as the months went by, into a continuing chain of humanity with similar problems and mannerisms, in one town after another. She made hundreds of acquaintances, but had few friends in whom she could confide. With such an immensity of new impressions bringing with them reiterated conclusions, and with little opportunity to express them verbally, she began to write.

She wrote, at first, because she wanted to translate what she was learning into a definite form; she wrote because she liked to read it aloud to Arthur, and share his merriment or understanding. Much of his work was carried on under a severe emotional strain, so that, subconsciously, she wrote for his delight and relaxation. He was a most satisfactory audience.

Her mind sharpened with interest. Each day brought its quota of new experience and she interpreted the life around her in her large easy script on any paper she could find. With no permanent desk, no routine for work, but writing something every day, she reached for the backs of letters, announcements, papers—anything which was available. All she needed by way of equipment was a table somewhere in her room.

It followed naturally that the more she wrote, the more she developed her natural aptitude for spontaneous questioning of those she met. Her friendliness was as artless as in her childhood; now she began to cultivate her innate ease with people, so that she might discover new truths. It was a gift of the gods, she discovered, to be able to put people at their ease when you wanted to know how they felt and what they were thinking.

Her daily notes became one of her dominating interests. When new triumphs came and Arthur was invited to take his family and preach as a Missioner in England, she was writing in diary form, every day, as a matter of course. It had become a necessity to her.

II

On a July afternoon in 1898, Emily Murphy stood at the rail of S.S. *Gallia* and watched the gaunt grey rock of Quebec slip into the dusk. They were all together, huddled in half-tearful homesickness. Emily pulled Kathleen and Evelyn closer to her as they stood under the darkening sky, and her eyes lifted in momentary panic to the elfin Doris, perched on her father's shoulder. It was a long journey they were taking, and the life would be unsettled. They were leaving security again. Since that fateful evening under the linden tree in the Ingersoll garden, when Arthur had asked her to give up their home for Mission adventuring, they had been drifting farther and farther away from their original way of life. Was this trip to England a mistake? Was it unwise to take such young children on so long an adventure? Was Arthur working too hard?

Her mother had insisted that the answer to all the questions was an emphatic "Yes." She dreaded the journey as a further break-up of Emily's home associations. There seemed to be too much of the traipsing-around in it for the children's good. She cried about it, and told Emily that she felt, with the end of the century, had come the end of holding back young people. They were off and away on any wild scheme that beckoned them.

The future lay under the blank immutable skies ahead. There was little sense in worrying now, but that night as the Murphys knelt to pray in their cabin, both Emily and Arthur wished themselves safely back in the known routine.

Emily was in her early thirties when the English adventure began. The years as a rector's wife had thickened her figure, and she wore an air of matronliness which then was expected with the thirtieth birthday. Her smooth brown hair was coiled high on her head, and her hazel eyes were still full of a rapturous contemplation of anything new and strange.

Here was a freedom greater than any she had yet sampled. Beyond the seas lay a world she had known in books, which she was to tread under ideal conditions.

An incident occurred a few days after they lost sight of the brooding Labrador coast-line, which had important repercussions. The tall Padre and his plump little wife were sitting in the lounge with a group of English visitors who were returning after a short visit to Ontario and Quebec. They talked of Canada, if not quite as the "blawsted colony", still with very much that attitude of mind.

One of them quoted Mrs. Jameson's book on Canada, referring to it as a "small community of fourth-rate, half-educated people, where local politics of the meanest kind engross the men, and petty gossip and household affairs the women."

Someone mentioned "Canadian gruffness and bad manners".

Mrs. Murphy, the parson's wife, listened in silence as the talk went round the group, until one man said that the Canadians were much more akin to Americans than to the British. They had, he pointed out, the same nasal monotone and tiresome habit of bragging as the Americans.

Then Mrs. Murphy leaned forward, and said bluntly: "Maybe. But do you recall that one of your own countrywomen—Miss Isabelle Baird, who has travelled the world for many years—gave the interesting decision that while the Americans are *naturally* assumptive, the English are *personally* so!"

The group roared and someone said, "There's a Canuck for you!"

She talked it over with Arthur in their cabin. "I'm glad they called me a Canuck. That's just what I felt like. And if there's a Jack Canuck there certainly should be a . . . a woman Canuck. Jack and Jill. Jack and Jane . . . Janey Canuck!"

Noting the name in her diary that night, she added: "They spoke tonight of our gruff Canadian manners. I have not seen enough of the world to institute comparisons, and it may be that we Canadians need the warmth of a more genial atmosphere to soften our brusquerie."

She knew almost complete freedom from household

routine in the two years she spent in England. While she accompanied Arthur on many of his Mission trips to the old Cathedral towns of England, to the soldiers, the sailors, the poor-houses and hospitals, she still had many, many days entirely her own. The girls were put in a boarding-school at St. Albans, and she, with Doris and a nurse, found a central lodging in London, Liverpool, or one of the larger cities, while Arthur travelled on his work.

With characteristic energy she set out to see as much as she could, and, night after night, noted her adventures in her diary. She tramped through the dungeons she had read about with shivering horror, when reading of them in Foxe's *Book of Martyrs* deep in the wood-pile lair at home. In one dungeon a guard was persuaded to put her in the chains which still hung from the ancient wall, and to leave her alone in the dark for a little while—so that she might actually feel what it was like.

She went to the inns she knew through her Dickens —at the Great White Horse in Ipswich, for instance, she ordered the very same dinner that Mr. Pickwick and Mr. Peter Magnus had enjoyed. Following the hours she had spent in copying some of Carlyle's ideas into the big sermon book as a bride, she found every inch of his home absorbing, and was finally abandoned by an irritated guard to her own explorations. She asked so many questions, and looked into so many details, that the rest of the party grew impatient.

For a month, she went every day to the British Museum and wandered through its misty halls, studying its garnered treasures. She became a familiar figure to the guards.

The release from a restraint she had known as minister's wife in a conservative community was one of the most exhilarating phases of her explorations. Time and again, she noted its delights in her diary. To be able to walk about, unknown, unnoticed, without the nagging realization that critical eyes were watching every move she made, meant a new delight for her.

III

A saucy independence of thought runs through her comments of what she saw in England. When she listened to the Archbishop of Canterbury preach, she noted "His Grace preached with the aid of an excessively ornate staff which in no way improved a monotonous discourse. I have a shrewd suspicion that a Canadian parish in the back counties would probably starve him out . . ."

When she was a guest, with Arthur, at a house-party for the opening of the grouse season, her hosts remembered a jolly woman with an American turn to her phrasing. They felt that a glimpse into the inner circle of hunting-life would be a real thrill to the Colonials. But Emily remembered the sport as savouring much of the "potting" of chickens in a farm-yard, since the game was so plentiful. When she had been a year in England, she had definite opinions of Englishmen. Listen:

"An Englishman must be always up and doing. He can only sit at dinner, or over hot punch. If he is rich he wears Balmorals and hunts tame deer. If poor, he wears hobnails and kicks his wife. It is sport anyway, for it causes suffering to others and amusement to himself."

Caustic comments, these, but at the same time she wrote with glowing appreciation of the hospitality and kindness she found everywhere.

She loved the holiday crowds, too, and wandered among them with unflagging interest. She tramped for hours along the docks of Liverpool and London, absorbed in the eager, struggling crowds that jabbered and jostled around the big hauls of fish. She had known, heretofore, only the homogeneous people of Ontario towns. There had been little poverty, little misery, few foreigners.

In the long summer weeks she spent on the sea-coast, she learned anew what a world it is for resting and dreaming. She did little all day but lie supine on the beach in tranquil indolence, learning what she called a charming variety of ways of doing nothing. Hours slid by every day in a lazily contented fashion, as she watched the children at play, or the flight of gulls above the waters. She grew relaxed and surfeited with beauty, walking through wheat fields gay with crimson poppies. The summer air hung heavy with fragrance of celandine, honeysuckle, rosemary and rue. Yet, being Emily, she turned her thoughts homewards and began to long for the bold features and sun-blistered hills of her own country.

The pattern of her life gave her this peaceful interval, in the prettiness of English meadows and the majesty of the English sea-coast, before the onslaught she was to know on the Western prairies. All unknowing, she made full use of the rest period.

She was also treading a world where there was un-

happiness and degradation. It was a world that beckoned to her with compelling force. She was catapulted
into a realization of the force of poverty, evil and relentless exploitation, and lashed out in fury at what
she saw.

It was all material to be studied closely. When, on
a river steamer, she saw a girl with "matchmaker's"
leprosy, she did not turn aside as everyone else on board
did, but began to chat with the girl, and presently asked her directly what caused such leprosy. Her findings
went into her notebook. "It is caused by inhaling the
fumes of the phosphorus used in tipping matches. The
teeth ache and then drop out. She is now at this stage
of the disease. Later the loathsome leprosy eats its way
into the roof of the mouth, and inside the nose, and
then the jaw drops off. They sometimes lose their
sight before death. The girl's wages were $1.92 a week.
Who is responsible?" Throughout the months, like the
deepening chords of an organ prelude, the question
began to dominate her mind. Who was at fault? What
could be done to help those who were seemingly helpless?

When Arthur went visiting in the slums of White-
chapel with a local curate, Emily went with them.
Loud-voiced, bold-looking women lounged in doorways and eyed them sharply as they passed. In an alley-
way a drunken slut lay prostrate on the ground. Her
hair was hopelessly matted. A sack tied around her
body alone covered her nakedness. She was loathsome
with disease and filth. As they passed from one wretched room to another, Emily was sickened at the misery
about her. On a sudden, they were in a place where an
old woman lay dying. It seemed to Emily as if her very

moments were numbered and their slumming became suddenly an impertinent intrusion, an ugly curiosity. They were, she felt, looking at people as if they were fossils in a museum.

Arthur knelt on the dirty floor beside the dying creature to commit her passing soul to its Maker, and Emily knelt beside him, clenching her eyes tight, as a child might, her mind filled with a woman's sorrow.

The curate was non-committal. These people, he said, rarely went to church, but he called and left a tract in their rooms once a year. "Really, Mrs. Murphy," he assured her blandly, "it does not do to get too familiar with these people." Her arm linked tightly in Arthur's, Emily hurried through the miserable streets and into broader paths where the sun shone on those who walked. Deeply disturbed, they travelled home in silence.

She wrote that night in a cold fury:

"There is not much use in preaching to people whose spirits are deadened by hardships and starvation, and who are struggling to keep their footing in a quicksand. Some of them are crying ominously in the night. The working brutes in England's backyard are growling and it would not be strange if, one day, they broke their chains. The whole matter is not of today only; it casts a lurid darkness over the future."

Preparation, all of it, for her rendezvous with destiny under Western skies.

IV

Arthur's preaching was so successful that it swept him to a popular acclaim throughout England. It culminated in a rare triumph for the Canadian Missioner. He was invited to preach for the season at Homburg, Germany, in the church where English-speaking congregations gathered.

Emily was ecstatic. She knew it meant fresh laurels for her husband, for only the most impressive preachers were asked to go to this famous German Spa, known, during the season, as the worldliest in Europe. To it came men and women from every country on the Continent, to drink the waters and to watch its colourful life.

Arthur went alone, at first, for Emily did not want to leave the girls. But the English weather was playing havoc with the trouble which still lingered after her bout with malarial fever in Chatham and, after a few weeks, she answered Arthur's entreaties by bringing Doris with her and travelling to Homburg.

She was swept into a world of people who, apparently, had everything. She saw life in the beautiful city at its most glittering, for the ladies were charmed by her fresh zestfulness, and invited her to many of their parties.

See her then, a small, sedate figure, with a massive head, sipping the waters at the spring, thronged with people chattering in all known and unknown tongues. She watched princesses with costumes wonderfully and fearfully made; the wives and daughters of Ambassadors; English duchesses, beautifully-dressed Americans and wealthy Jewesses. Down the long walk, too, came Adelina Patti and her boy-husband. Her hair, noted Emily, was dyed the new shade, Tuscan Red.

Now she knelt at Morning Prayer and Evensong in a wealthy and beautiful church, in a city that had a

fabulous quality to it. A fine choir of superbly trained
voices sang the old chants that she loved so well. She
knew Arthur's inflections in the prayers, as though she
were saying them herself. But, though she tried to
concentrate on her devotions, it was more than ordinarily difficult. People came and went during the service in a queer Continental fashion. Some came only for
the prayers, others for the sermon, others, again, for the
Communion. There was a Royal Pew, and when the
Padre prayed for the Royal Family, oftentimes he
could look down and see them there. On one occasion,
the Empress Frederick and the Crown Princess of
Greece were present, and after the service chatted
with Arthur for some time, questioning him about his
country, Canada. Emily observed that he patted a
small boy on the head—a little chap who was to be
king of Greece.

But the Padre preached to all these grandees as if
they were very simple people, and regulation everyday sinners, given to gambling, lying, sensuality and
hypocrisy . . . "which is most likely," added Emily, in
noting these details.

On holidays, she and Arthur wandered through the
forests of the Tanus Mountains, which lay about Homburg. Emily knew what she described as a "delirious
glamour" to her mood, as she and Arthur threaded the
dark languor of the woods, or lay on the pine-needles
that covered the ground. Arthur carried with him
Law's *Serious Call to a Devout and Holy Life*, from
which he read aloud to his wife. When tired of the
doings of Flavia and Miranda, leading characters in
this two-hundred-year-old book, they dozed their
weariness away, or walked to the Swiss chalet at the

edge of the pinery, to buy rusks which crackled in their teeth. "Like silly children!" wrote Emily, "and like silly children of the woods we made believe we were Canadian red squirrels, eating beech-nuts, and laughed with the sheer bliss of being alive!"

It was all a fairy-tale and, after all, the magic talisman to "live happily ever after" was given to them. For Arthur was asked to stay permanently, and make Homburg his home.

No, no! Neither Arthur nor Emily wanted it. For Arthur the work presented no problem, no difficulty to surmount. These people were too suave and comfortable, too sure of themselves and too careless of anything else. Emily knew that Arthur was too much of a rover to stay in so comfortable a setting.

Above all, home was calling. They both yearned for their own land. Their work was in Canada; their life bound up in its provinces. They must go back.

There remained a few weeks in England to fill Arthur's engagements—and then the Murphys stood again at the prow of a vessel sailing, this time, for home.

The crowd of friends and co-workers who had gathered saw a light-hearted family. Arthur was returning with two years of brilliant work behind him. Emily, beside him, her arms filled with red roses, was in the prime of her womanliness. She had changed during the past months. The impact of all that she had experienced was shown in her increased poise and serenity. The three girls clustered beside them, taller, healthier than ever, full of delight.

Only two years before, they had come to this tight little island, strangers, fearful of their dreams. But now the loved home life lay ahead of them under widening skies; and behind them were memories of hundreds of friends made; of understanding given and received. The world which had been conjured from books, had become a tangible reality that had taught them all much.

Watching the island which she was never to see again, slip into the shadows, Emily knew that her years there had altered the whole trend of her thought. She could never be the same again. She had seen so much, and learned so much that, surely, there must be some use for it, back home?

Yet, even as she yearned towards intangible dreams of service to her own people, she knew a haunting doubt. What opportunities could there be for her in the conservative and organized towns of Eastern Canada?

She pushed the doubt away and set about her usual duties, accompanying her husband on his work. He had been appointed chaplain of the boat, and part of his duties entailed regular visits to the steerage. In those days, horses were carried to England in the steerage, and immigrants brought back in the same quarters.

Emily called them the cave-dwellers, and on her first visit was driven back by the soul-sickening reek of poverty. They could not talk to many, for she found it a strife of many tongues, except for the querulous cries of the children—one language the world over.

She watched them with a haunted interest. Here were dreamers, coming to a strange land—a land she knew so well. Where would they find the material they longed for? Where could they build a new world from their old despair? Was there any place for them in the ordered existence of the Eastern provinces?

"No, lady," a steward told her. "These people are going further. They're heading out West. Far as they can get!"

The Murphys went to visit them, again and again.

They were in a putrid dormitory, with the stench of unwashed bodies and sea-sickness thick upon the air. Arthur was speaking gently to some of the poor souls, who lay white and wasted, on the bunks, dead to all feeling for life—until the gates of the New World opened to them. Arthur moved among them, giving what Emily described as the oil and wine of spiritual comfort. But now she no longer walked beside him with empty hands. She carried a bag of fruit on her arm, and, following Arthur, gave the women oranges and apples. "For I have a clear well-defined idea," she wrote that night, "that women are not all soul; that they have a way of hungering after bread, even before they hunger after righteousness . . ."

Emily Murphy, Missioner's wife, returning from the Old World to the comfort and haven of her dear homeland, had learned much.

CHAPTER V

Disaster

Only the light sorrows are clamorous; the
deadly griefs are silent. They bleed inwardly.

JANEY CANUCK.

I

ARTHUR MURPHY, in an east-bound train for Toronto, sat turning the leaves of a small green book.
On the cover was the picture of a young woman in the
fashions of the nineties—wasp-waisted, immense of
sleeve, with preposterously tiny feet and ankles peep-
ing from a swirling skirt.

It was his wife's book, *Impressions of Janey Canuck
Abroad,* by Emily Ferguson, dedicated "To my fellow-
traveller, the Padre". There was a brief note on the title
page: "Entered according to Act of Parliament in Canada, in the year 1901 by Emily Ferguson, at the Department of Agriculture."

Arthur realized that the book was poorly printed,
badly proof-read, the pages roughly treated in a slip-
shod binding. But it was Emily's own book, and its
pages were so full of her vivid tempo of living that it
had won high praise in England and the United States.
Arthur chuckled, again and again, as he dipped into
it. How fiercely she felt about matters; how indignant
she could get—and how funny! It was sheer delight to

turn the pages and recall the days as they had been lived.

In addition to this book, Arthur had published a volume of his sermons, *The Way of Life,* which was making quite a stir, and had already gone into a second edition. He and his wife had been happy in the planning and preparations of the two books.

Since their return from England, Arthur, who was still on the staff of the Church Parochial Mission Society in England, at a comfortable salary, had been continuing his Mission work in Canada. This entailed longer journeys to the Maritimes and to the Western provinces. Emily accompanied him on some of his Missions, but she spent most of the time in Toronto. Kathleen and Evelyn were attending Havergal College and Doris, of course, was at home.

"Little Girl Blue", Emily called her adoringly. It was natural, Arthur realized, for Emily to feel intense love for this little one, because, in a way, she represented the fairy-tale magic which had always been so strong in her childhood. Emily herself was always of robust vigorous build, small though she was, and the two older children were both fine stalwart girls. Doris was a chubby little thing, with flaxen hair and enormous blue eyes. Emily had told him once, laughing, that when she was a child, her secret longing was to be of the Doris type. Moreover, since babyhood, Doris had been constantly with Emily, when Emily had had little of the usual home associations, and this had heightened the mother's devotion.

Their home was near High Park, Toronto, and for a few weeks the family had been dining at a private club nearby, run by the president of the York County Loan

Company, one of the big promoters of the day. He had started a magazine called *National Monthly,* and Emily was writing a great deal for it. Arthur had the latest copy with him.

It contained over twenty consecutive pages written by his wife. There were some of the "Impressions" from England; a page or two on household economy; a bit on manners and fashions; on home decoration; and a treatise "About Kisses" that was as gay and amusing as Emily herself. Finally, came a number of book reviews —Emily loved writing them. Arthur grinned again as he noticed some of her *nom de plumes*—how she loved to dress up, even in the names she used . . . Lady Jane, The Duchess, Earlie York. The same Emily, this, who used to pose so often in costume before the old parlour mirror!

A mosquito moved to the window-pane, and Arthur watched it idly; unusual to have one so late in the year, for already it was autumn, and his big speech in Toronto near at hand. In a day or so, he was scheduled to be the main speaker at an important rally in Massey Hall. Toronto was a difficult place in which to speak, its people overly critical and hard to reach. He had preached in many of the churches there, but it was because of his brilliant successes in England and on the Continent that this mass meeting for him had been arranged. The feeling of those who were sponsoring it, however, was very clearly one of "We'll have to show Toronto something special. Think you can do it?"

The mosquito, hovering over the window, settled on Arthur's neck, just behind his ear, and stung him with a sudden stabbing pain that startled him from his reverie. This prick, the doctors said later, examining the sore and swollen wound, was probably at the root of the whole trouble.

II

Emily sat half-way down the curving rows of seats in Massey Hall. It was a high and gloomy building, with elaborate frescoes of carved dadoes above its enormous stage, and two broad semi-circular balconies. The palms, piano, rug and a row of chairs were in place on the stage, with a small table, and the inevitable jug of water.

At least two thousand men and women crowded the hall. Good, thought Emily, remembering the committee's fear that Toronto people would not come to hear an Ontario preacher. Here they were, in their hundreds, rustling their programmes with restless fingers.

It was pleasant to sit quietly, aware of the expectancy about her. She had such a serene confidence in Arthur, firmly rooted in the years past. This meeting marked another high moment—for somehow, no matter how successful one was in the four corners of the world it is *home* that matters. Toronto was Emily's spiritual home. In St. James' cemetery, north of the city, lay her grandfather, Ogle R. Gowan, and his wife. In the neighbourhood were the homes of her uncles and aunts. Because of her school-days at Bishop Strachan's, she had many associations and friends in the city.

Now, too, her mother was here, and the boys, all practising at the Ontario bar excepting Gowan who had become a medical doctor and was in Great Falls, Montana, after his studies in Europe. It was fun hav-

ing her mother in the city to be a grandmother to her
lively girls. Emily Gowan Ferguson still loved to dress
meticulously, and had taken to wearing black silk
dresses, beautifully tailored, and with a glove-like fit.
Emily chuckled suddenly, remembering the moment
last night, at their family gathering. Her mother had
come into the sitting-room very conscious of a new
frock, and Will had whispered, loudly, behind his hand,
"Some class to the cows in our pasture!" Her mother
had purred in delight, amidst their laughter, and, somehow, they were all young again, in the friendly family
circle at Cookstown. Only now the circle included Arthur, and the girls.

Thinking of Arthur, a little frown crowded her eyes.
He was working too hard. He had had no respite for
years. He was too intense. Since that last trip, when
they had been out West, he seemed more tired than
ever. Whiter . . . strained. He had promised her,
however, that after this big meeting he would take a
few weeks off for a real holiday. Perhaps they might
yet get up to Manitoulin for some fishing.

Arthur moved to the centre of the stage with his
committee. He towered over the others, the light shining on his fair hair, his calm and gentle face. And yet
. . . Emily, who had listened to him hundreds of
times, sensed now an apprehension in his bearing. She
leaned forward, subconsciously frightened, tensing herself for the moment when he would begin to speak.

She knew something was wrong when he stood up,
and she paled, watching him. He was obviously nervous, standing with his hand on the table as if afraid
to leave it. His apprehension conveyed itself to the
audience and all about Emily, people shuffled uncom-

fortably. Her heart began to thud as she realized that
something was troubling Arthur. Usually, he swung
into his talk with a naturalness that caught at the
imagination of his listeners; now he was groping for
words, speaking as if his mind were on other things.

"This meant so much to him," worried Emily. "He's
been working too hard. He wanted this to be a success
so badly. If only he would let go . . ."

But Arthur fought on to the end, until even he could
feel the listlessness of the audience. He sat down heavily and bowed his head in his hands, as the people rose
to sing the last hymn.

Pushing against the crowds as they streamed out,
Emily worked her way to the front of the hall and
across the empty space before the orchestra pit, towards the stage-door at the side. As she went she could
hear the murmured comments. "What's there about him
that's so good?" And another: "He may have been all
right for the counties—but you expect something more
in Toronto."

Eyes smarting, face burning, she pushed back the
heavy curtains, to find Arthur on a couch, his eyes
closed, and the committee in anxious consultation.

It proved to be typhoid; probably contracted, the
doctors said, from a mosquito bite.

Emily nursed him for weeks, for Arthur was danger-
ously ill. The strain under which he had been working
for years had lowered his resistance. The doctor came
once or twice every day, and there was a trained nurse
with him constantly.

Financial worries became frightening, and the brunt
of them fell upon Emily. The Church Parochial Mission
Society, struggling against financial losses for some

years, wrote regretting that they must curtail their Mission work. In spite of the fact that their plans to send him to Australia were practically completed, they had been forced, unhappily, to cut their staff to a minimum. They would have to terminate their arrangement with the Rev. Arthur Murphy. Emily tucked the letter inside her desk, and said nothing to Arthur, until he was stronger.

Somehow she managed to keep on with her writing throughout his illness. The *National Monthly* paid her well, and clamoured for as much material as she could give them. The fact that she must write under the difficult conditions of her home life somehow gave her a greater power, and she found that her ideas flowed fully and easily from her pen. She began to write far into the night, when Arthur was in restless sleep. The days were pyramided with work; but, praise be, as midnight approached, there were precious quiet hours, when she could sit at her untidy desk, and write, and write, and write.

The time came when Arthur was up for a few hours each day—pale and exhausted, fretting terribly at the cessation of his income and at the unpaid bills. The Mission Society had sent him $500, with their sympathies, to help cover the cost of his illness, but with nothing coming in they were facing apparently insurmountable debts. He strained against his weakness, and planned every day, new work, new enterprises.

Then Emily went down with the typhoid. It struck her with terrible force, and, as is often the case with healthy people lacking many body toxins, she was very ill indeed. For weeks she lay in hospital, hardly conscious, but in her convalescence, propped on her pil-

lows, she wrote "The Diary of a Typhoid Patient". The
cheque it evoked helped with her hospital bills.

III

Up once more, a pale and thinner Emily returned
to the house on Wright Avenue, where a pale and thinner Arthur was making arrangements to carry on more
Missions. He could not, the doctors said, undertake
work that was too heavy. He must avoid the larger
towns, and preach in smaller communities where the
strain would not be so great. It was questionable,
whether he could handle even that. One could not, they
warned him, pour out one's energies for years without
facing just the risk he had taken—collapse from a sudden attack, too overwhelming in its after-effects to be
quickly mastered.

Emily, still weak and tremulous, wrote her regular assignments for the magazine. She had been appointed
women's editor, and the work entailed a great many
letters to readers, in addition to her regular columns.
But she enjoyed it, and found in it freedom from the
too-pressing problems of her daily life.

She had more time than ever with Doris, and spent
many hours on park benches in the sun, on doctor's orders. Happy memories crowded back, as they fed the
squirrels in High Park, or coaxed the friendly pigeons
. . . memories of Arthur and herself in the forests of
Tanus, eating their rusks like Canadian squirrels.
Watching Doris laboriously climb the low trees, she
saw her again in the arms of a laughing sailor who had
run so nimbly aloft with the child, on one of their visits
to the English navy . . . Doris must continue dancing

lessons too—lessons which had been started in the Golden Hall at Homburg, when the little rough-and-tumble girl from Ontario had learned her first steps under the glittering, mirrored walls, among classes of Italian, French, English and Spanish children. . . .

On autumn afternoons, when Doris had been particularly good, they wandered through the toylands in down-town stores. Clerks grew to look for the fair child, and her mother, who both gazed at the dolls with the same delight. As the afternoon sun settled low over the rambling city on its half-moon of harbour, the two stepped into the dusk, to ride home in the slow-moving old horse cars.

And so to bed, and sweet, sweet dreams, little maid!

On a morning in November, 1902, Emily noted a feverish flush on her little girl's cheek, and laid her hand tenderly against it. Hot! burning hot!

The doctor diagnosed the trouble as diphtheria, but assured the frightened Emily that with proper care the child should be all right. There was no need, he felt, to summon Arthur back from the village of Beeton, where he was holding one of his first Missions since his collapse. They would watch the child. She was in perfect physical health normally, and had plenty of resistance to fight the malady.

Emily tortured herself with fear, but tried to master it, feeling that much of it was due perhaps to her own weakness. She seldom left the child's side but, with the nurse, watched every breath, or busied herself with the endless details inherent in caring for diphtheria patients.

Doris, in her fever, was endlessly demanding. Emily sat, hour after hour, comforting her with the child-talk she and Doris loved; singing to her; holding her small hand tightly, fiercely.

On a darkening afternoon, on November 23rd, the doctor looked worried. Complications were threatening. They were the dread of diphtheria. So far this case had been in the clear, but now, suddenly, his patient was slipping.

Doris whispered something through her choking throat. No one knew what she wanted, except her mother. Emily knew. It was Doris' word for the old Christmas lullaby.

Low and gently she began to croon—over and over and over. Then the song broke. Emily lifted startled eyes, intuitively, to where the doctor stood, fingers on the little one's pulse. With a terrible cry she sank to her knees beside the bed, her arms flung, futilely, across the small form; her head buried by the heart that had stopped beating.

Later she wrote the telegram to Arthur: *"Doris just died. Come. Membraneous croup. Emily.*

Arthur came. The telegram was still in his pocketbook, and Emily put it away with the papers in her desk. It was there when she died; and I have it before me now.

Together they comforted the overwhelming grief of the girls, and together they went for the second time to Cookstown with a small coffin. The old home had been destroyed by fire but the pasture field, where Emily had raced in laughter as a child, was there, now a carefully tended village cemetery. The rectangle of earth was hollowed, facing the luminous Caledon hills, and husband and wife stood, hand in hand, to hear the triumphant prayers of their faith cover the dreadful knocking of brown earth on a white box.

It was a grief from which Emily never fully recovered. Years later, returning to visit Cookstown, she wrote:

"I dread going out to the cemetery, and yet I long to go. It was to visit this place that I have come across the continent; but I never told anybody. And now that I am here, I dally indoors and laugh. Presently I will go out; but I would rather be alone then. There are two small graves out there, and the sight of them will sting my dull ache into torture. This is why I dally and am gay. Gaiety and grief are the extremes that meet. . . . The small girl who occupies one of these graves had asked me to sing to her of 'the little Lord Jesus asleep in the hay', and while I sang, she too, fell asleep. She did not hear the last lines, unless the angels sang them to her when she woke again. Or maybe old Luther who wrote the hymn, finished it himself for her. I have often wondered about it.

"And once she worked a little motto with thread on cardboard. It contained all the ethics she had been taught—'Be Good'. Afterwards I found this pitiful thing among her toys and had it framed. It hangs where I can see it every day. It is the summary of my creed. I know other and longer ones; but they may all be reduced to these words. After all, creeds do not differ; it is only the people. It is a pity—even a mistake, that Christianity does not permit our burning cedarwood, honey cakes and a measure of barley for a sweet savour to our dead. It seems heartless just to look and turn away—perhaps forever."

IV

Back in Toronto, the Murphys tried to pick up the life they had known; but it proved impossible for many reasons. The added grief of their child's death affected Arthur's frail health, so that the doctors insisted that both he and Emily should move away from Ontario, preferably to the Western plains.

A few years previously Arthur had purchased a small, unsurveyed timber-limit, in the confines of Jackfish Creek and Swan River, in Manitoba, about two days' journey north of Winnipeg. The family physician urged Arthur to take up work on the timber-limit, so that he could be in the open as much as possible. Such a life was imperative.

It seemed a logical idea to Arthur and Emily, and plans were made accordingly; but the family were very much upset at the change. The Murphys pointed out the wonderful prospects in the new provinces; the new opportunities Emily would have for her writing.

Emily's mother was greatly distressed. She had been patient over the other moves but could no longer contain her anxiety. With her background of traditional security in home life, she was panic-stricken at the sight of her elder daughter tearing up the roots of her home again, and leaving for the wilderness of the West; taking the girls away from their school to goodness knows what dreadful place; encouraging Arthur to leave his influential friends to traipse out to a wilderness full of foreigners and Indians. Her final, dire prediction was: "And mark my words, Kathleen will grow up and marry an Indian!"

Arthur went out first, and bought a house in Swan

River, as being the most suitable settlement near his timber-limits, in which the family could live. Emily and the girls packed, seemingly, for weeks.

On the last night in her Toronto home she sat to write on top of a huge up-ended trunk. She was turning her back on her own world, which had collapsed about her. She would be glad to be free of this house and its insistent memories of Doris. She must turn to the new life ahead in the unknown West. She had taken one trip across the Dominion with Arthur on his Mission tour, but there had been little opportunity to see much of the people, or the lands beyond the railways and the cities. She realized how all-pervading would be the change in her life.

The house was hollow and echoing. The relatives had gone home; the family was asleep. Praise be, there was an hour in which she could write. This was the end of a phase; and there could be no turning back.

"To move means a review of your whole life," she wrote: "Inside one little hour you laugh, swell with pride, cry, grovel with humility, and burn with indignation as the fingers of still-born projects, dead joys or foolish frolics reach out and touch you from the past. . . . There are compensations, though. Things get cleaned up. You lose fifteen pounds of absolutely useless flesh. There is the secret and blissful consciousness of removing mountains and making things happen."

Removing mountains and making things happen. In saying farewell to one phase of her life, she was hailing the next, with a phrase which was to prove her fundamental *motif* in all the years ahead.

PART II

New Horizons

CHAPTER I

How unfortunate are the ones who live in the
Eastern provinces. Existence there is only
canned life. We of the West, belong to the elect
few.

JANEY CANUCK.

I

SLOWLY, persistently, their train nosed its way
northward through the province of Manitoba—
named for its Indian original, *Manitou napa,* "Land
of the Great Spirit."

For two wretched days, and two equally wretched
nights, heading north of Winnipeg, Emily and her
family sat in the close and airless coaches, watching
their new horizons wheel by. Between them they
identified their travelling companions—a judge on
circuit: a fur dealer: lumber-jacks: a peddling Hebrew:
a woman with a brand-new baby going home; inves-
tors from the United States; railway officials on con-
truction work, and a couple of contractors.

At Portage La Prairie and Dauphin the conductor
obligingly held the train for them while they finished
gobbling their meal. For the rest, they grabbed thick

sandwiches when they could, and sipped scalding coffee in thick mugs.

Somewhere over the sky-line, Arthur promised them, was the settlement of Swan River. In the middle of it was a house, unfinished as yet; but paid for. Nothing much—but their own.

Towards this minute speck the somnolent rhythm of the train was bearing them. Most of the stations were tiny wooden boxes, with a cluster of simple dwellings about them. Some of them had logs piled so high beside them that, from the train windows, they hid the sky. Most of the villages had sprung up in the past eighteen months. Along this new line of the Canadian Northern Railway were Indian names painted to the cross-pieces and nailed to posts at the stations, names which Emily sounded aloud, listening to their music: Minitonas, Mistatim, Kinistino. Or descriptive names like Birch River, Crooked River, Pine River, Riding Mountain. Or important names like Kitchener, Durban, Emerson, Mafeking, Roosevelt, Gladstone.

At a weary midnight the train lurched to a stop, the door was flung open and the four Murphys stepped onto the wooden platform of Swan River.

There was no one to welcome them. They were strangers, utterly alone. The girls sank onto their bags while Arthur went to clear their trunks from the baggage-car. Emily stood beside her daughters, tired, but responsive to the sweetness of the air. Short and rather thick-set, she made an indomitable silhouette against the yellow windows of the station.

The engine panted beside her, its white smoke jerking into the air. Huddled forms sagged in the train windows, asleep through the brief stop. About them the low roof-tops of the settlement clustered along the track and the slender threads of the railway pointing still northward into the darkness.

Small, rough, isolated, was the settlement, but above and around it, infinitudes of time and space curved beneath the blazing stars. Subconsciously Emily sensed the distances beyond this cuddled group of houses, this noisy engine. Here was the immediate minutiae of daily living, set in a new world of eternal beckoning. Mysterious, hidden from her, lay the trails and forests she was to know so well. Out under the brooding silences men and women of every nationality moved in the lonely circles of their home lights. She was to know hundreds of them; to interpret them to the world she had left behind.

Emily Murphy, crusader, straightened her tired back. With an indrawn breath, and lifted chin, she saluted the future.

II

The path led along wooden sidewalks pocked with holes to a dirty hotel, a room with a sad-coloured carpet and a looking-glass that distorted their faces. They slept, Emily noted in her diary, with some pestilential insects, un-Christian in temper, and carnivorous in habit.

The first morning opened to a meal served on a cloth which she described as a map of the world done with washes of yellow, brown and blue. "The tea is a copperas-tasting decoction. The steak chews like the pneumatic tire of a bicycle, and I expect to see the boarders die on their chairs by my side."

Born in a village that was typical of old Ontario, Emily found herself now, in the beginnings of her new life, in a settlement which was the pattern of all Western communities at the turn of the century.

They mushroomed in the wake of the railroad, fastened around mines; formed the core of newly-opened territory. The houses were hideous in their inexorable utility. Stiff and ugly, the false fronts on the buildings of the main street reared blind windows over the emptiness behind. Hotels and stores were finished, outside and in, with embossed and painted tin. In the stores, Emily found, you could get anything —except the article you sought at that identical moment.

The Murphys' house was white, with a sunset painted on the peaked front. In it were three bedrooms, parlour, study, dining-room, kitchen and maid's room. When they moved in there was no lath or plaster on the walls, because there were no plasterers available. The paper was put on over stretched cheesecloth, and every time one of them leaned against it, they could see daylight through the chinks of the outer shell.

But men were soon at work, and with the Murphys' furniture brought from the East, the plain house soon became a home. Emily loved the lively wood fires that blazed throughout the long winter months, and the luxury of placing great logs in them to roar up the chimneys.

The girls were sent to Havergal College in Winnipeg, a branch of the Toronto Havergal. Arthur started to work on plans for developing his timber-limit over sixty miles away—plans which meant his absence for weeks at a time. There was not much personal friendship for Emily among the people of the settlement, although she soon knew them all, and most of their troubles. Her own best friend and confidante, she said, was the milkman.

Lacking individual affiliations, she viewed the district and its people collectively. Soon, before her ardent and eager eyes, the folk of Swan River and the territory round about became a panorama of absorbing interest. She learned to know the homesteaders by name, and loved to watch them ploughing the virgin lands of their farms. She recognized the lumber-jacks in their river boots and gay sashes; the English chappies in riding leggings and peaked caps; long-haired Indians who lived in tepees and tents at the outskirts of the village. There were Doukhobors from neighbouring villages, wearing flounced jackets and wide-seated trousers; Germans, Ukrainians, Swedes, Frenchmen, Icelanders.

Everyone in Swan River seemed to be in real estate. Business opportunities never ran out, for the villagers sold to immigrants, to each other, "and periodically the loan companies would swoop down and give a helping hand."

There were five churches serving the three hundred souls who lived in the village, as well as the students from the theological college, who came each summer to take, according to Emily, the spiritual pulse of the people. "Our mission boards must really make an endeavour to spend the money contributed by the very generous people back East."

With this multi-coloured life of a new country as background, she filled her own days with energy and interest.

III

She was reviewing books for *The Winnipeg Tribune*, and every week the baggage-man tossed a bundle of them on the platform. For a period of nine months, Evelyn counted her total—one hundred and ninety books—or an average of twenty-one a month.

The books filled all the shelves and table-tops and began to creep up the sides of the study. As each book was reviewed, Emily cut out the published notice and pasted it into the back of the book.

She wrote in a small study off the bedroom upstairs. She loved to work up here, and it became increasingly difficult to get her to bed, for she utilized the peaceful hours around midnight which she had discovered in the later years in Toronto.

Down in the sitting-room was the large desk Arthur had set up for her. There, as a natural follow-up of her close association with Arthur in his ministry, she helped with the book-keeping for the timber-limits, and the planning of supplies from Winnipeg.

Her inherited liking for buying in large quantities had now a new impetus, for Emily undertook to handle the buying of supplies for the men on Arthur's timber-limit. This was in the tempo she loved. She made occasional trips to Winnipeg to select many of the supplies herself. Arthur bought the heavy equipment, but Emily handled the rest.

She became an expert in lumber-jacks' outfits, judging the most satisfactory qualities to buy in moccasins, rubber boots lined with red eiderdown, gay lombard stockings with the coloured cord running round the knees, corduroy knickers, mackinaw trousers and

fleece-lined shirts. For outer wear she bought sweaters
and sheep-lined jackets of tan duck, caps of blue felt
lined at the back with fur, two pairs of mittens for each
man, one of wool, and one of unlined moosehide. The
men, she found, did not mind paying well for their
clothing; but it must be of the best quality.

For the "grub pile," she bought quarters of beef,
sacks of rolled oats, rice, beans and flour; large bags
of raisins, prunes, peaches and syrup, barrels of sugar,
tins of coffee, chests of tea, sacks of potatoes, crates of
condensed milk, boxes of tinned tomatoes, tubs of
butter, pails of lard, and plenty more. "They keep open
house in the camp," she wrote, "to the music of knives
and forks."

This lavish ordering suited her dramatic and generous temperament. Here was housekeeping with a grand
flourish; here was living and reckoning on a scale
that was worth while!

But, night after night, her work in her home and
the timber-limit finished for the day, she sat in the
glow of her lamp in the little study upstairs, and
listened to the silences before she began to write her
own sketches of the daily routine. Afterwards, these
were to appear as *Janey Canuck in the West,* one of
her most enchanting and successful books. Now they
were just the continuation of her day-to-day notes.

On winter evenings she could see far across the
moonlit snowy wastes and hear the crying of wolves,
like souls in purgatory. The village was so silent that
often she would feel as if she had dropped into a pit
of silence, seeming to hear beyond it the far-off call of
the city. With letters on her desk from sympathetic
friends back East, mourning her exile in the wilder-

ness, she wrote one evening that she was lonely sometimes for the pushing crowds, the velvety sweep of
feet, the whir of the automobile, the long rows of
houses "and all else that I once hated. But I am beginning to learn how much I can drop out of life without
being unhappy. I find almost as much joy in losing
my knowledge as in acquiring it. The ologies and
osophies, the big causes, cultures and cants are not
so sweet to my taste, as the life in these new and
naked lands."

IV

So, as the weeks passed she found a healing of the
deep hurts of the past, and a fresh exhilaration she
had not known before.

There was, first, the garden that belted her house,
in which blossomed pinks, and pansies; nasturtiums
("chintz-faced, sprawling things") sweet peas, lilies,
poppies, morning glories.

Beyond the little village lay the trails that she loved
to follow. Always she carried a book with her, but she
never read it, for there was no time. As the seasons
swept over this virgin land, she walked or rode, watching and noting minutely the physical changes of nature.
With her eye for wide pictures, she revelled in the
cloth of gold that was spread for autumn; the glittering
snow wastes of winter; the time of singing birds when
the land was a paradise of blossoms; and the full hot
bloom of summer. "Surely the West *is* golden," she
chanted, "the sky, flowers, wheat, hearts."

At this time the Murphys normally kept five horses,
three mounts for Emily and the girls, and two for
Arthur to drive. He had bought a nearby farm and

Emily's rides of the prairie trails became a daily adventure.

She always rode astride, "For there's no sense," she said, "in a woman hanging to a clothes peg on the side of a horse." Her habit was meticulously tailored from heavy and sturdy cloth. When she swept the trails with her girls behind her, blonde and dark hair streaming to the wind, Emily Murphy knew well the attractive picture they made.

But there were hundreds of lonely rides, when Arthur and the girls were away and she explored her kingdom by herself. She came to a little cemetery one afternoon, and found a piece of paper tacked to a rough-cut wooden cross. Under the brilliant skies she stooped to read a new Canadian's lament for his bride, tapped out on a borrowed typewriter, with one clumsy finger.

"No more thou are, and none here are so to me in kindness. Such hearted breast, such lovely voice, no more on earth be found."

She took the words home in her memory and wrote them down for others to savour their tender poignancy.

During these rides among the homestead farms she recognized and put to words the "Song of the Wheat":

"Who so great as to pen the song of the wheat?

"Who can sum up its epic?

"From its sibilant swish on the wide-flung steppes, to its whir and crunch under the wheels of the mill, wheat sums up the tale of the race. Like love, wheat rules the court, the camp, the grove. It makes or breaks the world of men. Wheat is blood. Wheat is life. Who can sing its song?

"In China rice is life. In Canada life is wheat. We should throw wheat on our brides."

But even as she joined the surge of life that was the West, she warned of the woe to come.

"None of the farmers hereabouts have yet dreamed of putting manure on the land. They are not *growing* wheat; they are *mining* it. They are using the accumulated fertility of centuries and making no return. But Nature keeps strict tally with them and their draft will sooner or later be dishonoured and their future prosperity discounted."

V

She was absorbed in Arthur's adventures with his timber-limit. He had brought to his new life the same intensity of purpose which had made him so successful as a preacher; but as he jumped into it "green," there were many worrisome and troubled weeks.

Arthur's timber-limit was near the border of Saskatchewan, and a year after their arrival, in the winter of 1904, he took a cut of 700,000 feet of spruce. It was about sixty miles from the Swan River in a direct line, but to take the logs down the Swan to the settlement meant, with the turns of the river, about one hundred and fifty miles of journeying.

Arthur and Emily, poring over their maps, developed a plan. Jackfish Creek ran through their limit, and they had heard of the heavy rise in the creek when the spring freshet was on. On this flood they should be able to float the logs down into Swan River at a point only fourteen miles away. The lumber-jacks agreed that it was an idea worth trying.

That was a slow season, and in spring there was no freshet. The whole winter's cut of timber was locked in the limit, with apparently no way to get it out.

Arthur and the fifty men who had been cutting in his limit all winter, set to work to build dams in the creek. Perhaps by waiting patiently until each stretch of water before a dam filled up, they could float the logs down, step by step.

This again proved impossible. On a spring evening, Emily opened the door to a despondent Arthur, returning with his lumber-jacks. Each of them must be paid $3 a day for the weeks of work; and this, moreover, represented only a small part of the expense involved in the work. There was no chance of getting the timber out for another year.

The outlook was dark. Arthur prayed about it, and canvassed the district for a solution. Finally, a hardware firm in Swan River, named Ashdown and Bossons, offered $35,000 for all the cut of logs in Jackfish Creek, and the timber-limit as well.

This was the first hurdle. Arthur now covered the province and became expert at timber cruising. He could outwalk Indians in heavy timber, and learned to know as much about it as anyone up there. On a ranging trip in Saskatchewan with an Indian and a white man named Copperwaite, they became lost, and wandered for days; but they passed under magnificent trees, and once safely home again, Arthur went to Ottawa to make a tender for the land. His offer was accepted, and with a partner on a 50-50 basis he went into it the following winter. With him were ten men and a cook; and the temperature was

50 below zero. For one hundred miles they cut through heavy timber; and in the spring, Arthur sold his share of it for $86,000.

The excitement of real estate, too, was so heady that neither Arthur nor Emily could pass it by. The railway was pushing steadily north, and around Carrot River in Saskatchewan was land which Arthur felt to be the finest in Canada. He bought up sections of land at $7 an acre in the country near the present town of Melfort. In all, he bought 8,000 acres, selling it soon after at $14 an acre. A few years later the same land sold at $100 an acre.

VI

Besides the book-keeping and buying which she did for the timber-limits, Emily was as interested in Arthur's management, and as eager to see everything, as she had been in their early days of parochial duties. Once, in the depth of winter when log-cutting was at its busiest season, she journeyed with him to the logging-camp in the heart of their private forest.

The thermometer stood at 48 degrees below zero the morning that he tucked her into the sleigh. It was a veritable bed of hay, rugs, furs and pillows. Emily, wrapped to her eyes in furs, clambered in with difficulty—and away they raced over the beaten trails, or across fluffy snowfields of dead white, where, Emily noted, "the wind brushed drifts into fantastic sculpturing." As they sped, they stopped only for occasional shots at a coyote, moose, wolves. Good companion always, Emily was ever ready to heave herself out of the sleigh and stand at the horses' heads, while Arthur tried his luck.

When, at noon, they stopped at a lonely shack to get warmed and eat a meal, they found the Tibble family inside. Thirteen children stood round-eyed in fascination as Emily and Arthur peeled off their layers of clothes and cooked their mid-day meal. When they left, Mrs. Tibble shyly presented the smiling visitor with a tatted collar; and Emily had promised to send her a bunch of literature monthly.

As the short afternoon darkened they were still travelling the eternities of snow; north and still north. At seven o'clock Arthur turned his horses into Vosnesenia, one of the Doukhobor villages of the province, set with its one-storied houses on either side of a wide street.

Out poured the friendly men and women, literally carrying the half-frozen Emily into a white-washed living-room. It was decorated with dadoes of brown and yellow, and hung with calendars and coloured pictures. Flowers filled the deep window-sills.

Here was the simple friendliness to which Emily always so gladly responded. She laughed with the women as they took off her coats and sweaters, her fur cap and extra clothes, and piled them in a mound. She cooked with enthusiasm the food from their grub-box carried in from the sleigh, and ate it, smiling happily at Arthur and their encircling audience. She divided strong cough-drops among the children, until at last they were quartering them, or passing around thin morsels for comradely sucking.

Fed and warm, she and Arthur must sit in state by the big stove while the girls of the village in their brilliant costumes of purples, reds and greens, bowed themselves into the room, and sang for their visitors—

weird and vagrant airs originating generations before in old Russia.

Their feather mattresses were as soft, she said, as marshmallows, but so short that they only held the body and not one's legs. Each one was set on a wooden bench, about five feet wide, which ran all round the room.

At last they were alone, with only a woman and a baby to sleep at their feet, a boy across the room, and a baby in a square box, hung like a bird-cage from the ceiling.

But there was no peace yet! The women of the house returned to examine Emily's underclothing in wonder. Dark heads bent over her golf skirt with the brilliant plaid lining; they rubbed her petticoats between their fingers, comparing notes on its weaving. They were delighted with the ribbon running through her lingerie, but shocked and amused at her corset. "They nudged each other, grinned and shrugged their shoulders . . . Then they showed me what they wore. Taking all things into consideration, I wouldn't exchange."

Next day, she and Arthur drove still farther north, hour after hour, and spent the next night in a Doukhobor lumber-camp.

There was so much to see that they were late in leaving and darkness fell while they were still on the trail. They were nine hours that day travelling by sleigh through the open distances, with the temperature 50 below zero.

Arthur tried to light the lantern as a foot-warmer, but the oil had frozen and refused to ignite. He put the flask of brandy wine to Emily's lips, but they froze on the metal. So he bundled her out to walk for a bit.

Heavy and clumsy in her sub-zero wrappings, her moccasined feet cut on the frozen roots of the trees, she staggered along, getting wrathier every minute. The horses walked faster than she could, and Arthur wouldn't wait. Between her anger and her exercise she did get warmer. Huddled in her blankets once more, she planned to be hateful for the rest of the way, and did not speak to Arthur.

But, suddenly, she forgot her rage, for there on the trails were the streamers she herself had made in Swan River!

Now they were on a trail that was barely three months old, cut by their own men through the heavy timber. Andrew, the Indian, had tied the streamers to show the muskegs. Over her head was a filigree of bare branches, in a forest of towering, spear-headed spruce. "This is a log-road, and these are all your own trees . . . miles of them! Look up, sweetheart!"

She recorded, "Only a few twists in the road till I hear voices, and quicker than I can tell it, two lumber-jacks have me out of the sleigh and into a wide, low cabin that is bright and warm, where there is an odour of fresh wheaten bread, and where a man moves among the pots and pans, with the air of one conducting a religious ceremony."

VII

She awoke to a strange world of men, set in the isolation of timbered acres that seemed to stretch in long, straight lines across the world. She was, however, as much at home as in any spot she had found yet. She chatted by the hour with the cook in the comfortable log cabin where the men ate—a cabin with wide, sunny windows. There were heavily-stocked shelves, and rows of red-skinned onions, hams and bacons pendant from the rafters.

She found a horse that pleased her, and rode the trails to watch the men felling trees, rolling the logs with canthooks up the spiked inclines, or piling them on huge skidways ready to send down to the river when the ice broke.

On a sunny noon, she came to a group of the men sitting round a fire, eating their lunch, and gladly accepted their invitation to eat with them.

Perched on a log, her short legs dangling, the fur hat close about her merry face, she ate "with transcendant delight" and an enormous appetite their fried pork, bread, butter and syrup, and drank great quantities of tea.

When the men had finished and were away to their work, she still sat, a solitary figure, staring into the fire, poking the big logs and watching the changing embers. About her curved the spires and arches and pillars of the forest. She sat listening for a few moments to the sound of the trees, "like the swish of silken skirts on a stairway; like the wash on a far-off shingle; like the slur of stealthy footsteps."

She wrote down the memory of it in her journal, sitting that evening in the cook's camp, with half a dozen of the men gathered about the stove, yarning in the easy half-languid manner of people who are resting after hours spent in outdoor work.

In camp at the Sunday service she sang "Jerusalem

the Golden" lustily, revelling in the setting. She was the first woman, white, red or black who had travelled the trail to the camp, and as she bowed her head over her hands to repeat the prayers of her faith, her mind must have flashed back to other times and other places. Arthur preached that day—as she had heard him preach in country churches, in cathedrals and on the sea. To the men who for months had been carving out these wilderness roads, he spoke of the great path-finders of the Canadian woods—Pierre Radisson, Groseillers, Mackenzie, Hudson and MacDonald.

"The Padre has not preached for months," she wrote. "He is resting his throat. Perhaps this is why the subject took such a hold of him. Be that as it may, some way or other, this little company of men seemed to move him strangely, and he, in turn, moved them to tears."

VIII

They lived in Swan River for four years, and came to feel that the world which stretched so wide and free to the horizons was all theirs. The sense of creating new territories, of merging with the peoples of the world who, somehow, were all neighbours here, was inspiring. Emily's insatiable interest in people gave her the gift of friendship with them. It did not matter if they could not talk the same language. They were all human, and a smile was potent conversation.

She found a new invigoration in her writing. The ill-printed little book, *Janey Canuck Abroad,* was winning praise from many critics, and a publisher was interested already in her coming book *Janey Canuck in the West.* She was writing for magazines in the East, and enjoying her book-reviewing assignments. Much of what she wrote she disliked, and there's a family story anent the afternoon she took great stacks of her work down to the Swan River for the men who were blasting its banks, to use as wadding in their powder shots. "I'm really becoming a rising author!" she told the girls that night.

They were very much a part of the village life, and when they left, two community buildings were there because of them. Arthur had presented a skating-rink for the young people. Emily, as she sat in her study at night, could see a large yellow light winking across the river—the new Victorian Order of Nurses' hospital. It had been brought to Swan River through Emily's efforts, and it is important in this chronicle as it marks her first community project. There were times, watching its activity, seeing how much it meant in the lives of the people for miles around, when Emily wondered at the ease with which the hospital had become a reality. Just a sound basis in need, a lot of agitation and an unflagging persistency—and there it stood!

They gave much to Swan River, and, in return, Emily gained a great deal that enriched the years ahead. She had come to know intimately the young West and the heterogeneous peoples who formed its population. Having seen their life so closely, having experienced herself many of their problems and hardships, and having learned to love the lusty country, and adopted it,—even as they, she developed a sympathetic understanding which surely helped to fit her for the unique post she was to fill. Where else in

Canada could be found a woman of similar intelligence and training who had touched so nearly the life of the early homesteader?

The years at Swan River were good, and Emily loved the home she and Arthur had founded there. A river of thought to and from the world outside flowed past her desk. Arthur was vigorous and happy. They had more money than ever before, and this entailed a generosity of living which was in the manner she loved. She enjoyed the healthy outdoor life, the riding, the woods, the widening spaces.

Time and again she noted her contentment, coming home of an evening in a radiant glow, to revel in a good dinner and stretch herself afterwards on the rug before the fire, blissfully absorbing its caressing warmth. Behind the door stood a barrel of apples, red-skinned, white-fleshed, sweet-blended. In the corner lay a pile of the newest books from her publishers, awaiting her exploration. Ah . . . thought Emily, they are good, these long winter evenings!

But Arthur, true pioneer, began to grow restless. This part of the world was explored, he felt. It was becoming too well settled. What lay farther west?

What lay, he wondered, in the new province of Alberta? There was land which had only just joined the Dominion of Canada, becoming a province in 1904. What was life like there? Would Emily like to go and see?

Emily watched his mind move in the old, familiar direction. There was no use arguing with him, threatening, or beseeching him.

"I have been observing the Padre's head," she wrote. "On the spot phrenologists have located inhabitiveness

—instead of a bump, he has a hollow. He has sold everything saleable, and wants to have a look at Edmonton."

And later,

"The Padre has decided to live in Edmonton, and I have decided to remain in Swan River. We will compromise on Edmonton."

CHAPTER II

Open Trails

I tell you there is magic in this land, and you
can hear unsung things. My heart is on tip-toe
for the reach of them.

JANEY CANUCK.

I

ON A HOT AFTERNOON in August, 1907, Emily
Murphy stood in the doorway of an Edmonton
store, watching the crowds that surged down Jasper
Avenue. She wore a white starched frock flaring to the
ground, and a white sailor hat, tied beneath her chin
with a long veil. A pink sunshade, tilted against the
sun, shed a radiance about her.

Jasper Avenue, lying under heat that rose like vapour
from the pavement, was worth watching so intently.
It had been a morass of mud three years before, over
which horses strained. A scant century since it was a
trail, snaking to the fort set high on the banks of the
great Saskatchewan River—a trail beaten by Indians
bringing skins of buffalo, marten, lynx, fox, bear and
beaver which would be carried by the Gentlemen Adventurers of the Hudson's Bay Company to the shores
of Hudson Bay, and the markets of the world.

Just before Alberta joined the Confederation of
Provinces at the turn of the century, four thousand

people lived in Edmonton. Seven short years later, the city's population, joined with Strathcona across the river, was fourteen thousand. Ten thousand people a month, it was said, were pouring into the province and most of them came to, or passed through, the capital, one of the most cosmopolitan cities on the continent. Most of them trod the broad Jasper Avenue that lay where the trail had been; and to this great main stem of the West came Emily Murphy also, in her fortieth year.

Two-thirds of her life had already been passed on other roads. Now, for the twenty-odd years remaining to her, Jasper Avenue was to be her thoroughfare to depths undreamed in the lives of the people it served. These pavements she was to tread in exhilaration and in despair; to cover lightly in vibrant health, to measure slowly in weakness. At times she was to sweep down the Avenue feeling mistress of her world; again she was to find in the contact of its people comfort for a heart's load almost too heavy to bear.

But now, as she stood there, in the rosy aureole of her little parasol, the Avenue presented to her fascinated eyes a place of wonder, where met Cree and Christian, trader, trapper, cowboy, judge, soldier and senator, engineer and explorer, priest, professor and pioneer—each doing his part, as Emily was to do hers, in the building of a great and growing city.

She watched a pow-wow of Indians in front of the Hudson's Bay store. They had received their treaty money yesterday, and were come from the nearby Reserve to pay their respects to the Governor of the Company. Among them were braves in scarlet paint, shells and ribbons, and men in red, green and purple. Subconsciously her mind formed phrases, moulding her impressions of foreigners in sheepskin coats and scarlet head wraps; negro porters and a row of sallow China-men, nuns—"little sisters in black with hearts of gold". There were vaudeville actresses with tawny hair and a direct manner, heavy-necked business men; horses and riders from the paper-chases; contractors moving camp; fifty dumping carts in line, besides drays with tents, groceries or blankets and hardware; cowboys keeping the cattle in line. There were coaches pulling out to Athabasca Landing in the north; settlers' carts for the Peace River; big drays for the British Columbia fruit districts.

It was a river of life which she was to know pro-foundly, a high flood-tide of young people in a new world; people from Japan, China, Russia, California, New Zealand. She contemplated it with rapture, and loved its violent extremes, its crudities; for under all, she sensed, lay the fabric of symbolism from the Old World.

Emily Murphy leaned forward intently, whispered passionately to the hurrying throngs:

"Learn to hope! Learn to rest! Learn to pray!"

II

She settled very quickly into the new life. She was busy finishing the last few chapters in the book of sketches she had written in Swan River, *Janey Canuck in the West*, published so successfully in 1910.

Word had travelled ahead, and Edmonton knew Mrs. Arthur Murphy as an author of note. She stepped into the gay and hospitable life in the new capital with delight. It was a happy change from the years she had just known, when there was little opportunity for the social camaraderie she loved so well.

"It's a great place, this Canadian West," she wrote. "It's a country of strong men, straight living, and hard riding. Tut, who wants to go to Heaven? . . . Too, we're very socially inclined with teas, tennis, 'mobiling, dancing, dining, and wild riding across the hills. When people are healthy and prosperous, they are instinctively hospitable and always in a big-handed, big-hearted way."

So many visitors of note passed through Edmonton, served as it was with three railroads, that there were many excuses for celebrations. Up at the new Government House, there was not always enough silverware for the larger receptions that were sometimes held. The ladies of Edmonton solved the problem easily. A number of them brought their own silverware—each piece marked with a distinguishing thread. Visitors to this surprising land may have noticed, without comment, the tiny strand of cotton tied about their forks and spoons. Did they guess the casual ease with which, the party over, guests picked out their own pieces, and toted them cheerfully home?

Filling the mammoth scrap-books with newspaper clippings of the Murphys' life began in earnest. Emily had faithfully kept all notes on Arthur's work and the reviews of her own books. Now there came page after page of receptions, dinners, luncheons. Through all of them pass Mrs. Arthur Murphy in a variety of notable costumes, relishing every minute.

When the Governor-General of Canada, Earl Grey, came a year or so after the Murphys had reached Edmonton, to lay the cornerstone for the new Legislative

Buildings, a great Ball was held in his honour in Thistle
Rink. It had been transformed with potted palms and
tiny Indian tepees around the dance floor for "sitting-
out" two-somes. It was Mrs. Arthur Murphy, "in white
lace with cream roses," who introduced the season's
debutantes to His Excellency—among them her own
Evelyn. During this period, in addition to the open
house the Murphys kept, Arthur and Emily were hosts
at two balls which were landmarks in the social tradition of the city. Hundreds of friends enjoyed the
Murphy hospitality in the lavish scale of those days.

Every Tuesday afternoon, Mrs. Murphy was "At
Home", with two kinds of cake and plates of small
sandwiches in readiness on the kitchen tables. To her
doors came the interesting young women who were, as
the years passed, to work with her in her social reforms.
There were young wives who had followed their husbands into new adventure; daughters of old-timers who
carried with them traditions that were still a-building.
Older women, too, had come with sons, or accompanied
their husbands in promotions to responsible positions.
All of them enjoyed meeting at Emily's home and, as
the years passed, worked with her in unceasing efforts
at reform.

Experienced in working with women through her
church affiliations, Emily knew, from the start, how
vitally important it was to any project to have the right
women leading it. One of her most effective natural
gifts was an aptitude, throughout her life, for getting
socially prominent women in the community to work
with her in bettering the general status of their sex.

With all this social interest, and in addition to her
writing, she still spent many days driving or riding over

the trails with Arthur. When they first came to Edmonton, he had planned to buy about four sections of land, and on them to create a home. He decided that the district about Clover Bar would be the ideal setting, but found nothing available under $80 an acre.

In any excursion about the Edmonton district the most notable aspect was its apparently lavish supply of coal. Nature was so generous in this valley of the Saskatchewan, that little boys could pick up pailfuls of the coal lying on the surface of the ground. It was, literally, kicking around underfoot.

Coal was selling at $5 a ton. Arthur learned that the actual cost of mining averaged $1 a ton.

The Murphys began to figure.

When Arthur found that it would take about $5,000 to put down a small shaft, Emily protested that he would be undertaking too great an expense. Arthur admitted cheerfully, "What I know about coal, you could put on a postage stamp. And what I don't know would fill volumes round the world . . . But still, it sounds like an idea to me!"

He bought land in a subdivision where coal was reported in a 6-foot seam, and paid $600 an acre.

But the shaft hadn't gone down more than 30 feet, before the men struck quicksands. Arthur had spent a lot of money on the shaft, but his jaw tilted at an angle that Emily knew. He fired his foreman and engaged another who eventually drilled through the quicksand, using a very expensive process. They reached coal about seventy feet down, and began to mine it. Arthur found he was spending more money than he had dreamed possible in putting up the tipple, screens, engines, boiler and cages for the mine. Moreover, he had to build a boarding-house for the men on his property.

Until there were entry corridors, or rooms opened up in the seam of coal, very few men could work at one time, and for many weeks the mine was only producing about a ton a day. The cost above ground was five times what the actual coal, as mined, was worth.

Then the price of coal dropped to $3 a ton, and Arthur realized that he must mine a hundred tons of coal a day to pay for his investment—a feat that was impossible until a year's work had been completed. He persisted, and, eventually, he was mining one hundred and fifty tons a day. The mine was named the Rosedale, and the Murphys had a man on the road selling their coal throughout the province.

The family liked to ride out to inspect their mine, Arthur and Emily with the team, each girl on her own mount. It was an exciting life, thought Emily, and eminently satisfying in spite of its worries. They knew a few weeks of exhilaration with, apparently, another battle won.

The Rosedale, however, had more cruel blows for its romantic owners. The coal petered out at four and a half feet, and the miners had to take out a foot and a half of solid clay. Heavy timbering costs followed. Then, one morning, the foreman discovered water to within twenty feet of the top of the shaft. By a miracle of good fortune no men had been down the mine the night before. Fifty feet of water had poured in over night. Arthur set two pumps to work for a fortnight but could not budge the water an inch. Government authorities condemned the mine.

The Murphys were mystified, until they realized that, as they were mining below the surface of the river, on the site of what is today the Highlands Golf Course, the river had entered the mine through some underground opening.

Arthur had been trying to pump up the river for two weeks!

Totting figures with Emily, Arthur estimated that he was the poorer by one hundred thousand dollars after that experience. But there were, of course, so many reasons for that failure; so many more why the next one should be successful.

He bought another mine with fifteen miles of coal, one mile wide, along Lake Wabamum, about fifty miles from Edmonton; and sold it a few years later for a handsome profit. However, he took his price in real estate, not cash.

Those were the boom days when many people lost their heads and their fortunes over land. Quick turnovers were the rule. Arthur bought and sold with the rest, making thousands; losing more.

III

Year by year Emily followed that impulse for exploring the country around her; for days at a time she would travel the open trails where, she said, "nothing met but the four winds; nothing passed but the clouds." Everywhere she went she dropped in casually to see the homesteaders, to hear what they were thinking and doing. While Arthur was about his business of land prospecting, Emily was absorbing information about the people of her new world.

She became good friends with the Mormons in southern Alberta, and wrote a series of articles in their de-

fence, for national magazines. People were accusing
the Mormons in Canada of plural marriages. Emily
wrote of these people with understanding and sympathy. One evening she attended a public meeting,
where, with Kathleen, she sat in the balcony expecting some exciting abuse as a result of her article, but
it was very dull. Later, a Woodstock minister, down in
Old Ontario, referring to her defence of the Mormons,
thundered in the *Sentinel-Review*, to Emily's delight:
"Mrs. Murphy is a person of poor intelligence, and very
ignorant."

She often visited the Roman Catholic schools, for
she knew the work that the nuns were doing so patiently with the Indian children of the districts. She
liked to play with the little ones and wrote many notes
on her hours with them. "It is good to rest in the shade
of the trees," she wrote one evening, "while these
chocolate-coloured babies jabber about me in soft
Cree, and finger my hair and clothes. Truly I am very
fortunate and have much fullness of pleasure."

The jails too, were a never-ending source of interest.
Wherever she was, somehow she always found time to
drop in on the local jail; perhaps to chat with some
prisoners and tell of her latest adventures in the outside world. There were always some who enjoyed talking to her, and who learned to look for her coming.

Her entrance into communities was made as if there
were unseen martial music about her. She was treated
as a guest of rare honour everywhere. So warm was
her smile, so direct her friendliness, so natural her interest that, year after year, the people offered her
their choicest experiences.

Thus, for instance, when she attended service in a

little Ruthenian church she was not left to sit in the body of the church, but was brought, with all honour, to sit beside the altar. She pasted a print of the church in her scrap-book. To us, it looks nothing but a bare frame building set on the bleak prairies. To Emily it harboured a miracle:

"I have always desired to see the mysterious sacrifice known as the 'elevation of the host', but now that I am an arm's stretch from the altar, I do not look, but cover my face with my hands. Only I see that dull ruby flame behind the man's ear when he takes the wafer, and the veins of his neck swell as if they hurt.

"But I look into the faces of the women and the men in the front line, who receive the sacred essence from the golden cup and golden spoon, and almost I can hear what their eyes are saying. What odds about low foreheads, thick lips and necks brown like the brown earth, when each has the god within? The Ruthenians—or Galicians, if you like the name better— may be a sullen folk of unstable and misanthropical temper. They may be uncouth of manner, and un- cleanly of morals, but I shall always think of them as on this day when I saw the strange glamour on their faces that cannot be described, except that it came from a marvellous song hidden in their hearts."

Sometimes, on these trips, she was with Arthur, or one of her women friends. Again, she was alone, on journalistic explorations to nearby centres which were springing up with startling rapidity. She was notable and remembered wherever she went, for her voice was deep, her laughter penetrating and infectious. She loved to set her enthusiasms rocketing off on others' minds; to see people sparkle in response to her vigour.

See her, on a typical jaunt, sitting in the office of the *Athabasca Journal,* up north of Edmonton, being interviewed by a very much impressed young editor. The interview was splashed on the front page of the *Journal* next day, closing with one of Emily's swash-buckling exhortations:

"And a parting word of advice. See to it that your city fathers don't linger around unnecessarily about the sewage, electric lights and street improvements. These things cannot be delayed without serious injury to the place. If they linger, don't hesitate to give them the same medicine as the croakers. Swat them hard, till they get busy and get out!" Exit Mrs. Murphy, with a slight swagger to her walk; a gleam in her eyes, and a growing sense of power. And then, at the door, a flashed smile, a wave of the hand that seemed to each of the staff watching her, intended particularly for him. They were hers from that moment.

It was the same vigorous enthusiasm for all things Western that made her open the door to an astonished Englishwoman with a comment that was to be published in England. For the Englishwoman was a journalist, much impressed by *Janey Canuck in the West.* On her Canadian trip she had made a special point of coming to meet Mrs. Murphy at her own home.

The address given her was 11011—88th avenue. Eleven thousand and eleven! The Englishwoman searched the little street for the rest of the houses, and blurted out her question as Emily opened the door: "If this is 11011—where are the other hundreds?"

"Oh, them? Going to be built!" cried Emily, and ushered her guest to the fireside to pour out her enthusiasms and belief in the country for a couple of hours. "They're going to be built!"

Of course, Emily!

IV

One of her best-loved memories was her trip to Grouard Landing in 1912, on commission by *Collier's Magazine* for a series of articles. Her invitation to attend Bishop Grouard's Jubilee was given by the Provincial Member in the Legislature for Peace River— Mr. Jim Cornwall. With Emily went one other woman and three other writers.

The trip took four or five days, although it was only one hundred and sixty miles north of Edmonton as the crow flies. They travelled by steamer down the Athabasca River, crossed a portage of fourteen miles, embarked on another steamer which carried them across Lesser Slave Lake to the northern shore, where the town of Grouard overlooks Buffalo Bay.

The boats were small and uncomfortable, but there was plenty to eat. The first night, after dinner, Emily paced the deck with her companion after facing a menu of macaroni and cheese, pork with beans, white fish, stewed tomatoes, escalloped corn, boiled potatoes, walnut pickles, catsup, soda biscuits, pumpkin pie, currant buns, cocoanut cake, cheese, stewed figs and coffee.

The Purser met them and, after polite generalities, said:

"My errand is to remind you, ladies, that there are sixteen bunks on this boat, and only eight mattresses.

"You will, of course, use your own blankets and pil-

THE MURPHYS IN SWAN RIVER, 1907.

EMILY, KATHLEEN AND EVELYN, EDMONTON, 1912

EMILY AS AN EARLY SAXON, ON MAJOR, EDMONTON HORSE SHOW, 1919

EMILY, AT A FANCY-DRESS PARTY IN EDMONTON, 1926, AS TOM MOORE, THE POET

lows, but I see you have not brought your own mattresses. On this boat are a group of priests travelling
north to Bishop Grouard's Jubilee, too, as you have
seen. . . . It would be wonderfully easy for you to
carry one, or even two, mattresses from the priests'
staterooms, for at this very minute the priests are saying their prayers on the lower deck.

"And believe me," he added, with what Emily described as a highly chivalrous manner, "you two ladies
have an unquestionable right to the mattresses, so that
I shall consider your act to be one of perfect propriety."

"Thus encouraged by the purser," Emily wrote, "I
proceeded with my room-mate to seize our 'unques-
tioned rights'. But approaching the priests' door, my
heart failed me, and our undertaking seemed a plain
and undeniable demonstration of wickedness, like rob-
bing a child's bank. They are such quiet, well-deserv-
ing men, these eight black-smocked brothers who are
going north to share the Jubilee of the great Bishop.
Also, they are very polite, and the one who is an astron-
omer and came from Italy, picked out the tenderest
cut of beef for me at supper.

" 'Don't be silly!' snorted my companion. 'The rules
of their Order say distinctly they shall deny themselves, and not sleep softly. Besides, when men take
terrible vows that they will never get married, it is a
woman's stoutest duty to steal their mattresses whenever the opportunity serves.'

"She also told me," reported Emily, "with rapid brevity, some names which Clement of Alexandria, a Father
of the Church, applied to women in the early days
of the Christian era. She had read about it in history.

"In the morning, when I told the Brothers how I

had taken their mattresses, and how sorry I was, being a bitter sinner and unlovely of heart, I explained that I had done so because I disapproved of their vows concerning marriage, and because of the unseemly remarks Clement of Alexandria had applied to women in the early days of the Christian era. They laughed again and again with much hilarity. Indeed, one of the Brothers said he applauded my moderation and marvelled that I was good enough to leave their blankets and pillows."

At Grouard Emily Murphy was present at all the solemn rites. She wandered among the people listening, talking, watching, analysing, turning it all into words.

On the last afternoon she bribed a guide to drive her across the hill to where the Anglican Bishop's empty house stood. She had known the Bishop well in earlier years. Now that the holiday he had at last taken with his family to England had ended in his tragic death, his wife and daughters could not afford to return and close up their home. Strangers were to sell its contents for what they would bring. The house was to be "done over" for another Bishop.

Emily walked softly through the empty rooms of the home which had been one of the most hospitable in the north. A mist was in her eyes and a painful tightness in her throat.

"I touch the chords of *Auld Lang Syne* on the piano, in honour of Madam, the mother. I kiss the houseflowers for the love of the young girls who carried them safely over the long, long winter. I finger the books in the library, with affection, in memory of the good Bishop who once told me kindly tales of these Indians who were his friends. . . . And when I, too, have

gone, may it happen that someone who understands
will touch my books in like manner, and say good-bye
to them for me. I could not so endure it of myself."

V

It was this personal intimate sympathy, plus her
insatiable interest in people and her enthusiasms, that
led her on, mile after mile, year after year, until, in
the decade after she moved to Edmonton, she became,
probably, the most informed authority on the actual
life *motifs* of the people in the West. Nothing was
ever too small on which to focus her interest; nothing
too impressive to frighten her away.

There's an interesting glimpse of her, in this period,
through the eyes of an old squatter along one of the
northern trails. One of the Western newspapermen,
on a story assignment, had dropped into the squatter's
homestead for a cup of tea and a chat. The man, pulling on his pipe, brought out his choicest experience
for this traveller from the world outside.

"Yep. A body sees tarnation many people passin'
on this trail. There's maybe one a day, besides the
regular freight people and that sort of thing. But the
one we remember best was a woman. Wonder if you
ever ran into her? Funny kind of woman she was, too.
Makes you feel when you're talkin' to her as if she's
more'n six feet. Her voice is big, and mild, and her
mind is too."

"And her heart, too," chimed in the squatter's wife.

"I reckon so. But though you think she's big when
you're talkin' to her, when she's gone, and you look
down the trail, why she's no more'n five feet!"

The newspaper man pressed questions. "What did she look like? Was she a squaw?"

"No! she ain't no squaw! You don't know that woman. Why, she just talks and makes you feel better, that's all. Ever know what it is to take a nip of something good after you've been on the trail, mushing for hours?"

It was Emily, of course. She had dropped in casually, as she loved to do, but found an ailing babe and a disheartened mother with an angry, depressed homesteader. Before she left, that night, the child was better and the parents too. The squatter, later, bought his wife a bit of luxury, to remember the day—an oil lamp for the table.

People, people; always the people.

"If you cross over the street you may talk with someone who tells you a piece of news or makes a proposition, or gives you a thought that may change the routine of your life. Indeed, which side of the street you take may be fraught with momentous issues."

And again:

"There is a sense of adventure in meeting people and talking with them; besides, there is so much to be learned from the unsophisticated."

Returning from her jaunts into the lands of Alberta, she wrote for hours late into the night. Another group of sketches was gathered and published under the title she liked best, *Open Trails*, in 1912. Two years later came *Seeds of Pine*.

As she journeyed up and down the countryside she flamed to the beauty about her. "I love these roses, and I kiss them fair on the mouth, over and over, till they blush to crimson." Yet, on the same journey, she spent some time at the dump of a railway camp, turning over the cans lying there, to see what the men ate most frequently . . .

One night, as a very special guest of honour, she sat with a group of old-timers as they drank the last bottle of champagne left from the longest and wildest spree the West had ever known.

Emily watched them lingering over the champagne, while she sipped her own lemonade with a cherry in it, and listened for the story.

It had to do with the Helpman Expedition, which arrived in Edmonton a little more than ten years previously to go to the Klondike.

On Christmas Eve, 1896, the party under the direction of Lord Avonmore arrived in Edmonton, last jumping-off place for the Gold Rush.

Promptly the local wiseacres dubbed it the Helpless Affair, and referred to Lord 'Ave-one-more, examining with awe the supplies the group had brought with them. Every item, except horses, was brought from England, and the duty alone had amounted to thousands of dollars. The party was provisioned under War Office approval, and the members travelled the wilderness as they felt English gentlemen should travel, with baled hay and hay choppers, baths, beds, tents, sanitary conveniences and other impediments transported by the trainload.

They had plenty of delicate food, egg powders, Westphalian hams, tinned ptarmigan, wood-cock, plum pudding; but nearly all these were spoiled by the long journey. When the boxes were finally opened most of it was unedible, and the party faced a diet of rice and beans.

With them, too, they brought liquor in barrels, cases, kegs, and demi-johns. There was brandy, benedictine, claret, champagne and canary. Arrived in Edmonton, the last link with civilization before the trek north, they discovered that the Klondike was prohibition country, and not one bottle could be taken in.

They had no permit to sell the liquor; so there was nothing left but to drink it. That was how Edmonton came to know the wildest and longest spree in the history of the West. It lasted a full six weeks, with increasing fury and many fights and arguments.

"Yes," recalled one old-timer, sipping the Koch Fils 1892, "they just fit and fit and fit."

The expedition was, of course, a failure. Some of the party got as far as Fort Simpson on the Mackenzie River, but their material was stolen, their horses died, and the few survivors finally trekked back to Edmonton, to wait there for months until their return passage money arrived from English relatives.

All this she loved—the countryside, its people, and the tales of their life; but, more and more, she was drawn into the details of city existence. As the years passed, her expeditions into the hinterlands grew farther apart. The old joyous eagerness of her forties, opening in a new land, was overlaid with the responsibilities and struggles she was finding in her club work and civic life. Coming back home she would write, again and again, in this strain:

"Oho! and oho! Why should I stay in town, I who only know the songs of the country? Why should anyone stay in a town which puts lines in her face; hardens her eyes; which spurs her feet and bridles her tongue?"

Yet, even as she loved the land and the wild, free

spaces, the other side of her life was fitting her, more and more, into its yoke. Increasingly, it seemed, the rapturous explorations into the world of the North and West were only undertaken when she could find time from her civic world.

Little by little, and year by year, as we shall see, she built a pattern which, eventually, enmeshed her completely, shutting out the laughter from her writing, the singing from her prose. During the ten years which followed her entry into Edmonton, Janey Canuck wrote her last book of the open spaces and of the people who lived therein; and at the end of the decade the first woman magistrate in the British Empire took up her work.

What happened to Janey Canuck of *Open Trails*, and *Seeds of Pine* to transform her into a magistrate? What details of living led her so naturally into a way of life so hard, so bounded by the sordid and unhappy?

With our knowledge of Janey Canuck exploring the open trails of the West, can we understand how Edmonton, the city, lured her, and won her, and bound her utterly?

Crescendo

It is good to live in these first days when the
foundations of things are being laid; to be able
to place a stone or carry the mortar to set it
good and true.

JANEY CANUCK.

I

AS WE PIECE TOGETHER the jig-saw of Emily
Murphy's life, the pattern grows true and clear.
The first impulses are maturing into habits of thought;
the outline for the final architectural majesty of her
life is limned.

Somewhere she wrote, "Wasn't it William the Con-
queror who put on his own crown? He is my favourite
hero."

In a sense, Emily did put on her own crown. She
wove it herself from the years she spent absorbed in
concerns of the little people she met. She bound it with
a love for humanity, and an insatiable curiosity for all
that affected it. She set it with her Irish devotion for
a bonnie fighter, and then found herself on a stage
made for her enthronement.

She walked onto the stage, arm-in-arm with her husband, on an early spring morning. They wandered the
streets of Edmonton, and looked across the wide val-

ley to Clover Bar, standing beneath an immense fir
tree.

On the rim of the valley lay the town, little more
than a rough settlement—the farthest north legislature
in the Dominion. To Emily a dream city was spread
below—the city she hoped one day to see. The crescendo and diminuendo of the lumber-mills floated up
to them from where the straw-coloured piles of lumber
lay in serried ranks.

"Out there, beyond the valley," said Emily, "there
are sunflowers. Drifts of gold over the meadows. And
there's more gold on the sands of this river . . . I like
this place, Arthur."

"At it again, Old Girl," said Arthur, "debauching
yourself with your emotions!"

Emily remembered the incident to note in her journal. "He was right—but I'd rather call it over-exhil-
arated. It is the fervour of living and the riot of the
senses that kill men."

But she saw, as the years passed, that the stage-
setting was, indeed, made for her. To walk the streets
of the town in the heady invigoration of the sub-zero
mornings was to sense a world that was almost too
beautiful. The sunshine that poured from the wide
skies seemed perpetual. The streets had a way of ending suddenly on open depths that flowed over the
valley; on autumn glory of scarlet and blue; on summer
shadows of green; and on the loveliest of all—white
frosted days when each tree was rimmed in silver and
the valley swam in a luminous glory.

All this Emily loved. It was the beauty of Canada
set to a high key of promise. She trod her new world
glowing, smiling, avid for every new experience. The

fervour of living and the riot of senses—of course, of course! Who would avoid them in this bright, golden world?

Vigorous and brilliant were the parties in the frame houses and frame halls. Here were men and women from round the world come to make their fortunes. In these early years Edmonton was probably the most cosmopolitan settlement in Canada, with money flowing through hands eager to spend and gather again. Doctors and scientists, adventurers and prospectors, timber men and mining men, with the gay, hearty women that such men marry, were making a vivid life for themselves in this northern post. At the balls— and the dinner parties that preceded them—women wore costumes imported from Paris and New York; furs and jewels and sumptuous fabrics. Gowns that had cost $300 were taken for granted at hotel banquets costing $15 a plate. Fortunes were made overnight in real estate; indeed, the little maid who opened the door for you at eight o'clock might be $200 the richer by midnight, with the transfer of a bit of property she had bought on speculation a day or two before.

So Emily and her daughters danced and dined, rode to the paper chases, crowded with everyone to the horse races. Arthur was adventuring in real estate, in oil, and coal, and, on most Sundays, he still preached gratuitously to help out his brother clergy. Tucked away in one of the scrap-books is a note from a Wetaskiwin paper in 1907: "The Rev. Arthur Murphy arrived here this morning by hand-car on the railway, to preach in St. James church. He left the same afternoon. You can't beat a hustler."

Emily travelled with him often and found rich ma-

CRESCENDO   119

terial for her articles and books. Publishers were increasingly demanding in their request for more sketches. Her ability to interpret this new Canada was making her writing universally popular. Two of her books, *Janey Canuck in the West* and *Open Trails* had run through popular editions and then been re-issued in "Wayfarer's Library".

She wrote at the big desk in her room, her plump little hand flying over the paper, gripping a blunt-pointed pen. Hour after hour was spent correcting proofs, checking details, answering her swelling cor-respondence.

II

Yet, already, the threads of Emily's public life ap-pear. As the years passed it assumed the gigantic proportions indicated on page 345 of this book.

It all began, I think, with the visits she loved to make to the homesteaders up and down the prairie trails. As she dropped in to chat over a cup of tea with the farm women, while Arthur was following up some new clue to adventure in the district, she sensed the loneliness that spurred their eagerness in welcoming her. She began to suggest group meetings at neighbour-ing farms, and often accepted their invitation to come herself. Always, she brought with her one of the latest books sent her for review. As they sat grouped around the warm kitchen, Emily read aloud to them some fragment that had pleased her—and saw their respon-sive pleasure.

She helped them to establish community halls, found herself sharing in problems for raising money, and other

community projects. Only a few years later she became
National President of the Federated Women's Institutes
of Canada.

As she worked with the women she saw the injustices
of their life. Alberta had been, until recently, one of
the Territories. No allowance was made at all for a
woman's property rights—because so many men in
the Territories had married Indian squaws. Any man,
under the Alberta law, could still sell his farm at will
and walk off with the proceeds, leaving his wife and
family to struggle on as best they might. Homesteaders,
too, could will away their entire property with no consideration for the part their wives had played in long,
tortuous years, to build up its value.

Again and again, Emily heard the bitter story of a
woman who had worked with her man for years on a
piece of land, only to have him sell out suddenly and go
off with some other woman. Holding close the sobbing
and bewildered wife, or watching her stoic misery,
Emily began to hark back to women's rights in other
provinces. Why should these Albertan women not have
the same security?

Home from such an interview, Emily found herself
enmeshed in the gay, careless life of her Edmonton
friends. It was a natural development that she should
start to tell them about their sisters who were facing
despair and defeat. She found a warm interest in response, for the women of Edmonton were always ready,
with a Western eagerness, to act in any emergency.

Their enthusiasm spurred her to start campaigning.
Talking to the women who came a-calling on Tuesday
afternoon was a natural prelude to talking to their husbands, and so to debating with the men she knew in

the Legislature. Three of her brothers were now lawyers, and Emily wrote often to them for advice in
planning her campaign.

She took to reading long-winded details of women's
property rights in the library, and the Legislative
Building. She began to visit the Legislature and sit
through the sessions, absorbing the way the men discussed the various bills. Many afternoons found her
in the gallery, listening to the passage of new statutes,
so that she might prepare herself for her own battle.

There was colour enough in the Legislature to satisfy
her writer's mind. At that time there were members
who had come from the Eastern and Western provinces, the United States, and from Europe. Among
them were farmers, ranchers, doctors, hotel-keepers,
real estate agents, editors, fur traders, mill men, coal
men.

She knew that to better the conditions of the women
in their struggle for property rights in their husbands'
estates she must have a new bill passed; however, she
could arouse little interest in it. The Hon. Charles W.
Cross, Attorney-General for the province, was frankly
antagonistic. "Why should women worry about pos-
sessing some of their husband's property during his
lifetime?" he asked. "Time enough after he's dead!"

Such attitudes only gave impetus to Emily's determination. "Whenever I don't know whether to fight or
not—I always fight," became one of her favourite
expressions.

The women were supporting her loyally; for she
was one of those rare women—a true friend of women.
From all parts of the province came letters of approval.
New ideas were welcomed in the West. With such

quick growth everywhere, how could any woman be apathetic in any just cause? Emily tucked away one letter in particular: "Go to it, Mrs. Murphy! I know what you're up against. I, too, have a troublesome husband!"

Doggedly she persisted with her lobbying until, finally, she came upon one young man who said that he was interested in her point of view and thought it just. He agreed to bring in the bill.

Thus it was that Mr. R. B. Bennett, member for Calgary in the House, first introduced the Married Women's Protective Act. It was sent to committee, and, one afternoon, Emily, learning that it was being roughly handled, asked if she might address the committee. With hours of study behind her, she came fully prepared to argue her case. For an hour and a half, the gentlemen listened politely to her impassioned pleading.

The bill went into its second reading, and was thrown out. Many of the men vowed they would never see it become a statute. Mr. Bennett was described as "a susceptible young man affected by the pleadings of the ladies."

But the day the bill was discarded, a reporter in the *Edmonton Journal* had this to say:

"Mrs. Murphy is so much in earnest over the bill, that its success is as good as accomplished. It may not be this year, nor the next, but this leader of women will keep hammering away until even the most obstinate man will be convinced that it is best to withdraw quietly and without further ado, and let down the bars."

Prophetic words, for the Act was finally passed a

year or so later. The Dower Act of 1911 provided that
a wife must get a third of her husband's estate, even
when he did not leave a will; and that it was impossible
for him to will away her third of the property.

III

Her love of old-world symbols, developed through
the years, brought her into the limelight with another
battle.

Placidly, a group of women told her that the Old
Fort was to be removed in order to landscape the
grounds about the handsome new Legislative Buildings.

Emily was horrified. The Fort had been built a
century ago. It was part of the grant of land made by
Charles II to his Cousin Rupert—for the Gentlemen
Adventurers of the Hudson's Bay Company. The little
cluster of logs set high on the banks of the river had a
history, practically analogous to that of the fur trade
in Canada. Now, it was to be tossed away to make
room for geranium beds and lawns!

What to do?

Emily found little response among her friends; they
were impressed mostly with the fact that the new
buildings were reputedly among the finest in Canada.
Of course their landscaping must be of the best. Why
worry about some old log buildings?

She went directly to Members of Parliament. She
called on them without self-consciousness to state her
case. She gathered influential groups of women to her
house and argued with them until she won their backing. She spoke of the outrage, at whatever meeting she

attended, so that her agitation made itself a tangible reality throughout Edmonton's society—and Legislature.

As a result, the Fort was taken carefully apart and stored in preparation for re-building on another site; but, as the years passed, and no definite stimulus was given to its re-building, nothing was ever done with it. Another heritage of Canadian history went a-mouldering for lack of public interest. Later, the timber used in the Fort gradually disappeared; and the remainder was burnt.

Other matters were crowding Emily's life—matters for urgent attention. She realized that when she went after a problem, she could find a matching interest among her associates. Between them, they could bring results. She began to sense the power that organized womanhood could have in fighting for their own rights and their own recognition as citizens.

As a result of her close interest with men and women through the outlying centres, her interest in hospitals became dominant. Early in her Edmonton career she was asked, one afternoon, as a popular social leader, and as a "name", to be a member of the Ladies' Committee which made an annual examination of the local hospital.

Each year, the Ladies' Committee made the little gesture of examination. They called, to find the staff in neat array, the work progressing smoothly. Their report was always pleasant, but vague.

The year that Mrs. Murphy was for the first time one of this committee, made history. The staff looked for the same routine but, from the outset, Mrs. Murphy startled both her committee and the staff by setting

off on her own, away from the carefully-guarded group
of ladies. Mrs. Murphy was opening doors. Mrs.
Murphy was chatting with absorbed interest to a patient down the ward, who seemed to be telling her
the story of his life. Mrs. Murphy was in the kitchen,
with the least of the cooks, asking questions with an
intentness that was bringing forth equally intent
answers.

As she looked, and questioned, and wondered, Emily
was remembering the dreary, dismal places she had
visited in England. She was remembering, now, her
vow never to encourage anything sloppy or inefficient
in her own country's management of hospitals or
asylums. So, her eyes bright with interest, her jawline
at an aggressive angle, she did her own investigating.

She wrote and re-wrote her report with a passionate
dedication. When she gave it before an ordinarily
lethargic board, and described what she had seen, she
launched an uproar which was to rock Edmonton for
years.

Access to the fire-escapes she noted, were blocked
by beds, invalid chairs and baby carriages.

Flushers for cleaning utensils were inadequate.
Nurses' quarters were very poor.

Vegetables were not properly kept. The nurses'
dining-room was next to the mortuary. ("Comment
unnecessary," said Mrs. Murphy.)

The hospital, in her opinion, was over-staffed. Yet
the bills were not properly collected; and the staff did
not handle its work well. The hospital was running
on a daily deficit of nearly a hundred dollars.

There was a great deal more of her report, published

for all the world to see, under a banner headline in the *Edmonton Bulletin*.

Furious meetings followed. The medical superintendent of the hospital vowed that as the paper had featured Mrs. Murphy's report, he would insist that it publish every word of his thirty-page report, presented as a rebuttal to the outrageous statements of "that Mrs. Murphy".

But at the conclusion of the board meeting, it was the unanimous decision of those present that the superintendent's report should not be made public. Mrs. Murphy's charges stood; for there was no way to disprove them.

Emily was constantly fighting for better conditions in the hospitals, for there seemed, always, some phase of the work which she wanted to see improved. She found herself facing, more and more, the resentment of men who objected strenuously to her insistence on her own point of view when she felt matters were wrong. Through page after page of her scrap-book are newspaper clippings telling of these stormy meetings. Through all of them, one finds the concentrated interest centring about Mrs. Murphy. She made many enemies as she grew more determined to better conditions. There were many who protested, "For Heaven's sake, don't let Mrs. Murphy in on it!" Who knew what would develop if she went to work? If Mrs. Murphy felt it necessary, precedents were broken. Private feelings must be ignored if it were for the common good. She never made a personal matter of a point of view. When she felt like it, she could lay about her with salty phrases and vigorous figures of speech which

were often the undoing of her adversaries, and she
was often so unexpectedly humorous that she dis-
armed her worst enemies. She had a manner of rocking slightly on her toes, with her hands clasped behind
her back and a quaint Irish intonation when she became very intense.

A newspaper report of a stormy meeting on the
hospital, in January, 1910, concluded:

"One may not always agree with Mrs. Murphy's
methods or conclusions, but in strict fairness, one
recognizes, and is bound to admit that she is terribly
in earnest and capable of playing any antagonist at
his own game.

"I was interested in watching the battle of wits
between Mrs. Murphy and some of the men ranged
on the other side of the house. Not all of the men spoke
or referred to her personally, but everyone felt that
back of almost every speech was an underlying sense
that she was there listening, and sizing the matter up.
It was rather an uncannily funny feeling, as if one
aimed a general remark straight at the head of one
particular person in the room, without caring to look
at her, or single her out.

"I noticed the men every little while looked to see
how she was taking matters. And I know that every
word she uttered was listened to with undivided attention."

IV

During the war years she became enmeshed in
working with women for various patriotic works. She
grew particularly interested in a plan for registering

Canadian women so that they could be called up quickly to take their place, as needed, in voluntary work or industry. The project was started, but never completed.

As her capacity and interest in public life increased, she saw about her many complex social and sexual questions awaiting solution—questions which always beset a new country. Many deputations came to her house, asking for her backing and interest in some phase of women's club work. From East and West came the same urging.

"You are the one to lead the campaign, Janey."

"People will listen to you—they won't to anyone else."

"Will you just start it? We'll give you a strong committee—and we'll do all the work."

"If you'll just head-up the campaign! We only want your name!"

So, beguiled and coaxed, seeing always the need, she accepted appointments on committees of all types, and, shortly, was working for them with all the energy she knew. Emily Murphy was never one to serve in a routine capacity. Her interest led her on to ever-expanding work, and to a correspondence that was becoming gargantuan for one in private life. She still answered her letters by long-hand, writing far into the night on them, instead of on her own literary work. Evelyn helped her many evenings and, on returning from long trips, she would hire a secretary for a day or so to catch up with her mail; but, in the main, it was in her own tireless handwriting that thousands of letters were answered, and thousands of reports given.

Times without number, some routine mimeographed slip requesting information would be sent from other parts of Canada. Emily Murphy always considered the question carefully—and gave of her best in answering. It was natural that, more and more, the people of the East and West should turn to Mrs. Murphy of Edmonton, as the one who would give, always, clear-thinking advice. Any notable who headed across Canada was advised, "Be sure to look up Mrs. Murphy!"

"Ask Mrs. Murphy" was so easy to say, but the hours spent in interviewing people, in answering letters, in sending reports, began to take a heavy toll on her energy.

When Emmeline Pankhurst, British suffragette, went west on a campaign for social hygiene, she was directed to Emily Murphy. The two of them spent many days travelling over Western Canada, speaking to meetings. On the long train journeys, the two women, so vividly contrasted, whiled away the tedious hours by playing solitaire with Mrs. Pankhurst's miniature packs of cards—her favourites. Similar cards had accompanied her during her first hunger strike in Holloway jail. Playing with them had comforted her so much that the matron, feeling the endless games of solitaire helped to assuage her pangs of hunger, confiscated them until Mrs. Pankhurst was released.

When Alberta became the first of the Canadian provinces to grant suffrage for women in 1916, Mrs. Pankhurst presented the packs to Emily as a souvenir of their work together. Emily adopted the habit of playing solitaire for relaxation and release from strain, and it became, in time, one of her chief escapes from the rigours of her work.

At the close of this first decade in Edmonton Emily began to feel the lapsing of her energies. Her health was troubling her for almost the first time in her life. The initial signs of that fatal weakness, diabetes, from which eventually she died, became apparent.

She began to take treatments, and journeyed to Rochester for a difficult operation.

In Kathleen's diary at this time is a brief note: "Mother is coming back from Rochester tomorrow, and we can hardly contain our excitement. Father keeps pacing up and down the sitting-room, saying over and over, 'Dear Old Girl. Dear Old Girl!' "

The family life, too, was meeting difficulties which darkened the horizon. In 1916 the real estate boom began to crumble, and fortunes were lost as quickly as they had been made. Some of Arthur's investments were in land—now he watched them fade as mortgage demands could not be met, for no one could raise money on real estate. Finances were increasingly difficult and, with the war blackening the world outside, and Emily's ill-health, the Murphy family found need for every bit of Irish courage and optimism they could muster.

Throughout these days, Emily's interest in the work to be done never slackened. She was finding more time for studying the legislative bills which outlined the solutions of many of the problems she was battling. She worked closely with R. B. Chadwick, superintendent for the Government's Department of Neglected Children, on a bill to be known as the Children's Protective Act, never dreaming that she would ultimately be called on to administer it.

Working back to the legislative bills that endeavoured to solve the complex social problems of her day, she came, naturally, to an interest in their trials in open court. From slipping into the legislative balconies to watch the members discuss the bills, she took to attending the Juvenile Courts, the District Courts, even venturing into the sacred precincts of the Supreme Court.

"Without being priggish or pedantic," she wrote in *Maclean's Magazine*, in 1919, "I can truthfully say that the pros and cons of the legal arguments I heard in these different courts were of greater pleasure to me than my visits to the theatre or horse ring, much as I appreciated the latter. This probably arose from the fact that I am descended from two families which have produced many eminent jurists, and that I have inherited a legal cast of mind."

V

On a spring morning, early in 1916, a routine case was tried in the Edmonton court, which was to change the whole course of her life.

About twenty girls had been arrested in a police round-up, charged with being common prostitutes and night-walkers, contrary to section 238, clause (i) of the Criminal Code. In the group were clerks, stenographers, maid-servants, housewives and some vagrants who, unquestionably, came under the description used in the code.

Rumour had it that stool pigeons had been used to gain evidence, and that the women had been given intoxicants prior to their arrest. Later, these rumours were proven to be false, and with no basis in fact whatever, but, at the time, some members of the Local Council of Women felt it was a matter that should be checked. Two delegates from the Law Committee of the Local Council of Women were asked to attend the case in the Guard-room of the Royal North-West Mounted Police, to hear the evidence and to make sure that the women were treated fairly.

With the exception of the girl prisoner who was in the dock at the moment, they were the only women in the room.

Seeing them, Counsel for the Crown asked the magistrate to request the women to withdraw from the Court, as the cases were unfit to be heard in a mixed audience.

The women stated that they came as representatives of a committee on laws pertaining to the protection of women and children, and wished to remain.

Counsel replied tartly that decent women, such as they appeared to be, could have no desire to hear the evidence in these cases.

Disconcerted, angry, the women withdrew, as the threat of not being "ladies" was one they could not face. Out in the hall, they telephoned the one woman whom, they knew, would give them sound advice.

Mrs. Murphy's telephone rang. The story was told her, and one of the women asked, "Should we return to court?"

Emily was on definite ground. "Agree with the magistrate," said she. "Such cases should not be heard by a mixed audience. And apply immediately to the government, urging that a court be established for the City of Edmonton in which women offenders may be tried by a woman in the presence of women!"

The women stayed away from the court; but, as always, they insisted that Emily be the one to apply to the Government urging a woman's court.

For several days she shirked the task, and then, timid and fearful of her reception, and without the solace that comes from even one companion, she tackled the Honourable the Attorney-General, Mr. C. W. Cross.

To her amazement, no argument was required. When she had outlined what had taken place, and her recommendation to the women, Mr. Cross agreed immediately that such a court was urgently needed.

Then he said, bluntly:

"When are you ready to be sworn in, Mrs. Murphy? The Governor-in-Council meets next week, and your appointment as Police Magistrate will doubtless be ratified."

"Ah! . . . no! . . . that is to say, I'm not ready at all!" said Emily in one gasping breath. "I never thought of this. I don't know anything. I have too much work at home; and my people won't let me!"

All the objections she had learned from women slackers, she reported later, came tumbling from her mind. The Minister only laughed and said, "Let me know in a week."

Arthur felt it was a role that she could assume with dignity and in which she could serve her country-women more closely. Her daughters were proud at the prospect. But Emily was in a state of violent contradiction. She remembered it vividly, later, for in writing about her appointment, she said:

"After concluding that I dare accept and that I dare

not, for half a dozen times, I decided to consult some trusted women friends, for it seemed that I was forcing myself along a hard and unaccustomed trail which might end in a slough.

"Besides, I was afraid of the nastiness of sex-pedlary that would have to be considered even before a court made up largely of women. In the days when I was a juvenile, it was not considered good form to mention an animal of the opposite sex by name, therefore equines and bovines were all of one sex to me . . . I have always been embarrassed because of this faulty education as a child, and while I could write of matters relating to sexual problems, I found it difficult to speak of them even to my own children."

The difficulties affecting her own personal life, her career as a writer, and her capabilities to handle the work kept her in a state of torture for days.

"Should a woman keep court?" she asked her friends.

"Of course she should," said one, who was a church deaconess. "There were women magistrates in the Roman Empire—why not in the British?"

Answered another, "Keeping court is not a man's nor a woman's job. It's a job for anyone who knows how."

A mother of six put it this way:

"A woman with a family can keep court better than a man, in that she has performed such work for years in the management of her family. In training her boys and girls she has had to do with false pretenses, assault, incitement to breach of peace, cruelty to animals, cheating at play, loitering, obstruction to justice, misappropriation, false evidence, trespass, forcible entry, idle and disorderly persons . . . and many other offences of an anti-social character."

The artist in her, recognizing, at last, the lengths to which her cumulative interest in people had brought her, was yet to be satisfied.

"How can I keep court when I am trying to be a writer?" she asked of another writer.

"The interruption, and not the task, may hold the angel," her friend replied, and added, "You must! We'll disown you, if you decline!"

Shortly after, Emily Murphy was sworn in as Police Magistrate in and for the City of Edmonton. Within a year she received her commission as Police Magistrate in and for the Province of Alberta.

She was the first woman in the British Empire to be appointed as a police magistrate. Little Emily Ferguson of the pig-tails and the mirror dramatics down in Cookstown; Janey Canuck of the open spaces and the passionate love for growing things and humble people; Mrs. Arthur Murphy, minister's wife, with the merry chuckle and the bright eyes.

Now, Emily Murphy, Police Magistrate.

PART III

Her Worship, Magistrate Murphy

CHAPTER I

My own petition? That of Tagore's—May I never lose the touch of the one, in the feel of the many.

EMILY MURPHY.

I

NEXT MORNING, word of her appointment was in newspapers around the globe; with it came an immediate transformation in her life. Telephones shrilled endlessly; neighbours dropped in to tell of their delight; telegrams crowded the study table. Whenever she set foot outside, she walked to the sound of rejoicing, saw shining eyes approving her new stature, friendly faces beaming their good will; old friends, many of them, but also hundreds who knew her only as a public figure. Strangers, too, who spoke timidly; "Aren't you the Mrs. Murphy they've made a judge? . . . A grand thing!"

As the days passed there were many editorials paying tribute to her as an individual; to Edmonton for its leadership in appointing the first woman magistrate in the British Empire; to womanhood with an upper case W. Letters poured in from the hundreds of people who called her friend. There were many, too, from those who knew her only through the Janey Canuck books or magazine articles. All these well-wishers focused on her a world of hope for better things, a promise of new leadership. All of them sounded one theme: "You can't imagine how proud we are that a woman has been chosen at last."

Emily faced the sudden blaze of publicity with an inherent dignity and a sense of the inevitable. For one thing, she was becoming used to being in the spotlight of interest. She had been decorated by King George V as a Lady of Grace of the Order of St. John of Jerusalem, a few years previously, in recognition of her writing, and of her welfare work. She was President of the Canadian Women's Press Club; had been first national president of the Federated Women's Institutes, and a senior executive member of many national organizations, as the list from *Who's Who* testifies. She was, indeed, a dominating figure not only in the West, but throughout Canada.

But, beyond the fact that Emily had become a distinguished figure in Canadian affairs, she knew that she had been prepared from childhood for just such a role as this. She might answer the routine questions on how she felt, facing such an appointment, with a correctly shaded "I feel very ignorant and inadequate— but I want to do it well." Nevertheless, there was a serenity in her heart as she undertook the new responsibility. "Nothing ever happens by chance," she wrote, "everything is pushed from behind."

"Pushed" . . . from far back down the years when
a pig-tailed youngster listened for long hours to the
lawyers of the family. The close companionship she
had with her three barrister brothers; the anecdotes,
the oft-discussed court cases, the arguments on fine
legal points, the debates on proper procedure, had all
been a part of her life from the earliest days back in
Simcoe County. More recently, because of her interest
in children's welfare work, she had spent long hours
in court. Her research into problems affecting women's
rights had familiarized her with many angles of the
law. The work ahead of her was already broadly
familiar to her. She was a traveller on a road, new in
detail, but whose general contours and direction she
had often glimpsed.

The fact that she was appointed to the bench with
no experience as a lawyer was not unusual twenty-five
years ago, when often magistrates were similarly in-
experienced. It was typical of Emily, however, that she
should start to read law immediately with the same
concentration she had always brought to any undertaking. She spent days in the court library poring over
legal volumes, studying evidence and the statutes. Her
brothers wrote her many pages of advice on the best
books to buy for herself. These books soon became
annotated in exactly the same manner as her school-
books at Bishop Strachan's, or her husband's volumes
of sermons.

She tucked into her desk the telegrams her brothers
sent her when news of her appointment first reached
them.

There was the one from the youngest Ferguson boy,
Harcourt, now a brilliant young barrister and King's

Counsel in Toronto, member of the firm of Miller, Ferguson and Hunter—the same Miller, who, later, left the "Stork Derby" Will.

"Let me offer my congratulations to Your Worship", Harcourt wired, "Try to temper your decisions with mercy, and do not hand out too much of your own medicine, namely, hard labour."

From her eldest brother T. R., now a King's Counsel in Winnipeg, came this word: "Well done. In fact, I say shake, Judge. The fact is that none of your brothers have yet been able to attain to a position on the bench, and as Fate had willed it that someone in the family must be a judge, you simply had to do it to save our face. Again, well done. You beat your brothers to it, and I say to them all they can put that in their pipe and smoke it. While I am at it, Emily, be easy on 'them wimmin'. That is the one thing I am afraid of—that you may not possess sufficient gallantry to pass over many things."

From her third lawyer brother: "Good morning, Judge. Common sense and mercy are necessary attributes; legal knowledge a valuable qualification; pride, and sometimes a bad liver, are curses of most legal administrations. Brother Bill."

Bill later sent her, also, a copy of a letter sent to him on his own appointment to the bench of the First Appellate Division of the Supreme Court of Ontario, by James Haverson, K.C. This noted criminal lawyer, with a character all his own, liked to dub himself the "Protector of the Wicked", and in writing to Bill on December 16th, 1916, said:

"I helped make you a Bencher. I unwittingly assist-

EMILY, ORGANIZER AND FIRST PRESIDENT OF WOMEN'S CANADIAN CLUB
OF EDMONTON, AT ITS INAUGURAL MEETING, 1911, WITH HER EXECUTIVE

CANADIAN WOMEN'S PRESS CLUB, 1913, TRIENNIAL CONFERENCE,
Three centre figures: Marjory MacMurchy—Lady Willison (Hon. Pres.),
Col. George Ham (Hon. Member), Emily (President).

NELLIE L. McCLUNG, M.L.A., EMMELINE PANKHURST, EMILY.
TAKEN AT EDMONTON

ed in your elevation to the bench. Now let me speak
from a safe position.

"You are the president of a wicked Tory club. You
are evidently the member of a church containing a
large percentage of wicked men. Your business partners are wicked, and you know you are the friend of
the Protector of the Wicked. I therefore ask you not
to forget your old friends when you come into your
kingdom.

"On the bench be fair, but in case of doubt, lean
somewhat to the wicked. They are grateful and human
people, and will appreciate your efforts."

Emily framed the letter and hung it on her office
wall.

II

We have Emily's own picture of that first day on
the bench. In *Maclean's Magazine* for January, 1920,
she wrote:

"My first day in court was as pleasant an experience
as running a rapids without a guide. Besides, the
lawyers and police officials looked so accustomed and
so terribly sophisticated. Indeed, I have never seen
brass buttons so bright and menacing as on this particular day.

"Presently all the men became embarrassed and
started to stammer over their manner of addressing
me. One said 'Your Worship' and another 'Your
Honour'. A negro said 'Your Majesty' and the rest
said 'Sir'.

"The unintelligible jargon known as the 'information and complaint' was rattled off by the Clerk of the Court to a red-faced type whose chiffon evening dress was hanging in tatters from her shoulders, it having been torn off her by 'a dog' the night before, while she was intoxicated on one of the city's main thoroughfares.

"The accused tells me that she was walking along quietly when this Bobby fellow came right up behind her and pinched her.

" 'Constable, did you pinch the lady'?" asked I. "It was most unbecoming conduct in an officer.'

"After a prodigious side wink at the police boys, he explains that he merely arrested her . . .

"The next case is also a breach of the Liquor Act. Before his client pleads, Counsel for the Defence gets to his feet and objects to my jurisdiction as a magistrate. On being requested to state his objection, he argues that I am not 'a person' within the meaning of the Statutes. His argument takes up quite ten minutes and in the end is duly noted. Whereupon the hearing of the case proceeds.

"On every subsequent case, this man, who is the most popular criminal lawyer in the city, persisted in raising the objection, while I persisted in hearing the whole argument, the thing appealing to my fancy immensely. Other barristers caught up the objection and we had a merry time of it. He was a poor fellow indeed, who could not put up a new aspect of the argument" . . .

Emily nodded briskly, and noted the objection to her jurisdiction as not being a "person", until, as the months passed, the matter died down. Emily, however, did not forget. The question was brought up on her first day in court in 1916. Looking back on her mem-

ories of that day, in 1920, she made it a focal point in
her story as we have seen. In 1927, she formally began
her efforts to have women declared "Persons". In 1938
a brass tablet, placed there by the Canadian Federation
of Professional and Business Women's Clubs, was unveiled in the Canadian Senate where it hangs, noting
her triumph for history. Her immediate recognition of
the challenge is the notable factor. The story back of
those dates, and the brass tablet, comes later. In meeting the challenge, she was to know one of her greatest
triumphs, a triumph holding within its cycle perhaps
her most bitter disappointment.

III

This objection that she was not a "person" within
the meaning of the British North America Act was
one of the very few public criticisms made of her appointment. The majority of lawyers welcomed her,
liking her direct good humour, respecting her conscientious approach to the need for knowledge, recognizing her judicial analysis of the facts in relation to
the men and women called before her. So, as men
will, under such circumstances, they gave her every
help and encouragement. Through the years her
popularity grew. She herself wrote always of the
forward-looking phases of her work; told repeatedly
of the humanities in her cases, and of the salvage
possible through understanding and good sense. On
the surface, from the day of her appointment, to the
eulogies in the press when she resigned from her post,
there was only good comradeship and progress to
report.

Back-stage, however, she fought for several years

a constant battle against petty tyrannies which wasted her time and energies and might have proved overwhelming to one of lesser spirit. She fought persistently and patiently, alone, drafting and redrafting arguments and claims, in the long evening hours when she might have been resting, or finding relaxation in pencilling more sketches of the life she was watching with such absorption.

These back-stage difficulties were small, endless, pinpricking obstacles, placed in her way by a few who resented the intrusion of a woman into the work she was now doing. Her appointment as Police Magistrate for Edmonton, and, later, for Alberta, was an invasion of a realm which had been man's absolute domain. A small group of anti-feminists waged a campaign of obstructionism, working always against her jurisdiction, humiliating her, belittling at every opportunity her standing and authority. It was not an open fight—she could have met that with her usual fire and gallantry. This engagement with niggardly minds was no stimulating contest, merely a weariness of the spirit.

Surely now she knew a full understanding of the Ferguson crest, a bee sucking honey from a thistle, "Sweetness from difficulty." Emily never allowed these bickerings in the background to assume undue proportions, nor detract one iota from the dignity of the position which women had won, as personified in herself. Always, she faced the public with a jollity, a steadfastness, a serene determination. Only her family and a few close friends knew the picayune mortifications that beset her daily path, and made her undertaking so much more difficult. Her public life as a Police Magistrate cannot be properly appreciated without a realization of the under-cover opposition she faced behind the scenes.

If she had objected too strenuously to these small incidents, which had the effect of belittling her role, or sought public condemnation of them, she faced the quick criticism awaiting all women working in a man's world—the claim that women are hard to work with, unreasonable, emotional over unimportant details. If she had given way meekly to the arrogance and casual treatment she received from various officers, she, and her work, would have been quickly relegated to a very secondary position. Her sphere of power would have been minimized, until she would have been declared ineffectual, and gradually eased out of her position.

Among her papers when she died were hundreds of letters and notes, carbon copies of originals or hand-written first drafts which testify how stubbornly she contested for the rights, not of herself alone, but of all women in public life. The letters are corrected and redrafted as meticulously as her literary work and illuminate a lonely, personal, and hitherto unknown struggle.

Trouble arose at the outset from the attitude of the other magistrate, and that of the chief of police. There was one other magistrate in Edmonton at the time of her appointment. When Emily protested over any action of these officials which she felt interfered with her work, she found nearly every man-jack in the department aligned against the rank outsider—a woman.

Indicative of these petty annoyances was the routine detail of obtaining a police badge. It should have been hers with the same organization which laid a blotter and inkwell on her table. She asked for it repeatedly and received repeated assurance that she would get it next day. Other matters pressing on her attention the badge would slip her mind, until some occasion arose when she felt the need of it. Then the procedure would be repeated all over again.

She could not obtain proper furniture for her office, nor sufficient staff without ceaseless effort. The matter of keys for her desk, of the court-room being used by others when her cases were scheduled, of her dockets being correctly filled, all presented small but very real annoyances over a period of five years. But scarce half a dozen people knew of what was happening behind the scenes. It was Emily's personal battle, and conditions were not righted until the appointment of a new Chief of Police in 1921.

IV

With the beginning of her work as Magistrate, a new Edmonton was unveiled to Emily's penetrating regard, a cruel and relentless world, set up back-stairs, behind the façades of conventional city life. Heretofore, her associations, wide as they had been, were largely with the open-hearted, simple folk. Whatever trouble had concerned them, they knew kindly impulses, and had ever before them a hope of better things. Now before her, came a steady procession of tragic figures, clothed in misery, set about with filth, disease, wretchedness and despair.

Because of her difficulties in getting adequate staff, and her habits of writing her own notes the majority of the records of her cases were handwritten by Emily. Under the pressure of her tasks, the facts were all she had time to note, and there is surprisingly little evidence in any of her writing, of the humanities she watched, day by day. Because she was concerned so personally with the salvation of those passing before her, and with the correction of the evils sweeping through her court, she had little time to write of them. We check, page by page, and see only her brief reporting of children neglected; of fourteen people found asleep in two small rooms; of husbands begging her to compel their wives to return home from another man's house to take care of the children. She recorded stark facts telling the necessary details of little girls, under fifteen, living with Chinamen; fathers' assaults on their daughters; soldiers' wives embroiled with men; drug addicts; mothers reporting their children as incorrigible. It was a daily pattern of misery following every curve in the bitter dregs of life, missing nothing of its squalor, knowing each down-beating horror with a familiarity bred of its repetition.

The artist in her was keenly alive to the dramatics of these characters she watched, day by day. The crusader pointed, always, to the reforms needed, and to the responsibility of the community for the misery hidden down its back alleys. Her woman's sympathies responded directly to the needs of those who came before her. It was impossible, she found, to sit coldly passing judgment on women, without making some attempt, however slight, to salvage them from disaster, to back them up in any attempt at repairing their broken lives.

The first woman she sent to jail went insane, and was transferred to an asylum where she committed suicide. She left four little children whose father had deserted them. Emily was horror-stricken and went herself to the asylum to inquire into the case. The superintendent told her that the woman had several strongly settled delusions, and was probably insane when first committed to jail.

"The magistrate does not sleep so easefully if she has misgivings concerning the irresponsible unfit whom she sends to prison," she wrote, "when these should properly be placed under custodial care of another kind . . ." From her first case she saw the need for an improved method of handling the men and women arraigned in court. Throughout her years as a magistrate she urged, repeatedly, that a better adult probation system was needed, and a more intensive study of the problems criminals represent. "The method now in vogue," she often said, "is as if one sent a smallpox case, a fractured limb, and a maternity case to a hospital and gave them all the same treatment, making them stay for an allotted period without any consideration as to whether they have recovered or not."

As her back-stage struggle for the establishment of her concurrent jurisdiction clarified, men, women and children passed before her in about the same ratio as those in the men's court. There were many times, too, when, because of conditions which made it difficult for some mentally-deficient woman to come to her court, Emily would take her clerk to the home and examine the poor soul there. She was every whit as dignified sitting in some small room, with a sewing-machine for a table, as she was in her own court.

The miseries of her cases were with her, always, dogging her mind with their complexities. Her interest followed many of those called before her, so that she was often troubled at some unsolvable situation, wondering if, and how, it could be bettered. An evening spent drafting her letters, reading evidence on some special case, preparing her reports on asylum visits, would end with Emily lying wide awake in bed, checking and re-checking on new angles of a young girl's prosecution. Too often, a restless sleep was pierced by the doorbell. Wrapped hastily in her dressing-gown, she signed many a search warrant and went back to bed, knowing that in some tawdry, miserable room, men and women were being rounded up and taken to jail, to appear before her a few hours hence, draggle-eyed and cringing, or arrogant and sullen. Many times, too, she went down to the police station to give bail to women who had children they could not leave.

She sat in court, on a big throne-like chair, set on a small platform, with the Union Jack draped on the wall behind her. Day by day, she confronted business men caught with pathetic little girls; women with sexual complexities and inhibitions which no one could solve for them; children whipped and ill-treated by mis-shapen ugly creatures, whom Emily found difficult to believe human. She watched trembling young girls with blank, frightened faces, and older women whose eyes were blank because they had learned to eliminate personal fear; bitter and shoddy women with no hope left; school-girls pregnant by some respected neighbour; servants hysterical in their accusations against employers; flower-faced youngsters with lying, cruel hearts. She came to know the meaning of disease, viciousness, insanity, cruelty.

"In the Court-house one learns sad things," she wrote, "terrible things that may not be written down on paper, and that many would fear to read. One feels that nothing can ever thrive again which is good or pure."

A very large percentage of her cases dealt with foreigners, and one of Emily's characteristics as a magistrate materialized as a steadfast refusal to hurry them through, as was often done, because those concerned understood no English. She recognized that, except for the court, the only place foreign women came in contact with Canadian officialdom was at the post office and the customs. While she had to penalize them often, she did her best to send them away with their self-respect intact and no root of bitterness in their hearts.

As Janey Canuck, Emily had made a habit of studying closely the way of life in the pioneer settlements of the West and her staunch interest in foreigners and their problems was shown, again and again, not only in her handling of their tragedies in court and mental hospital, but in her letters and later articles. Typical of her approach was a letter to the Hon. Ernest Lapointe, Minister of Justice, in which she interceded for a man who had killed his wife's lover with an axe: "Maybe if C . . . had not been a foreigner and had used a gun instead of an axe, and had pleaded 'the unwritten law' it might possibly have gone easier with him. It frequently happens because we do not know the mentality of foreign persons, or because we cannot speak their language, that we are inclined to put them safely out of the way and to keep them forever there, seldom re-opening the matter. Besides being easier, this is a summary method—but not entirely consonant with either justice or humanity."

Many a terrified immigrant, cringing in her chair before the unknown menace of the court, stared in unbelief at Emily's kindly face, or listened with surprise to the gentle intonations of her voice. They could not understand a word of what she was saying, but they recognized the contradiction of their fears in the nuances of her speech.

One day a poor old German woman who was brought into court, crouched in a corner, trembling with fear, and refused to be placed in a chair. The orderly and policewoman reasoned with her ineffectually, until Emily, motioning them to sit down, walked slowly to the prisoner, took her hand, and softly called her "Mutter". Reassured, the old woman submitted to court routine.

Evidence showed that she had spent eighteen years working on a Canadian farm, and had reared eight sons and a daughter. Her husband, investing foolishly in one of the real estate booms raging throughout that period, had mortgaged the farm heavily. Worry preyed on her mind until she became demented.

Presently she began to wander through the court, singing a song of her childhood and fingering things like a curious child. Emily knew the song she sang, "Thou are a fragrant flower . . . so beautiful; so sweet".

The last time she had heard it was from Fraulein Ana, in Bishop Strachan's school. "Perhaps that was why," said Emily, in telling the story, "I was not shocked like the clerk, the interpreter, orderly, Herr Pastor and weeping daughter, when the defendant, stealing up to the big official chair, quietly kissed me on the cheek. Pouf! She might kiss the court if she wanted to . . . Which may only go to show that a woman

magistrate is incapable of upholding the time-honoured
dignity of the bench in the generally approved manner
of the male occupants thereof."

V

As a woman magistrate Emily was fully conscious
of the latent power in women's organizations. She was
closely allied, throughout this period, with many of
them, and worked indefatigably for their interests,
drafting resolutions for sponsorship, and programmes
of work for development. She felt that if the great
women's organizations only cared enough they could
bring about the reforms she saw were so desperately
needed. Rehabilitation, for instance, was surely women's work. So, too, was the introduction of such
national programmes as the payment of wages to male
persons in jail—to be paid for the maintenance of their
families. If the prisoner had no family, she believed
the wages should be held until he was released. Why
should the city or municipality be obliged to support
a prisoner's family while the Government got the results from his labour? Besides, the fact that labour
is imposed as a penalty in itself, she declared, gives a
prisoner a wrong idea concerning it. Labour should be
a means to his redemption—something which makes
for a building-up, and a maintaining of his respect.

In presenting suggestions for reform, Emily's belief
in women, and her endeavours for their more responsible status, brought many improvements in the West,
and did much to give leadership in fields of education
and jurisprudence throughout Canada.

She held it as a cardinal principle that the dis-

tinguishing mark of a really fine woman is loyalty to
her sex, and reflected this faith and loyalty in all her
work. I have before me her report to the Attorney-
General's department of October 2nd, 1916:

"In the short time this court has been established
I have found that the burden of my work, while arising
out of the court, has actually been situated outside
its walls. While I am not in duty bound to perform
such work, I am, nevertheless, prompted to do so from
humanitarian motives . . . and because it is the wish
of the women back of the movement, that I do so."

No matter how detailed the minutiae of her daily
routine, she looked outwards, always, to the periphery
of her work, and its implications to the country as a
whole. She approached her task with the thought that
while she wanted to help individual cases, her total
efforts should benefit womanhood itself. Women, she
felt, were often ignorant of their duties as mothers,
wives and citizens. Many of them, because of bad
environment, lack of education, or poor pay, or some
queer mental slant, had fallen into evil ways. Such
women were a menace generally, and she felt that
the Woman's Court, properly established and conducted, helped to achieve these women's redemptions,
and so benefited the community.

She relied on women's intelligence and ability in all
her appointments. The orderly in her court was a
woman who had had many years of experience as
matron at the Headquarters in Alberta of the Royal
North-West Mounted Police. The orderly accompanied
all women to the court, served all summonses, and
frequently made arrests.

On the constabulary force in Edmonton, at this

time, were two women with full powers. Their work was of a preventive and protective nature, their special beats the cabarets, dance-halls and streets after the theatres had closed. Women probation officers attached to the Department of Neglected Children also had full constabulary powers.

Encouraged by Emily, many women came to sit in the court and learn what reforms were needed. Hearing the cases without embarrassment, as no men were allowed in, they gained a knowledge of the provisions of the Criminal Code, the Provincial Statutes, the City by-laws. They also learned what was happening in the cabarets, dance-halls, opium dens, cheap lodging-houses, and on the streets, and so were able to take definite action whenever required.

The band of friends Emily had gathered in her early Edmonton days were loyal allies now. Most of them, at one time or another, had found jobs for one of Emily's "girls". Many a one of them, knitting a khaki sock in her court-room, and listening to some girl's story was thinking a way out for the girl, with herself in the role of big sister. Not a few so-called society matrons slipped into the Black Maria beside a prisoner, or into the cells, where they might talk the matter over and come to a decision.

There were times, of course, when Mrs. Murphy thought the women of the city were not as deeply interested in the work of the court as the urgency seemed to demand; times when she felt alone and over-worked.

"But one day," she recalled in a magazine article, "I was startled to find how much the women valued their court, not as an exemplification of women's rights,

but as a spiritual force in the scheme of things. I found
out that at their weekly services in the churches, they
were offering prayers that all things which were pure
and lovely and of good report, might be demonstrated
in my life and that I might have the requisite strength
to carry on the work.

"Than this, nothing more beautiful has ever happened to me."

VI

Aggie and Florrie . . . Maggie and Louie . . . Annie
and Nellie . . . Lily and Pearl.

The same names were whispered before her, month
after month. The same types sat before her, facing
their moment in court with whatever defences they
could muster. The same charges were sonorously in-
toned by the orderly, involving vagrancy . . . keeping
a disorderly house . . . procuring . . . found-in- . . .
assault . . . rape . . . incest . . . cruelty . . . conspiring
to defraud . . . theft.

Every woman who came to her court was interviewed by Emily, or one of her helpers, in the dingy
little office where so much of her work was done. A
friendly comment, perhaps, set a girl at ease, or a
hand on the woman's shoulder, and a straightforward,
"Now, Pearl, tell me the name of the man responsible
for your condition." Perhaps an arm around a frightened girl's shoulder, and a whispered invitation, would
bring down the young head, deep-buried in shaking
hands, and the story, laboriously elicited, told in half
sentences and long, aching pauses. Emily was steadfastly patient, deeply concerned with each case in

which she felt there was any hope for betterment.

She found that girls were more amenable to advice on such an occasion, and more inclined to take advantage of a fresh start in life. There was nothing, she said, in all the world, quite so desolate and forlorn— or, indeed, more desperate—than a girl who stood for the first time, alone in the prisoner's dock, as a convicted criminal. She might resent advice or what, at some other time, she might term interference or patronage but, at that moment, it seemed like a glimpse of clear open skies for some woman to put an arm around her, and ask if she wanted another chance to make good in a fair field.

It was heart-breaking to find how small a cause had often brought about a girl's downfall. One such tragedy occurred when a mistress had locked the nursemaid out all night, because she was late returning home. Often a girl hadn't the price for her lodging, and so, for lack of a few cents, had been drawn into a life of infamy and disease. "There are some of us," Emily wrote once, "who think it is an odious scandal for huge sums to be expended on town halls or other municipal buildings when in many towns there is not a place in which homeless girls can sleep in safety."

Moreover, Emily found that one of her difficulties lay in uprooting from the minds of these girls the belief that they were now outcasts and irretrievably lost, so that no respectable occupation was open to them. Many a time she quoted to such a girl Adelaide Proctor's lines:

"No star is ever lost we once have seen,
"We always may be what we might have been."

Repeatedly, Emily pointed out that in fining a girl as a vagrant or night-walker, the State was virtually becoming a sharer in the traffic. The girl's fine, she said, became a licence fee until she was again apprehended, and another fine paid. This fine was usually borrowed from one of the men friends with whom she had become involved so that, too often, she stepped out of court with the entangling noose tied more tightly around her neck.

Describing this in a magazine article, Emily said: "These panderers and unspeakable harpies sit in court ready to pay the girl's fine, and to take her out to earn and repay the money again and again . . . There is no public defender for the girl; no man or woman to free her from the yoke of these evil ones who continue to batten and fatten upon her soul and body, because, forsooth, they have become her paymaster. No, for the most part the public are dead as brass to all this. Assuredly there is need of trumpeters here. Few, if any of us, seem to recognize that if we are to rescue and restore the girl, she must be treated quite otherwise than by the imposition of costs and fines."

Nothing pleased Emily more than a wedding arising out of one of her court cases. Her own wedding ring was used in such ceremonies time without number. The family never knew when to expect a wedding party at the house, with a purposeful Emily, a timid young girl and a tongue-tied lad. Something to eat, of course, was quickly assembled by whoever happened to be home and, if there were time, a wedding cake iced in silver and white.

She wrote hundreds of letters to girls she had sentenced, released, or who were out on bail. In her mail came crudely wrapped parcels, filled with elaborately crocheted camisole tops, cushion covers, doilies, lace edgings, made for her in jail by some of the women she had sentenced. Some of her friends sensed an opportunity for fun in these gifts; but to Emily they represented something deeper than the obvious, and she showed them only to those who would look at them with her own understanding.

Always, she was direct and forthright. With all her interest in her cases, she had little of the sentimental about her. "The best way a woman magistrate, or any other woman, can be a saviour, is not to stoop and save, but to stand by the girl and let her save herself."

Her work of rehabilitation with older prostitutes was discouraging in the extreme. Many of them preferred the ugly and obscene. "Vain, vulgar and intemperate," she wrote, "and bearing the physical stigmata of their type, they are willing to sacrifice the future—even their length of days—for the flare and flutter of the swallow pits described as the underworld."

The older women did not readily respond to the methods of the Women's Court. They might be moved to tears, and promise to do better things, but the experiences they had known, Emily felt, had registered on their nerves and very fibres, until they seemed powerless to help themselves. Their wills were weakened; their moral nature broken down, and they had become exiles from their common humanity. Such women, she said, became wreckers and treacherous trulls.

Most of the difficulty arose from the fact that these older women had become addicted to the use of habit-forming drugs. Many of them, with a twist of pain about their mouths, told her they would be wholly unequal to the physical strain of their lives without taking opium. The men responsible for the traffic in Edmonton, as elsewhere, persuaded the girls that drugs were necessary.

Many of the more experienced prostitutes objected to being tried in Emily's court claiming that she was hard. Emily, being a woman, knew instinctively when they were lying and, being used to tears, was unmoved by them. Before a liar, or faced with cold viciousness, Emily became equally cold and hard—even more so, as many a prisoner discovered. She had a habit of listening quietly to such a prisoner, then snapping her gold lorgnette and gazing steadily at the woman as she talked. A moment or two and then Emily's voice snapped also, relentless, convinced. "Stop your lying!" With such cases Emily was adamant, regarding her duty as involving the protection of the community. Her sentences were severe; her leniency non-existent.

As a magistrate she never claimed any particular privilege for women where crimes were concerned, for, as she put it, there could not be any sex in sin, or sex in soul. Yet, since it was harder for a woman to re-instate herself socially than for a man, the treatment had to be considered in that light.

During certain physical crises, she discovered, wo-men, through nervousness, were apt to be less respons-ible. There were periods in which they seemed to be hypnotized by their own hysteria and in which they seemed almost demented. These cases were most difficult for her to handle, and she felt, always, that they would never be treated properly until the courts had the assistance of psychologists and clinicians. An awareness of her ignorance in all such cases made her task at times seem burdensome beyond endurance. These difficult cases which, so her imagination told her, were beyond her power to help, came home with her at night, and troubled her through long wakeful hours.

She found considerable resentment among her prisoners. The majority of women, because they were of the same sex, expected sympathy and defence from a woman judge, rather than justice, and were surprised and chagrined that she should "side with" a man, on any grounds. This was particularly true in cases where women had beaten up their husbands. Perhaps, because the average woman in the northwest was vital, big and unafraid, husband-beating was fairly common. "He's able to take care of himself," these women told Emily, who felt that a man, beaten by his wife, while ludicrous, was also perhaps the most helpless and pitiable object in the world. If he struck her back, he knew that the result might be serious, and so he must, perforce, either stand up under the beating, or dodge as best he might.

Scores of men came to her office to discuss the crimes their wives had committed, but it was in rare cases that any charge was laid. One man with both thumbs broken by having them pressed back, explained how the "Missus" was "always trying to mess me abaht." Another, with a wicked gash in his eyebrows caused by a flying cup, asked Emily to "Just send for Violet and scare her a bit."

She became used to threats to her life. Drug addicts, severely sentenced, vowed they would shoot her;

several women threatened to have her officially disqualified because she was obviously "no woman's
judge". Anonymous letters contained threats. Telephone calls, with dark hints of vengeance from friends
of the accused became more or less routine.

"There is one distinct benefit, however, to being a
Police Magistrate in a woman's court", she wrote. "You
are saved from the risk of stagnancy. You will have the
distinction, too,—albeit a graceless one—of having
persecuted more perfectly pure, unoffending ladies than
any other woman in your city."

VII

The habits of years die hard. Emily's mind was en-
grossed with the realities of the living tragedies that
paraded before her. Her imagination was absorbed in
plans for the rehabilitation of broken girls, and her
energies spent in writing hundreds of letters. Yet, her
old instinct for gathering notes persisted. While she
wrote a few magazine articles on her work, scattered
through her papers are odd scraps of notes that give
other vivid sidelights—comments and memoranda
gathered with the old love which Janey Canuck had
given to the passing fragments of life.

Here, for instance, with its inevitable rusty pin, are
gathered notes on scraps of ruled paper, headed
"Tears".

"Dr. C— trying to work me not to prosecute for
drugs, cries.

". . . Oscar K——, —— Hotel, cried in my office
because he wanted to work me not to cancel his
mother's licence.

". . . Men and women who are under drugs, cry easily.

". . . Fathers cry over their young daughters who have been betrayed.

". . . The dry-eyed woman whose children are taken away from her forever, cries. (She pictures their past and future.) Very sad.

"The little girl who has grown attached to her baby and is giving it up forever, cries.

"The woman who strives to hold the tears back; whose face quivers under the stress of her emotions, or who restrains herself, except for the tell-tale crimson that spreads itself in patches on her throat and face, is usually a pretty good sort, in spite of her lapse from virtue, and is seldom irretrievably bad.

"Indeed . . . tears are more nearly to the surface where men are under pressure. This particularly applies when their protective instincts have been appealed to. A man will break horribly when told of the tragedy that has come into the life of his girl-child. Than this, life has no sadder happening.

"A son whose mother has become insane, or a young husband whose wife has wandered off into the badlands of the underworld, is filled with an amazement of sorrow, and finds his consolation in tears."

VIII

She could, on occasion, be bitterly scathing in her denunciation, whether it was in a verbal encounter or in one of her letters. Mrs. Ellen Robinson, for many years police matron in Emily's court, recalled, after Emily's death, one of these brief stinging moments:

"A very lovely girl," she recalled, "whose father was on the police force, was taken from a hotel with a married man, who had a good position in town. Next morning his lawyer asked that the man be excused from court as his wife was hourly expecting to become a mother. The girl was found to be terribly diseased and was also pregnant. Mrs. Murphy told me to bring the man into court. I'll never forget the quiet words she spoke. 'Good morning, Mr. —. I understand your wife is hourly expecting her baby!' 'Yes, your Worship.' 'Well, I had you brought in here just to express to you the contempt I feel for a man of your calibre'."

"The lawyer whispered to me," said Mrs. Robinson, " 'had that been me, I would have wished the floor to open and swallow me up'."

She believed in forthright honesty in her approach to those responsible for trouble. This letter, written to a father in a neighbouring town, to tell him of his daughter's condition, is typical of her method:

"The child is in a state of distraction, but agreed to leave her case in my hands until I decided what was best to be done. She is deeply concerned about her sister Blanche, also here in town, and asked me to see that nothing happened to her. I have made enquiries into the background of the girls . . . and feel that you, as their parents, have been extremely lax in your parental oversight . . . I do not mention these facts to wound your already lacerated feelings but that you may realize that this girl is not culpable for this sad affair so much as you and her mother. She is only a girl-child, with a girl-child's supreme ignorance of the world and her own sexual nature. Moreover, I desire to sting you awake in order that you may look better to her welfare in the future and to that of your other daughter. It is appalling beyond words, the ignorance that exists among parents as to the life lived by their own children and their apparent apathy to these matters."

Her innate appreciation of the dramatic moment was proverbial. The afternoon five unmarried mothers were in court, all requesting that their children be put out for adoption, is a case in point. Emily had the five young women brought into court and lined up before her, while the spectators watched in some bewilderment. Looking sternly from one to the other, Her Worship commented on the fact that the five of them were relinquishing all rights to their children. She denounced them as a group and then gave them a foretaste of their retributory isolation. "You have companionship in this crime but your punishment will come when you see a group of children playing in the street . . . and you will wonder if one of them is yours."

Her brother's vaunted fears that she might lack sympathy for her erring sisters, again and again proved groundless. There is an understanding often running parallel with her most vituperant denunciations. For example, listen as she speaks on a case just closed:

"I wish to talk to these two young men. Come here. I do not know what to say to you. You are both presumably intelligent men, and to me it is a hideous thing that you should have taken this little broken-backed, feeble-minded child and done this thing to her. If she were a year younger, you would both go to prison and get lashed; so you may consider yourself extremely lucky that the girl is turned sixteen. It is a terrible thing that she should have run away from home and taken refuge in your hotel and that she should have been betrayed there . . . The child evidently got into a den of vipers, and it may mean that she will be shut up for the rest of her life, as she has not the will-power, nor the mentality, to protect herself . . . You both look the part you have played. You had better stop drinking and brace up so that you are not all yellow cur."

Regarding the mentally unfit who ranged before her, she wrote, "With one's sense of decency outraged and anger uppermost in one's mind, it isn't easy to be tolerant with the fool, the criminal, the ingrate. It isn't easy to divine the human quality behind the dull or crafty faces of the neglected or the degenerate. And yet the most astonishing thing about these unfortunate persons is the ease with which they yield themselves to the healthy, affirmative forces, and how they absorb the fine spiritual quality in others."

IX

Some of the reforms she preached twenty years ago are needed as vitally today. She believed, for instance, that until a nation-wide system of industrial homes was set up, for teaching wayward girls work by which they could earn their own living, the problem of delinquency was not being met. There was little use, she contended, in shutting them up and teaching them almost nothing; in turning a girl out on the street no more capable of maintaining herself than before incarceration. "Where is the use of telling a girl to be good when we all know that goodness is largely a by-product of efficiency? In talking to girls, and inquiring into their habits, where feeble-mindedness was not a causative factor, I have found the bad girl to be the ignorant, lazy one who has not been taught to use her hands . . . The industrial side of redemptive work is one which requires the close and urgent attention on the part of all interested women. Much good work has been done in the past to reclaim the wayward girl but, after all, the struggles in life are not so much between the good and the bad, as between the good and the better."

This need for an intensive study of the possibilities in rehabilitation was uppermost in her mind throughout her years as a magistrate. The first step, in her mind, lay in a strong attempt to settle the case before it came into court, if at all possible. A patient and intensive study of a woman's history was often required in order to rehabilitate her in the light of her disabilities, capabilities and adaptabilities.

She felt that the woman magistrate, being used to the woman's task of applying remedies to the ailing, was more inclined to avail herself of the assistance offered by the psychopathic clinic, the venereal disease clinic, and the industrial or maternity home. Indeed, the idea of punishment, she often said, had little to do with courts—that of rehabilitation was uppermost. This process might mean a term in jail, or a period on parole—but on no occasion, whatever, should a woman's self-respect be lowered or destroyed.

"By and by, when our eyes have grown clearer, we shall see that all criminal courts must be casualty clearing-stations, when the offender's case must be carefully diagnosed and the proper remedy applied."

X

This personal interest of hers in what was happening in the minds of those who passed before her, meant that, in actuality, she was never free from the pressure arising out of her work. The telephone at home was always shrilling with someone calling for help, or perhaps insisting on giving information regarding a couple of neglected children; a case of immorality; some tragic insanity. There were, too, many threats of vengeance from friends of those she had sentenced, anonymous letters; or pleas for assistance from strangers who knew of her work. She received hundreds like these which follow.

"Dear Lady:
"I have heard of a home in Edmonton where girls can go who have gone wrong in life, and I understand they can leave their little one there if they wish . . . I hope you can give this a little of your precious attention, as you are the only one I know who would tell me about it . . ."

"Dear Madam:
"I am here in Killam and there is a friend of mine here, who would like to know if a woman who has been away from her husband for over seven years, and never heard from him and he has never supported or wrote her ever since, could she get married again to another man without having a divorce . . . ?"

"Dear Friend:
"I have been told that you would help me with

my trubble as I am a breed girl and I am 24 yrs old and got in trubble with a white man and he dont help me with my baby. I am all most destiu I stook the last two summer since I had my baby and traped in the winter and I cant catch nothing this winder would you please be kind enuff to let me know if I can collect for the support of the baby."

There is a thick file of letters beginning with one from a twenty-four-year-old Scandinavian girl, Johanna:

"You will allow me to write to you at least, and let you know all my sorrows and misery . . . About 7 months ago I had a child with our neighbor C . . . who promised to marry me. After the child was born he refused to do it and promised on a piece of paper to pay for the upkeep of the child 15 dollars a month until the child is big enough to earn a living for itself . . ."

Johanna's letter went on at length to tell how C . . . in spite of his promise on the piece of paper, had contributed nothing. He had married another woman, and was now enlisted. Johanna had sent her precious piece of paper to a firm of lawyers in the nearby town, asking them if, because of it, they could get some payment for her. They had done nothing—and would not return the paper, "Because," reasoned Johanna, "I am poor and cannot pay them so much as they need and C . . . 's father is rich and the lawyers will be more in favour to him than me. Your Honour . . . I am now lost and neglected from everybody. I am hungry and my child is with me. I have not got a piece of cloth to go out and seek the justice . . . I am not seeking anything

but justice and what the king and country guarantees
me in this country. Pray save myself and my child and
bring justice on tap . . ."

It was an appeal which Emily could not resist. She
knew the type of family from her years of association
throughout the West.

Next day a long letter went back to Johanna. As a
magistrate, the matter was beyond her jurisdiction, but
she could advise her. In part, she wrote:

"I have no jurisdiction over the crimes committed
by either men or boys, or on cases outside Edmonton.
[This was in her first year on the bench, before she
had been made Police Magistrate for Alberta as a
whole.] I therefore cannot give your case any official
attention but would be glad to help you in any way
possible as one woman might help another." Followed
practical advice on handling Johanna's problem and
then: "Do you need clothing for yourself or your
brothers and sisters? If so, let me know their ages and
which are girls, and I'll see if I can help you."

Over the months Johanna wrote regularly to Emily
telling of developments. Finally C— was tracked down
in England, and a promise extracted that he would
pay five dollars a month for his child's support. For
this service the lawyers exacted a very heavy fee which
Johanna could not possibly pay. Moreover, they would
not return the "piece of paper" until the bill was paid
in full. Emily advised the girl to pay something on
account, but even this proved difficult for the girl.
Whereupon the firm wrote direct to Emily: "Seeing
that you have interested yourself in this case, we think
that you might at least see that Miss B— pays us

for the work we did for her. Unless we hear from you in this matter, we intend to publish our correspondence."

Their letter and its threatening tone infuriated Emily, who was never easily cowed. She took counsel of Arthur as to what was best to be done. He was of the opinion that they might be so foolish as to try and publish the letters, so she wrote to the local paper asking to be informed of any such move in order that she might have the opportunity of replying. Then she wrote to the lawyers, outlining in brief the whole situation. On the last page of the file is her concluding blast:

"Why you should in any way hold me responsible for the account is beyond my wits' end. The girl was an entire stranger to me, and I only knew her as a helpless, ill-instructed girl who declared herself to be in distress as between solicitors who insisted on the payment of their fee, and the man who betrayed her. After all this you have the supreme impudence to say that if Miss B— does not pay you the balance you will publish my letters. My opinion of you—and believe me it is a well-matured opinion—might possibly have a salutary effect on the mending of your manners, but I will be content to say that such unwarranted action on your part would hardly add to your status as members of the bar in this province and certainly would in no way enhance your reputation with the general public. Personally I think I would be rather pleased if you did publish these letters in the interest of all concerned.

"In conclusion I would lay upon you an admonition which you will heed, if you are even remotely wise.

Don't you dare to write me such another communication as your last, unless you are prepared to take the consequences. It would take much better men than you would seem to be, to intimidate me by such paltry and currish threats . . .''

No further communication. Case closed.

Here is an eloquent letter, written to a woman who was in jail, sentenced by Emily for contributing to the neglect of her children. The letter is worth reading, apart from every other consideration, because it indicates the way in which her creative energies were being turned to practical applications, rather than to further "sketches" for book publication.

Writing to Mrs. P— Emily said:

"Because Easter should be a time of happiness and because I know you must be deeply unhappy, I am taking the liberty of writing to you, not as one who was obliged by her position to pass a painful sentence, but just as one Western woman to another. I have been counting the time till you will be back again in Edmonton and see that it will not be long now.

"I remember when I was a little girl at boarding-school, I used to cry a good deal from homesickness and kept a calendar to mark off each day as it passed. I imagine you must be feeling something the same way. But after all nothing matters in life, so long as it doesn't make us bitter. Some old chap said once, 'There lies no desert in the land of life,' and I have always found this to be true in my own experience. Indeed, I have always hoped and believed that the scapegoat which the Israelites sent out to the desert to die, didn't die, but found plenty of cool water and green grass.

"Of course you know that we arranged that your mother should take care of the children while you were away. When Mr. P— comes home, if you need my help in any way, it would give me much satisfaction to help you. The same applies to all the women at MacLeod from Edmonton. It does not necessarily follow that because a woman has slipped either wilfully or through an error in judgment, that she differs materially from the rest of us.

"We have heard here about the work the women are doing in the Guard-Room for the Red Cross, and think it splendid. It shows that while the women are shut in for a while they still kept the hearts of fine free women. We are working here to get a farm where the women and girls can grow things and make their own pats of butter and jars of jam without any guards, but just to stay there, on their honour, till their time is up. We hope to arrange, too, those who wish to learn millinery, book-keeping, shorthand, and things like that. Pray that we get it. All you women—pray that we get it.

"I do not know if Mrs. Emma L—or the others from Edmonton would care to hear from me (but indeed, I should hope so). If you think they would, please say I send a greeting over the miles, and that all I have said to you, is for them as well,

"Yours in all sincerity,"

Hundreds and hundreds of letters, written in the same spirit, went from Emily to prisoners and inmates. Many of them followed her visits to jail or asylum. For

EMILY, REVIEWING EDMONTON CITY POLICE FORCE, 1926.
First row. *Left to right*: Chief Constable A. G. Shute, Emily, Mayor
Ambrose Bury, Crown Prosecutor, Alan Harvey

EMILY CONDUCTING A JUVENILE COURT, WITH NO MAN PRESENT, 1918

LORD CHANCELLOR SANKEY OF HIS MAJESTY'S PRIVY COUNCIL, AT TEMPLE
BAR, 1929. ON HIS WAY TO DELIVER JUDGMENT RE THE STATUS OF
WOMEN AS "PERSONS" UNDER THE BRITISH NORTH AMERICA ACT

instance, this note went back to Ponoka after one inspection, at Ponoka asylum:

"You asked me yesterday to find out what had become of your children. I find they were brought in
from the county last week and are in the care of the
Government at the Edmonton shelter for children.
They are happy and quite well, so that you need not
worry about them at all. I called on Mrs. Guthrie
who has charge of them and she says the children
have always been together since you went away. They
are having a birthday party for the little boy on Saturday. The little girl has done particularly well at school,
and is very bright. I know you will be pleased to hear
this."

Written the very next day, and following a personal
visit by Emily, to see for herself how another woman's
children were faring, this letter might serve as the
basic pattern through the years of her public life.

In that pattern of vital personal concern, keyed to
her vision of things as they should be, lay the facts of
her genius. As the first woman Magistrate to be appointed in the British Empire, Mrs. Arthur Murphy
became an inspired woman in an inspired interpretation of her responsibilities.

CHAPTER II

Life in Death

Their's is a veritable life in death . . . The scene
has all the suffering of tragedy with none of its
dignity.

EMILY MURPHY.

I

ON A BRIGHT JUNE DAY in 1930, I walked with
Emily in the world she had come to know so well
since she was made Magistrate—a world set behind
the walls of penitentiaries and asylums.

We drove out from Edmonton to Fort Saskatchewan
jail while the sun was still low in the morning sky
and, later in the day, to the Ponoka Mental Hospital.
Although I did not know then of the years Emily had
spent on the prairie trails, I remember that as we
talked, her eyes constantly searched the horizon.
Imprisoned as she was, on the shuttle that ran from
her court to these great square buildings, set on their
flat acres, her spirit still yearned subconsciously for the
days when she rode "where nothing met but the four
winds; nothing passed but the high clouds".

She spoke of the people we were to see in the asylum.
So many of them, she said, were such fine-looking
folk—a mother in the flare of life, with perfect plans

174

for her family; the intelligent labourer whose wife and young children were stranded at home; the professional or business man with brilliant prospects. Emily knew the life each one had lived, and her thoughts reached, always, to the possibilities that might develop in finding a solution for each case.

In her handbag was a letter just received from one of the men in Lethbridge Jail, scrawled in pencil on the blue prison paper.

"Dear Madam:

"On behalf of the inmates of the Hospital Ward, permit me to thank you for the lovely roses which brought a double message—one of fragrance and beauty, the other like the violet ray, invisible but more powerful and direct to the heart.

"Shut in as we are, any token of kindness is doubly welcomed; not that we are worthy of it, possibly quite the contrary, yet because of this, an unexpected blessing. As I look at the petals falling, they remind me of the fading friendships with those on the outside, until at last we stand alone, dishonoured and forgotten. It is a terrible penalty we pay for wrong-doing, and alas, we realize it too late. It is not the penalty that hurts most, but the heartaches and the hopelessness that accompanies it.

"The wheel to which we are bound, rolls straight ahead, and knows only tears. Hysterically we laugh, and then we weep, until our fears are gone and then we fall in one long, deep sleep.

"Sincerely and gratefully yours,
"James F. H.——"

Emily folded the letter carefully and put it back in her bag. Eventually I read it again when I found it among the hundreds upon hundreds of letters which had been crowding her bedroom shelves for so long. "Many of them feel that way," she said, "but only one in a thousand is articulate."

I thought of James F. H—— again, as we walked slowly down the long, long corridors of the women's wing in the jail. Since it was Sunday, and a time of day in which the prisoners were in the cells, most of the little cubicles were occupied. Each woman was intent on some personal interest, with her back turned to the door for a measure of privacy. Emily stopped at each cell. She knew every inmate, and I could sense the subtle changes in her manner to fit the mood and type of each. Most of the prisoners were crocheting, reading, or staring into the vague sky beyond the bars. Nearly all turned with an ejaculation of pleasure at her low-sounded "Dollie . . . Hello there, Lily . . . Good morning, Pearl!" They came close to the door, paying no attention to the stranger with Mrs. Murphy, except for a quick flicker of eyes. Each looked at her eagerly, begging for some news of home, word of husband or children. Some asked her to take messages back; to ask relatives to send them personal possessions needed—a pink comb from the upper bureau drawer; a package of hair-pins; a new snapshot of the children. Emily left a word of hope with each of these petition-ers. "I saw your Bill not long ago. He was looking very well and told me he was counting the days till you got home." Or again: "I had your children in last week, Nellie. Jim has passed into the next grade, and the baby is learning to walk. Won't be long now before you're back!"

Some of the women remained sullenly where they were and paid no attention to Emily's call, or turned dark faces towards her, staring insolently. Now and then, there was flint and steel in Emily's voice; with others, she spoke gently. "No good sulking, Jennie. The sooner you make up your mind you're going to behave yourself, the sooner you'll be out."

We must drop in, too, and chat with a few of the staff officials, asking for information on prisoners in whom Emily is particularly interested. We must see the women file in for their mid-day meal, and check on how they find the food. As always, Judge Murphy was studying critically what she saw. I was conscious of several apprehensive officials in the background. What kind of a report would Mrs. Murphy take back? She could hit hard when she was displeased with what she saw.

Later, as we walked down the gravel path to the car, some of the prisoners saw us. Faces pressed close to the window bars; hands were waving through, and voices calling, "Goodbye, Mrs. Murphy. Goodbye, Ma'am! Tell my George I'm thinking of him . . . You won't forget the pink comb? . . . Ask Mamie to write to me . . ."

II

At the jail, I sensed the clinical honesty with which Emily faced the men and women sentenced for their crimes; but as we walked through the crowded halls

of Ponoka Insane Asylum that afternoon, I realized
the deep, aching pity she felt for these afflicted men
and women.

Emily showed little trace of sentimentality in her
approach to any phase of her work as Magistrate. She
had a penetrating, analytical interest in human life,
always, and searched behind the detail of each case
for the cause and possible solution. Because she concerned herself intensely with the curative aspects she
never allowed herself to be depressed by the tragedies
she watched, day by day,—with one exception, the
commitment of mothers to insane asylums. When she
could make it easier for the insane woman's family by
having the court enquiry in the woman's home, rather
than the police station, she would do so. Inevitably, on
her return home, her family found her still deeply
involved in the humanities of the case. She would tell
of the children's tears, and the husband's dazed misery;
recall every nuance in the evidence; plan, perhaps, for
some method of meeting the needs of the disrupted
family. After one of these mental cases, Emily could
not touch her dinner, and it would be two o'clock in
the morning before her family could finally get her
away from her desk, and into bed.

As we trod the wardroom floors, I glimpsed how
deep and personal was her feeling for the wrecked
lives and the bitter, wanton losses gathered at Ponoka.

The patients were grouped in three buildings according to the degree of their insanity. In the bright rooms
of the first, the patients were quiet, since most of them
were only seized occasionally. Here was a real eagerness for her coming, and she was followed closely with
welcoming eyes wherever she walked.

A handsome boy lifted his cue from the billiard table to speak to her. "An alcoholic," Janey explained, as we moved towards him.

"I'm going home next week, Mrs. Murphy," he said. "The doctors declare it. The last time we met was in Edmonton. Remember? You fined me $3.25 for speeding on Jasper Avenue. The fine was much too small."

"You're not ready to go out yet, Lad," said Her Honour, twinkling. "No man who was normal ever acknowledged the like before."

This was Emily's world by right of her active fellowship, her interest and sympathy. She was really concerned with the progress the women had made in their embroidery, the men with their carpentry. She had a joke or two for some, and was quietly intent during a long babbled explanation or halting enquiry for those at home.

As the shadows lengthened, we passed into the third building where men and women moved in ever-restless currents, or sat, lost and hopeless, on the benches that circled the rooms.

"No matter how immured the outsider has become," she wrote once, "one must steel oneself stoutly for the hurt of the wards. One walks past the sorely distracted patients and notes the profound depression, fumbling hands, worn eyes and tightly pinched faces. Apprehensive, delirious, exalted, furiously maniacal, unstable or melancholic—theirs is a veritable life in death. The scene has all the suffering of tragedy, with none of its dignity."

As we walked slowly through this last building, I noticed a very tall figure with a full red beard, draped in a white sheet-like affair, with sandals on his bare

feet, following us carefully. As we turned at the door
for one last glance back, he was hovering near, waiting
patiently for Emily to speak to him. Quickly she moved
to him. For some moments they stood together, the
short thick-set little figure in black with her earnest
face up-turned to the calm blankness of the tall figure
in white. His large, very blue eyes shone on her with
a radiant calm; the highlights on the bony contours of
his cheek-bones gave his face an unearthly glow. Behind the two of them weaved the melancholy pattern
of the empty-minded.

I watched, absorbed, until the tall man smiled
gently, and moved off, pacing slowly through the
chaotic rhythms about him. After a moment, Emily led
me outside, past the guards. "He believes that he is
the Christ," she explained. "He was once one of the
smartest business men in Edmonton. He wanted to
buy too many things for his very pretty wife and
daughters. He struggled and worried—until he cracked
up. Now the family is destitute, living off relatives.
But, as you can see, he is happy. And it's strange how
he quiets the patients . . ."

III

It was characteristic of Emily that in all her work
as Magistrate and Judge, she sought, always, for the
significant truths behind her cases, dissatisfied merely
to deal with them, day after day, clearing the docket
and taking up the next day's list as a matter of routine.
It was not enough that she sit in judgment on those
who came before her; she worked, always, on the
wider implications of what she handled.

Wherever possible she found jobs for the girls ranged before her, and wrote to hundreds of them until they became established in life again. It was a common thing for a friend who had taken one of "Emily's girls", as they were called, into her home as a domestic, to have "the Judge" telephone of an evening to make personal enquiries as to how the girl was coming along. Was she happy? Was there anything special she needed? "Be a good girl now," sounded over and over again. "Be a good girl. I want things to turn out well for you."

Similarly, in the cases of insanity she handled, her insatiable interest in the victim and the social problem involved drove her to activity far beyond the normal. She became one of the most influential and authoritative students of the best methods applied in mental hospitals and jails. So, too, she studied the drug menace, realizing from the beginning of her work on the bench that drugs lay at the root of many of the tragedies before her. She spent years on intensive research into the whole problem and, as we shall see, waged an intensive and enduring fight against it.

Her breadth of vision and vigour of mind drove her continually, and she was concerned with all the major developments in the Province of Alberta which placed it in the forefront in so many social programmes. So intense, for instance, was her interest in the asylums, that only two years after her appointment, the Minister of Public Works, the Hon. A. J. MacLean, asked her to visit the provincial hospital at Ponoka, to give her impressions and conclusions. He asked for an informal report; a study made by an interested but impersonal official.

He expected a fairly routine formula, but so helpful

was her analysis that, shortly thereafter, she was asked
to become a member of a Visiting Committee to study
conditions in all the provincial jails and mental institutions.

This first informal report is interesting since it is
typical of her approach to any challenge. She drafted
and re-drafted her direct and simple statement, so that
it became a clear-cut analysis of the whole organization. She made no criticism without giving a very
definite suggestion as to how it might be overcome.
She never suggested the spending of increased money,
without also giving her ideas as to where the necessary
sums might be obtained.

On this, her very first semi-official inspection of
Ponoka, she was perturbed by the lack of employment
among many of the inmates, and suggested that no
one who was not occupied could be happy, especially
if he were introspective and unduly self-conscious.

She noted that the patients' evening supper consisted of two slices of brown bread, buttered, and a
small portion of corn syrup, while the staff supped on
sausages, boiled cabbage and potatoes. She recommended that the opposite condition should exist, if
there had to be contrast, since tests had shown that
insane persons who were properly fed, had a much
more rapid recovery than those who were poorly, or
even moderately, well fed. Many of the patients, she
realized from her own two years' experience in court,
had come to the hospital in the first place suffering from
malnutrition caused by their poverty, ignorance, or
physical disease.

In time, Emily was asked to act as Secretary to the
Visiting Committee, and to her other work added the

labour of writing the long, detailed reports. As a member of this group of five, she made exhaustive surveys of the grounds and buildings, equipment, patient strength, medical staff, nursing and housekeeping arrangements, treatment of inmates, follow-up treatment. Inmates or prisoners were permitted to come before the Committee with any complaint dealing with the insufficiency or poor quality of food, lack of warm clothing, general discontent with the administration, or the attitude of officials. Much time was spent in questioning the patients, probing for details when any injustice was feared, soothing them when none was indicated. These regular visits meant many nights spent at the small adjacent hotels, with ensuing inconvenience and weariness; but as usual the evenings were filled with her writing on what she had heard and seen during the day.

When the Committee members were visiting at Ponoka, special rooms were assigned to them. It became a habit, with Emily, to slip out after midnight and walk through the wards to see how the patients she was concerned about were sleeping. If they were asleep she took hope that they were on their way to recovery; if they were restless she sat beside them, talking quietly, listening carefully, trying to find some further clue as to where their main trouble lay. One of the Committee members, Mrs. J. W. Field, describing these nocturnal visits, said to Evelyn, after her mother's death:

"I wouldn't have had the courage to do that in a million years, as it was such a fearful, scary place at night. Your mother seemed to be absolutely without fear, and impervious to the danger she ran, as she her-

self had committed many of the patients and they were
very vengeful sometimes. But Mrs. Murphy seemed
quite at home with them. I wish you could have seen
her dancing with the patients, when we happened to
be there on a social evening! She had a knack of making them enjoy it all very much."

Emily Murphy's reports were direct and very much
to the point. Typical of them is the terse account of
an unexpected visit to an old people's hostel.

"On the arrival of your Board, the noon meal was
being served. This consisted of roast beef, potatoes,
carrots, and tapioca pudding. The beef was tough and
badly cooked, thus rendering it unfit for elderly persons who would have difficulty in mastication . . . The
pudding was unappetizing and of a gluey consistency.
The food was served up some time before the inmates
entered the dining-room, so was cold. The kitchen was
neither clean nor tidy."

Her ability for encouraging people to talk was of
very real value in the long investigations the Committee
held into certain occurrences in the institutions. For
one thing, Emily knew these people of old. For ten
years she had been dropping casually in on them, on
her visits with the Padre to the prairie districts. She
knew how they thought, and how they felt, and how
to win their confidence. In the stenographic reports of
scores of investigations it is easy to see how the direct
and friendly questioning of the little woman with the
hazel eyes brought a response.

But her interest did not end with the evidence. She
must write for herself on the humanitarian aspect of
what she had heard. Here is a fragment of her thinking, selected from hundreds of similar notes, on scores

of investigations as an illustration of her method. For days she had sat with the Committee studying a brutal affair in which a mentally-deficient patient had first, it was alleged, been put into a strait-jacket, and then kicked to death. One of the guards was sentenced to five years in the penitentiary for manslaughter as a result. One of the witnesses was a young guard. Not content with the routine and official evidence, Emily wrote for clearance of her own thinking, many pages of notes. Among them, this:

"C—, who assaulted L—, says he only carried him to the bath but did not hit him. He is a University student and son of C—. If he were approached in jail, or after he gets out, and told that he has a chance to redeem himself in the eyes of the Government by telling how the patients are ill-treated and what knowledge he has of this, or of slackness, it is probable that he would do so.

"He should be told that he is not being asked for names, but only to tell how the patients can be protected in the future . . . what he would do if he were superintendent.

"If it could be pointed out to him that we realize he was only a youth who, through an unfortunate chance, was jolted into manhood in an hour . . . He can redeem himself by an interest in and care of those unfortunate patients for the rest of his life. This does not mean that he is to 'squeal' on S—, or anything like that, but just help the Government in its task of cure and protection."

" . . . Its task of cure and protection."

This was the responsibility Emily shouldered, day after day, crusading in her own work, and through whatever avenues she could reach, for an ever-increasing awareness on the part of the public and of the government for its responsibility in both the cure and the protection so badly needed.

IV

Vehemently and repeatedly Emily reminded those in authority that insanity was not a crime, and that the qualities required in dealing with it were wisdom and humanity rather than a harsh, unthinking officialism.

However, in dealing with the problem arising out of insanity, she was equally firm in upholding the need for sterilization of the mentally unfit. The weak-minded, she felt, are more to be feared than the wicked, in that there is no hope for them. She would not allow the imbecile or the feeble-minded criminal to increase the burden of the workers, lest the nation become weak. Emily believed, always, that they should be segregated until they became less numerous, making them as happy as circumstances permitted and, if possible, self-supporting. "To the criminal who is only vicious and not feeble-minded, jails are often sanatoria where they recover their nerves and their physical strength. Many would die years sooner, if it were not for the rest and healing of the prison. Besides, it gives them a chance to break with the old companions and to start afresh if so disposed."

At a time when few women would discuss the principles involved in sterilization, she was striving vigorously for its practice, and was a key worker in arousing favourable public opinion prior to the passing of the Alberta Sexual Sterilization Act in 1928.

She realized that because, very properly, no reports
of individual cases were given, the public was in complete ignorance of the menace. In her work as Magistrate she had re-committed one woman three times to
an insane asylum. In the intervals between her commitment the woman gave birth to three children, the
last one having to be taken from her arms in the cell
where she had been placed, awaiting removal to the
asylum.

On any suitable occasion, Emily drove home the
truth behind the cases she witnessed, telling, for instance, of the woman who wrote to her from a settlement near Edmonton, asking that her husband might
be sterilized as she had borne him numerous children
during his six periods of release from the mental hospital. "If the doctors refuse this," she wrote to Magistrate Murphy, "it is my intention to undergo the
operation myself."

She pointed out the implications, too, of the letter
from another woman in the province, who in writing
to the Bursar of Ponoka Mental Hospital regarding an
account for two of her children, said "I have no money
for you . . . but I have nine more children." The official
who went to investigate reported that this woman
had actually had nineteen children in all stages from
idiocy to imbecility—in mental stages of from three
years to twelve. All were liable to become charges on
provincial institutions.

"For a surety," she wrote, "the condition of mentality
in which either men or women are discharged from
the psychopathic hospitals and permitted to re-enter
the community life, will, in the future, be unintelligible
to humanity . . . Some of the opponents to the Steriliza-

tion Act had a good deal to say about private liberty, quite forgetful of the fact that social necessity is one of infinitely greater moment. Since I know of no way of driving home a nail other than by hammering at it, let me emphasize again that insane people are not entitled to progeny."

Her direct, forceful thinking on this complicated problem, which was bound up with much fuzzy thinking on the part of the public, made Emily battle steadfastly for basic principles. Yet she was just as quick to see the injustices involved in unnecessary hardships on the victims of insanity.

Most of these defensive measures were behind the scenes—yet were none the less effective. There was the occasion, for instance, when a suggestion was made in 1918 that the Provincial Police should insist, for purposes of economy, that all cases of insanity be heard in the particular village or district from whence they came.

Emily rose to the issue with banners flying, and wrote a long letter to the Attorney-General, calling for wisdom and humanity rather than this type of "harsh unthinking officialism"—a favourite phrase of hers.

No woman, Magistrate Murphy reasoned, whatsoever her status, should be charged with insanity in her home community, if it were a rural one. So searching and intimate were the questions as set forth under the provision of the Insanity Act, that it was neither fair nor discreet to expose anyone to the gossip of the countryside ensuing from a knowledge of the answers given. Moreover, she said, the personal details arising out of the evidence, the doctor's testimony, the personal problems, should all be guarded with the greatest secrecy, for the sake of the patient's family.

Owing to the polyglot population and other causes peculiar to pioneering, the incidence of insanity in Canada, Emily felt, was becoming alarmingly high, and called for an inordinate expenditure of public funds. In 1932 it was estimated that four per cent of the population of Alberta was either insane, or feeble-minded, making the quota of insane persons about 30,000. Of this number, only 1,700 were able to receive treatment in the over-crowded institutions.

Allied with the problem of public expense was that of the spread of tuberculosis. For years, Emily made a special study of the problem. She became Vice-President of the Board of Control for the Alberta Association for the Prevention of Tuberculosis. She approached this problem with the same philosophy which motivated all her work, insisting that the conservation of life should be an integral part of social politics. The State realized that it could no longer leave to philanthropy the feeding and care of prisoners nor the care of the insane. She believed that the day was rapidly approaching when the care of the sick would be neither an ill-regulated whim nor a "society rage that exhausted itself in a ball".

V

For over twenty years, Emily Murphy laboured in this way, striving to arouse public opinion to a realization of its responsibilities. She sounded her warnings, and cried aloud her ideas whenever the opportunity arose. She was just as emphatic and forceful in some small gathering, as she was before a great audience. She would write a "letter to the editor" with the same impassioned force she concentrated in any article for a national magazine.

She knew from bitter experience how apathetic was public interest in any of the reforms advocated by forward-thinking social workers, but she felt that this apathy was, in a large measure, due to the fact that the average man or woman who worked closely with the problems was too busy to write or speak in public about them. Always, in working for "more direct and positive action" from the public and the Government alike she contributed an astonishing amount of it herself. With her own life and work, burdened so heavily, it would have been only natural for her to be too busy for any public education, in addition to her own work.

The record is there, however, not only in the memories of all who knew her, and heard her speak; but in the articles she wrote, in her thousands of notes and bulky journals. Alberta's forward-looking programme itself has, within its development, much of the thinking and experience of Emily Murphy. In all the preliminary activity leading to government action in an enlightened treatment of the insane, in sterilization of the mentally unfit, in health education generally, "among those present" at the heart of the struggle, was Her Honour, Judge Emily Murphy.

She faced her responsibilities in the social betterment programme of her province at whatever stage she met them. It might be that they lay most heavily upon her as she sat in her great chair, beneath the draped flag, carefully probing the examination of the insane—a procedure necessary in Alberta before one could be committed to an asylum. Perhaps it was as she listened to the dreary details in a woman's home, taking back into her own home-life the misery of the children. Week after week, as she worked in government institutions, as a member of the Board of Visitors, listening for endless hours to the painfully elicited details of prisoners' complaints, or public investigations into some catastrophe, her thoughts turned to the impact of these cases on the community without.

So, too, she measured out the infinite detail of her personal responsibilities for direct and positive action in her personal visits to jails and mental institutions, carrying many a cheerful word from home with her; and, on her return, writing to relatives and telling them of the progress made.

Her nation-wide association with women's organizations and welfare agencies, was also, for her, an instrument for service. She urged her fellow-members continually to action in setting up reforms, or to an intensive study of the social problems involved. Her published articles are only a small indication of the labour involved. She squandered her energies magnificently in the tireless notation of facts and persuasive arguments on thousands of scraps of paper, all because of her sense of personal endeavour.

Yet, where did the maximum of her strength lie? Was it in the stimulation of public thinking; in the analytical judgment she brought to her court decisions; in the gentleness with which she questioned an unhappy inmate at Ponoka? Or was it, perhaps, in the disciplined compassion I glimpsed that day when I trod the Asylum halls with her—a self-discipline enabling her to move in that tortured world, with the confidence of one who can, in very truth, encompass tragedy?

The Breath of the Poppy

There is only one thing worse than a guilty
custom and that is a guilty acquiescence.

EMILY MURPHY.

I

HEART-SICK, revolted, appalled, Emily became
aware of the traffic in narcotics in watching, day
by day, its effect on the slack-jawed, sodden creatures
who were hauled before her.

Before this, her only knowledge of opiates had been
in the blessed lessening of pain. Once, when she had
suffered for weeks before a major operation in Rochester, she had written:

"Poppy is the beneficent fairy that has soothed the
hurt of a world. She slows the living engine, cools the
flaming wheels and banks up the fires, so that the flow
of force is only passive. Thus she proves herself a defender of vitality, a repairer of waste and a balm for
hurt minds. Good Princess Poppy!"

She had felt vaguely that there was a traffic in drugs,
but associated it, in the main, with Orientals in Vancouver and a few lost souls here and there. With all
her interest in the life of Edmonton, she and her friends
had been utterly ignorant of its tragedies in the illicit

192

drug traffic. Here was a phase of life, she discovered, corrupting, debauching, menacing; and the people were all uncaring, wilfully ignorant of what was happening; or, perhaps, only carelessly so.

A well-known corner on Jasper Avenue, which she passed every day, proved to contain a secret underground parlour for opium, with numerous bunks. Several hundred people in Edmonton attended "snow" parties every week.

In a city café, where she sometimes dropped in for a cup of coffee, all the staff were found to be drug addicts; four of them were arrested as pedlars.

A negro tailor patronized by people she knew, turned out to be a drug pedlar of the most vicious type. Most of the dance halls and cheap places of amusement purveyed drugs to the initiated.

In one prairie city of about 30,000, she learned that the police found, upon investigation, hundreds of young men and women, many of them not out of their teens, who were addicted to the habit. The city would have indignantly denied this, she knew. Police, clergy, teachers and parents, not looking for addiction, and not knowing the symptoms, would have said, "Impossible!! We do not know of any drug users . . . not more than three or four!" But before the Federal police left, they had convicted fifty men of peddling drugs.

She passed sentence on frightening semblances of humanity, named as if in the most lurid fiction: Hophead Joe; Limpy Lil; Winnipeg Dutch; Dopey Bennie.

Here were wretched men and women from whom everything seemed to be gone but the terrific poison in their veins; toneless, half-awake creatures with what Emily called "a kind of zig-zag appearance".

A bride of three months, married to an addict, who had herself become one, appeared in court one morning. During her trial for having opium in her possession, she became hysterical and began to beg piteously for the morphine which had been denied her since the previous day. On stripping her for a hypodermic injection the physician and matron found her body to be covered with angry-looking carbuncles, which, the doctor told Emily, were due to infection from the needle. "Her husband's chest," as Emily described it, "looked more like a perforated milk skimmer than anything else."

On another day, a woman with "a drooling mouth and body emaciated and juiceless", reminded Her Worship, that years and years ago, two thousand miles to the East, they two were girls together. "You have often been to my home—remember the garden parties? Won't you release me for the sake of old times—and my mother?"

Even a magistrate, Emily reflected, may suffer soul-ache and feel a piteous perplexity. What would the mother want done with this dreadful creature who once was her daughter? She should, of course, be freed from drug habituation and from the poignancy of her suffering. But how? There was no institution to which she could be sent for hospitalization, and cure. All the Magistrate could do was to sentence such a prisoner to jail—to be fed and housed after a fashion, to be denied the drug, but to have little hope of restorative care.

"They were bitter words this woman uttered when I imposed a term of months upon her," Emily wrote, "but these fell scathless upon me for I knew that this severe and unrelenting treatment was, after all, only a demonstration of kindness, and maybe of love, for the victim herself."

In her work as magistrate, Emily came to know the satisfaction of salvaging young girls from a life of bitterness; she was comforted with the care and attention given to the mentally unfit. For the drug addict, however, she early learned that there was little hope of reclamation without proper hospitalization. Two years after her appointment, she, who was customarily so optimistic, so buoyant in her point of view, was writing of women drug addicts:

"Realizing that no woman may become or remain degraded without all women suffering, you may attempt something in the way of salvage, only to find that to reform her would be about as difficult as making Eve from the original rib. Unrestrained by decorum, void of delicacy of soul, moulded by vice, the companion of debauchees and drabs, she seems to be one of those desperately 'down-and-out' women who, for her life dictum, has taken the words *Evil, be thou my good*. Sometimes, her husband takes her to another city, or the police may gather her in for a term in jail. Sometimes she goes to the asylum, and sometimes she dies . . . but more often she is just a burden and a heart-scald at home and abroad."

Sitting erect and imperturbable in her big chair, Emily studied what she saw, and probed deep into the minds of those who stood sullenly or fearfully before her. She noted young women centuries old in misery; questioned white girls found insensate with black or yellow men; talked pityingly with a hag-faced girl in her teens, found smoking opium with a Chinaman, in a piano box, with a curtain of sacking across the opening to deaden the fumes. Almost every prostitute, she found, used narcotics in some form or another.

She herself summed it up for us:

"Here are men of all colours. Shuffle-gaited, foundered fellows who have started on a downward course, from which, to most of them, there is no retreat; black men, who, from likely lads, have become derelict in body and soul. These are the irredeemables—abandoned, dangerous men who are more than a match for justice.

"If you look longer upon these scenes of ignominy and shame, it will be to marvel at the numbers who suffer and who are palpably insane; men and women with pain-smirched faces and senile bodies full of festering sores. Others, who are brain-sick, stare upon you with ape-like expression or glare and gnash and gibber.

"The talk? Where is the pen that could set it down—*or dare to set it down?* This babble-talk of incontinent tongues—these hideous cursings of guttural throats, the direful pleadings, the self-recriminations or, worse than all, the hard, soul-blasting and horrific laughter.

"These are they who die by what they live upon."

II

Emily went to work.

It was impossible for her to be an observer only, before such wanton destruction. She must search for answers to the questions pressing her intelligence. Whose was the responsibility for this traffic in a living death? What chance was there of staying it? What methods should be adopted to lessen its power? Characteristically, she saw no victim but what she searched for the cause of his downfall, and looked toward his possible cure.

She must first embark on a comprehensive study of the background to this hitherto unappreciated problem. During the early years of her appointment she read and indexed practically every publication dealing in any way with the drug traffic, in both ancient and modern times. She searched the publishers' lists, the libraries, the book stores for reference material from Great Britain, America, India, China.

There was, she found, no book of general education on the drug menace. So far as the average public was affected, there were only a few brochures, a medical work or two, and some books on the details of specific drugs. Patiently, steadfastly, in her spare time, she assembled the scientific, or analytical discussions, the personal experiences of men and women throughout the world, in every century, and every clime, underlining, annotating, filing for reference.

As she worked, she began to visualize the role she might fulfil in revealing the horror that walked in every city—so that the people might comprehend its menace, and take action to avert it.

She wrote voluminously to the Federal and Provincial Governments and received, in return, hundreds of reports, import statistics, summaries, letters. Each one was carefully studied, and cross-checked for material she could use.

In the course of a year she wrote two thousand letters to the Chiefs of Police in cities and towns throughout Canada and the United States, asking for

their experience and factual data on the situation in
their centre. Letters went to legislators, to social workers, to philanthropists, to wardens of the big jails.
She broadcast her questions, searching, always, for
truth, her mind burning with her own horrific discovery
of this evil, which, all unwittingly, she had condoned
through her very ignorance.

The questionnaire she sent to the Chief of Police
was clear-cut and direct. She asked:

1. Is the traffic growing?

2. What drugs are most used?

3. Is there any considerable addiction among children?

4. Are prohibitory liquor laws contributory causes?

5. What nationalities are most concerned with the
   sale of narcotics?

6. Have you knowledge of any drug rings, local or
   national?

7. Have you anything to say regarding the relations
   of the following classes to the traffic: smugglers,
   prostitutes, custom officials, railway porters, or
   taxi drivers?

8. Have you anything to say regarding the prescribing of narcotics by druggists?

9. Approximately how many convictions were made
   in your centre last year?

Answers arrived by the hundreds, and varied from
many pages of exhaustive information to that received
from the Warden at Kingston Penitentiary.

"Dear Madam:

"In reply to your different questions the following particulars are submitted.

1. I do not know.
2. Morphine and cocaine.
3. Yes.
4. I do not know.
5. Chinese.
6. No.
7. No.
8. No set rule. Each case would be dealt with on its own merit.
9. I do not know.

Much of the material she received was useless; but, gradually, as the months passed, she began to assemble a comprehensive story. In gathering this information and in planning her educative campaign, Emily realized that she was in a unique position as a writer, with her opportunities for first-hand studies on the effect of narcotics, and for the continual questioning of its victims. Writing, studying, making her own deductions from what she saw and read, she used every opportunity in her work to familiarize herself with the thinking of hop-heads, drug-takers, cocainists, and drug-fiends.

"Because I have known some of you in your hours of deepest depression," she wrote, "and have looked into your lives with closest scrutiny, I cannot but suffer with you. To have seen your tears of shame and sorrow,—yes, and to have seen your anger—means that, at least, I understand."

III

All this voluminous and detailed "paper work" was not enough. Mental and physical activity was always integrated in Emily Murphy's life. Thus, she herself went, time and again, with the matron or physician to check on the prisoners. She used her talent for questioning, whether in court, or in private discussion in the cells, or her office, to explore deep into the causative forces.

She went often beyond the routine court interrogation; for instance, time and again she asked:

"How do you feel when the drug has loosened its spell?"

One day she was told, "I feel as though squirrels were walking over my back . . . My super-optimism is superseded by a feeling of terror or doom . . . Out of doors, more than once, I have been chased far down the street by terribly hostile trees."

Or again, when she asked, "How do you suffer? What are the pangs of a cocaine user?" The answer came jerked from bitter lips: "Starvation! When using coke for several days, I don't eat. No addict does . . . I get low in vitality, so low, that if you put out your hands and touched me suddenly, I would feel as if bolts of electricity has passed through me . . . the magnetism of your body would hurt me!"

Again she questioned a man of position and marked ability. He told her that he did not use morphine for the pleasure it afforded but because he suffered so much when it was taken away.

"There is, too, Mrs. Murphy," he explained, "a fascination with the hypodermic syringe which is almost inexplicable . . . I think men like to take a bit of pain with their pleasure, just as a mountain climber strains his muscles, freezes his face, and endangers his life for the 'something hidden' behind the hills."

"But the pain is so terribly out of proportion to the pleasure, that its use is stupid," Emily argued. "Why lick honey from such ugly thorns?"

A lifting of the eyebrows, a shrug of the shoulders, silence, and then a careless, "Oh well . . . I stay with it always, this peaceable remedy of human life."

Emily persisted: "It is no remedy. Instead of being a surcease from cares, the suicide of morphine addicts has grown enormously."

"Yes . . . perhaps . . . But I have not reached that stage!"

There was the morning she questioned Betty:

"When you take cocaine, Betty, what does it feel like?"

"Coke bugs," Betty explained, intent on giving an exact picture to this sympathetic woman judge with the kind voice. "I get them under the skin, generally in the back. I do silly things then. That was how I came to take those things from Mrs. K—. I didn't want them, but was just goofy."

"Why do you smoke?" She asked each one.

"Forgetfulness," was the usual answer, given in one form or another. Emily noted, however, that "one has only to come closely in touch with the smoker to know that his vaunted pipe-dreams are more often of tremendous glooms and fatal slopes, and that he cries for help with a voiceless throat."

She wrote: "A woman who is deeply under the thraldom has told me how, in each successive indulgence, she passes through strange transmutations and across wide lands that have no horizons. Sometimes, in the narcotic stupor, there comes to her a black sun that expands and contracts, and the rays of which cause her head to ache intolerably . . . On her recovering, she suffers from an appalling introversion when the chain of her bondage ceases to be anything but golden. This must, too, be true about her pain for, as she tells the story of it, her voice becomes thin like a fret-saw and her face seems to shrink as though she were ill and very, very old."

Early in 1921 she went to Vancouver and worked closely in co-operation with the police force of that city, to see for herself what the background of the traffic was. With the plainclothes men, she saw sights and settings that no other woman who was not herself an addict had known. Impelled by her compassion and her longing to shake the people awake, and show them the stark facts, she followed the police fearlessly. She has told of one such visit in quiet prose that is unforgetable:

"In entering Shanghai Alley, I was warned to stand clear of the doorways lest a rush be made from inside, when I would be trampled upon.

"In passing up a narrow staircase of unplaned boards, one detective walked ahead and one behind me, each carrying a flashlight. 'Why do you keep me between you?' I asked. 'Gentlemen should precede a lady up a stairway.'

"Without replying, the head man stopped about mid-way up, and inserted a long key into a board when, to my amazement, a door opened where no door had been visible. Here, in a small cupboard, without a

window—a kennel of a place—lay four opium debauchees or, as the police designate them, 'hop-heads'.

"The hole was absolutely dark, and the men slept
heavily. Although plainly narcotised, the police might
not apprehend the sleepers. One may only arrest those
found in the act of smoking. It would seem that here,
as in the best English circles, the eleventh command-
ment is 'never interrupt'.

"And so, in like manner, several doors were opened
for me, to show how I was being protected from a
stealthily opened panel, and all this might mean to a
witless, worthless lamb like me. As you looked and
looked again on these prostrate, open-eyed insensates,
it began to dawn on you what Bret Harte meant when
he spoke of 'The dread valley of the shadow of the
drug'.

"In one of these dens, the detective suddenly pointed
like a dog on game. 'Opium!' he said. 'I smell opium!'

"Almost immediately from over our heads, we heard
the pad of running soft-shod feet, for the game was
up and afield. Upon entering the room above, no one
was to be seen, but the room was filled with the sickly
fumes of cooked opium. Only the month before, a
half-dazed unhappy wretch, in an attempt to escape
from the police, threw himself off the roof of a building
and died on the pavement beneath. The other China-
men, to have revenge, swore that one of these detec-
tives had thrown the man off. The detective charged
with this crime was the one ahead of me with the
long key."

It was in Vancouver, too, that she heard of the tip-
off police had received about a certain Chinaman who
was selling drugs. There were many alley-ways, back

rooms, hidden staircases and secret doorways to be traversed before one came to the heavy door set with a panel. A pre-arranged knock and the panel opened. You put your money into the yellow fist which came through, and gave your order. You waited outside the closed panel until, in time, it slid open again and the drug was put into your hands.

The police planned to follow all procedure—but to have a pair of handcuffs ready to clasp around the wrist. Everything went according to schedule, until the police officer grabbed at the yellow hand protruding through the hole in the door. It slipped through his fingers like a piece of fat pork—for it proved to be heavily greased. When the heavily barred door was broken open, there was a long and difficult chase through cellarways and passages, until the man was found cowering behind a barrel.

For all its sordidness, this was the high adventure of the chase to which Emily responded eagerly. She made copious notes of such adventures, and listened with a full appreciation to descriptions of how carrier pigeons were sometimes used to send the narcotics; of how small power-boats slipped out at night in the wake of in-coming steamers from the East, to pick up the narcotics, which were tossed overboard in floating containers.

As word of her investigation into the drug traffic grew, there were many who came to her office or, on occasion, to her house, asking advice, pleading for help, telling what they knew. The girls were frightened at the type of men and women who sometimes stood outside their door, but obeyed their mother's strict orders, to show each one up to the study. There was

Emily Murphy, 1914

one evening when Kathleen, spending the evening at home, showed an emaciated young man upstairs. Turning at the stair-head, she saw him, sleeve rolled up, giving himself a hypodermic injection.

There were often mysterious telephone calls with tip-offs as to pedlars, opium dens, addicts. Threatening voices warned her to "lay-off", with promises of quick revenge if she did not stop her researches.

She worked closely with the members of the Narcotic Division of the Mounted Police, and discussed her deductions and findings with many of them. She was astonished, as the months went past, at the opposition given from persons she would never have suspected. It was, she found, of a very determined nature, though usually under cover. She believed that much of it came from those interested in the liquor traffic, who did not wish the narcotic traffic interfered with, as they were trying to persuade the public that it was the result of prohibition, thus hoping to gain public support for a return to the old system. "I notice too," she wrote in one of her letters, "that officials who start out intending to fight the drug traffic, have the quietus put upon them before they go very far—not universally so, but more nearly so than we think."

She found that the lack of public interest was general; opinions as to the extent of the traffic were confused and contradictory. All this, however, but stirred her interest, gave impetus to her mission. Had she not been in the same situation herself, until she had the opportunity for seeing the traffic? Did not the public need only to be told the truth? Her task as an educational force was clear-cut and challenging.

IV

What she found in her investigations was startling. In 1919, on a per capita basis, Canada led the world in the narcotic drug traffic.

The traffic had gained a big foothold in the Dominion during the previous decade. In 1912, for instance, there were only 35 ounces of cocaine imported into Canada; seven years later it had jumped to 12,333 ounces. Similarly in 1907, Canadians had imported 1,523 ounces of morphine. In 1917 the import total was 30,000 ounces.

It was true that the licensing system which the Federal Government had introduced in 1919, lowered imports considerably—on the record. Emily was convinced, however, from all that she found, that the illicit traffic was growing enormously.

With her mass of evidence assembled from hundreds of city police courts, with her own insatiable reading, and the knowledge she had gained in her years of magisterial work, she wrote five articles exposing the drug menace in Canada, for *Maclean's Magazine*.

The results of her exposé on the increased traffic in Canada were instantaneous. Newspapers throughout Canada published editorials or followed up Emily's comments with local stories indicating how true they were. In school and college, from pulpit and platform the facts of addiction were presented, stripped of the spectacular.

"Clean-up squads" went to work in towns and cities throughout Canada, and Emily co-operated closely with those in her own province. In one letter she notes her method of helping a plainclothes man who was investigating a southern settlement. "Almost every day I sent M—a letter with notes gleaned during the twenty-four hours, on the narcotic situation . . . who is selling, using, or being convicted, also, who is likely to give information."

With the publication of the articles, she received hundreds of letters, many of them from drug addicts, asking help, or telling their own experiences. One of them, in particular, wrote such a vivid letter, that Emily became interested in helping him to conquer the habit. Within a year he was at work with the police force, as an under-cover man. For a year or two he corresponded often with Emily, outlining the results of his investigation. On one occasion, when he was in a small Alberta town, he wrote to Emily:

"I placed the book you loaned me in the top drawer of the bureau in my hotel room, forgetting that it had your autograph in it. Last night, several big drug-pedlars came to my room. Joe discovered your book. If I had shown a bulldog a life-sized picture of a Tom-cat, I might have produced the same effect . . . In desperation I told them that I had burglarized your home in Edmonton . . . I told them I was trying to find evidence on which you could be cinched, so as to stop your anti-drug activities. After I caught my breath, I became very eloquent and managed to turn the incident to good advantage. It was very nasty while it lasted. You will notice that the fly-leaf has been partly cut. One of the bunch started to cut it out, to show his headquarters evidence of my perfidy. As the leaf is still there, it means that I talked him out of it."

So keen was the national interest in what she had

to say, that in 1922, *The Black Candle* was published. It was the first general summary of the drug traffic for the average reader published in Canada, or, for that matter, in the United States. For the first half of the book Emily used the articles she had published in *Maclean's*. For the second portion, she assembled the added information she had garnered from letters and interviews following the magazine presentation.

Her whole object was to present the facts without sentimentalizing over them. They should, she felt, be given fully and truthfully to the public. She struggled to keep her writing free from the mystery with which, she felt, writers were prone to surround drug addiction and to discuss it, so far as possible, as a deplorable and disgusting habit, one in which the addicts could be pitied and controlled. It was her responsibility to give these facts to the public, leaving it to make its own deductions.

There were, however, certain recommendations she made which were echoed in the press, among women's organizations, and from the public platform, for many years.

She asked for hospitals to cure drug addiction, and urged that institutional treatment be available in every province.

Penalties should be more severe, with the option of a fine withdrawn.

All drugs should be procured from the Government, and a record kept of every grain from the time it left the importer until it reached the ultimate consumer.

She felt that the practice of some physicians in prescribing narcotics in large quantities for their patients, to be administered by themselves, was unwise. More-

over, the Criminal Code was too indefinite, and gave
doctors too wide a privilege in prescribing drugs. There
were those who were thus enabled to dispense drugs,
yet slip out of any conviction when brought before the
court.

But above and beyond all her practical suggestions,
was her compelling reiteration of the need for education. Until the people knew fully where the menace
lay, what the symptoms were, how youth was en-
snared, and to what an extent the vicious traffic was
increasing, there was little hope of staying it.

She had dedicated *The Black Candle* to the members of the "Rotary, Kiwanis and Gyro Clubs, and to
the White Cross Associations who are rendering valiant
service in impeding the spread of drug addiction".
Following its publication she worked with them vigorously to increase their educational programme. In all
her associations with women's clubs, and welfare
organizations, she pounded home the need for an
active, unrelenting fight against the traffic. There was
no subject, she reminded them, upon which philanthropy could better expend its forces, than to the
education on the addiction, disease, and the humane
help possible to its sufferers.

She had the satisfaction of seeing very definite
results following the publication of *The Black
Candle,* symbolic, in its title, of the opium pipe. Not
only were its contents the focal point for a nation-
wide resurgence of public education, but the material
she had assembled was used in countless ways. The
Secretariat of the League of Nations ordered a great
many copies, one for each member of its committees
interested, in any way, in the traffic in narcotics. Pro-

vincial Departments of Justice, in many instances, circularized the magistrates within their jurisdiction urging penalties that were more severe. Statutes in many provinces were amended to include some of her recommendations.

Its impact on her personal life, too, was manifold. A prominent American working in Europe recommended that Emily be added to the Advisory Committee of the League of Nations on the Opium Section. Sir Robert Borden, who was president of the Canadian League of Nations, asked her to serve on one of the committees. She was also invited, together with practically all the governors of the Western States, to sit on the advisory committee of the White Cross Association in Seattle. Emily herself spoke in practically every province on the traffic in narcotics.

Mrs. Wallace Reid, following the much-publicized death of her movie star husband, planned to use *The Black Candle* as the basis for a film, and came to Edmonton to discuss it with Emily. The film company concerned, interviewed T. R. Ferguson in Toronto, but the matter was never cleared. It was Emily's secret opinion that her brother's grandiose idea of what the film rights were worth, had discouraged the promoters of the idea. T. R. had checked her manuscript carefully for her and, in writing to her about it, illustrated, again, the close brotherly devotion there was between the family. "I thought," he wrote, "how many a time you must have laid your pen aside, utterly wearied mentally and physically. Disheartened too. You have handled a monumental subject in a masterly way. I am more than proud of you."

The book, signed by "Judge Emily Murphy", with

"Janey Canuck" this time in brackets beneath, received a world-wide press approval of the critics for its effective handling of an appalling subject. In it, however, Janey Canuck, and her delicate craftsmanship, were not much in evidence. This was Judge Murphy slashing hard at a seemingly hopeless problem, urging reforms in the face of a disinterested, careless public.

She knew, however, that she had accomplished much of what she had hoped, and kept to her crusade, year after year. Among her papers, when she died, were some unfinished articles on the drug traffic; but in revealing its danger to the people and in stirring up some positive educational action, Emily Murphy knew she could count her work a success.

One doctor in California criticized the book on petty grounds. Emily came back in fine fettle in a letter with five pages of single-spaced typewritten argument. In it is this sentence:

"*The Black Candle* deals with the moral, physical, mental, social, curative, legal, criminal, punitive, causative, historical, tragical, medical, financial, and even grimly humorous phases of the subject. There is absolutely no other book which does this."

Writing to W. A. Deacon, the young literary critic in Winnipeg, who was to become one of her very real friends, she said:

"One of the compensations of the years, is an increasing immunity to praise or blame. One gets too busy to bother. I have always felt it to be a sign of weakness to explain over-much. I did not write the book for money, fame, or dis-fame . . . The results I have had, have been eminently satisfactory . . . Do you know that this hard-headed old villain actually prayed that she would live to put over the story of the drug menace in Canada? (And a fool doctor told me I wouldn't) . . . Having lived and accomplished it, nothing else matters. Only myself knows what I suffered in the whole undertaking, but that is past now, and the public have the story as they should have it.

"I am sure that there will be scores of better written and more interesting books on your table from Canada and England, but probably nothing that is of more vital importance to our people at this time. Indeed, I feel quite sure that there is not, and you can call me a conceited body if you like . . . This thing came to me as a revelation, and I believe its knowledge will come to Canadians in the same way."

Today, as vivid as it was twenty years ago, Judge Emily Murphy's battle cry is one to challenge Canada:

"Public opinion destroyed slavery; public opinion can destroy this new slavery.

"Our people have both the conscience and the courage.

"It is poor policy for one part of the Empire to produce the poison which destroys another part of it. Our responsibility cannot be relegated to experts, philanthropists, legislators, or the League of Nations.

"There is only one thing worse than a guilty custom —and that is a guilty acquiescence."

PART IV

CHAPTER I

Preliminary

She who would put on gloves must learn how to spar.

JANEY CANUCK.

HIS MAJESTY KING GEORGE V, was humbly advised in October, 1929, by his most learned counsellors, the Law Lords of the Privy Council of England, that women should properly be considered "persons", within the meaning of the British North America Act.

There are now two Honourable members of the Senate of Canada who are women; and a brass tablet in the Lobby of the Red Chamber bears testimony that they sit there as a result of the initiative of five women in the Province of Alberta.

But if we wanted to be really fair, we should have to recognize that the advice given His Majesty on the status of women, the presence of the two feminine Senators in Ottawa, and the brass plaque in the Senate, came about because at the time when the British North America Act was passed, a country gentleman near the shores of Lake Simcoe, was teaching his boys and girls to share responsibilities.

In the early pages of this book, we have seen how

213

Isaac Ferguson taught his daughters, as well as his sons, to play cricket, to ride, to hitch and drive a team, to carve properly, and to cast accounts. While Eastern Canada was nurturing Victorian proprieties in the upbringing of its girls, the young Fergusons were also learning that whatever the work to be done, boys and girls should learn equally well to master it.

Cradled in a realization of this mutual responsibility and with its forcefulness as a basis for thinking, Emily Ferguson Murphy faced up to its challenge throughout her life, whether in her work as Magistrate, as crusader against the illicit drug traffic, as writer, or as an active citizen of her community.

The question of a woman's right to share responsibility with men in public appointments was raised on her first day, as she presided in court. She liked to tell the story, and, referring to the long struggle to have women declared eligible to sit in the Senate, would say, "This was a woman's fight started by a man . . ."

The "man who started the fight" was the defence lawyer who questioned Emily's appointment on her first day in court, since women were not "persons" within the meaning of the British North America Act— foundation of all Canada's constitutional laws. The issue was always a live one, and Emily kept it so, insisting on a full argument, always. When a Women's Court was opened in Calgary, under Judge Alice Jamieson, the same cry was raised, until finally, in 1920, in an appeal arising out of a case from the Calgary court, the Honourable Mr. Justice Scott of the Supreme Court of Alberta, silenced it as far as that province was concerned by ruling that, in his opinion, women were "persons".

That was victory at the provincial level. It took twelve years to win similar recognition from the Dominion. The question as to whether women were "persons" and so eligible for the Canadian Senate was argued back and forth from coast to coast in the Dominion. It passed without decision, over the desks of five prime ministers—Sir Robert Borden, The Right Honourable Arthur Meighen, Viscount R. B. Bennett, and the Honourable W. L. Mackenzie King, in both his periods of legislative leadership.

At last five intrepid women from scattered centres in the prairie Province of Alberta carried the matter, step by step, to the very highest officers of the Realm; and the world listened as His Majesty's Privy Councillors at Number One, Downing Street, at last pronounced the advice they would give the King.

It was, of course, a national question, and Emily always considered it so. Hers was an impersonal crusade for a new charter of liberty for Canadian women. In addition, it was inevitably a personal matter for her, founded on the core of her own upbringing and standards, and invested, as the years passed, with measureless quantities of her generous and boundless energies. During the twelve years the question was under debate, she amassed an immense file of correspondence, and made literally thousands of notes on her scraps of paper—notes and comments which no one ever saw. She kept the fervour of her personal feeling under restraint, taking care never to embarrass those who worked with her for the same end, nor to let it become a political issue; but those who were close to her knew how deeply she cared, how fierce was her desire for this national vindication of her personal working philosophy.

II

It was in 1920 that Emily Murphy, as an aside to her work in Court-house, asylum and jail, wrote to the editor of the Canadian publication, *Women's Century,* suggesting that as one of its editorial features it press for the appointment of a woman to the Senate. "I am sure," she added, "that you will find a woman in the East who would be the ideal appointee."

She did not consider such an appointment for herself until she received a letter from Gertrude E. Budd, secretary of the Montreal Women's Club, on January 7th, 1921, asking that she allow her name to stand as their nominee for the Senate. This letter is before me now, and to it is pinned a torn paper on which Emily wrote, "How it started!! You will see that it didn't emanate from me. They just knew I had fought the "person" disability in Alberta and had won out. Mrs. Budd was formerly a Calgary woman."

At first glance, it might seem strange that a Montreal Women's Club, in a province which did not grant the provincial vote to women until 1940, should approach a Western woman as their nominee for Senatorship. But the link is clear and direct, as Emily showed on her bit of paper. Mrs. Budd, moving from Calgary to Montreal, knew Emily's work well, and had watched her campaign to have women declared persons in regard to the application of the British North America Act, in Alberta. In Montreal, being a forward-looking feminist, she gravitated naturally to the Montreal Women's Club, which, under the guidance of its vigorous little president, Mrs. John Scott, was doing all in its power to increase women's franchise.

Interest in the Montreal Women's Club turned to

the thought of a woman Senator and Mrs. Budd wrote to Emily asking if she would favour being appointed to the Senate.

Emily agreed to have her name suggested. The results were not long in forthcoming. Sir Robert Borden acknowledged receipt of the resolution, but was of the opinion that women could not be appointed to the Senate, since they were not persons within the meaning of the Act.

One can imagine Emily's chagrin at meeting the same excuse which had hounded her ever since her appointment to the Magistrate's Court in Edmonton! Her eyes were glinting with challenge as she wrote to Mrs. Scott recounting her experiences over this "person" business. Her letter closed with this paragraph:

"And now, after five years of quietude on the Saskatchewan, along comes the memorandum from the office of the Minister of Justice, with the same old rigmarole. It is almost unbelievable. Do you wonder that when I read it, I laughed and felt relieved?"

Somewhere in the letter, she noted, with a chuckle, that she was not much a person, perhaps, but still one, *de facto* because of Alberta's interpretation of the word.

The Montreal Women's Club was not easily discouraged and, presently, another resolution went forward to the new Prime Minister, Arthur Meighen. Just before he retired from office, a few months after his appointment, he announced that he would like to see a woman in the Senate but, his advisors declared, one could not be appointed *without an amendment to the British North America Act.*

The idea caught at the imagination of men and women throughout Canada and, presently, petitions were crowding the desks of government officials. The National Council of Women, and the Federated Women's Institutes, in session, forwarded resolutions requesting the appointment of a Woman Senator. Both of these great organizations asked Emily to allow her name to be associated with their resolution but as she was the National President of the one, and the National Vice-President of the other, she felt that this would not be seemly.

Tens of thousands of men and women signed the petitions which were circulated throughout all the provinces. Over the years, fresh outbursts of interest and energy arose with each of the half-dozen Senate vacancies which occurred in Alberta.

The resolutions signed and forwarded repeatedly over the years, are significant in that they sum up the feeling of Canadian women who were interested in the idea.

"Whereas the women of Canada are without representation in the Senate of Canada,

"And whereas, measures affecting the welfare of women and children, together with private statutes relating to divorce are considered by the said Senate, without the advice and assistance of any representative of women,

"And whereas there is at present a vacancy in the said Senate in Alberta which requires to be filled,

"And whereas Mrs. Emily Murphy is well qualified to fill such a position of trust by virtue of her training and experience acquired as police magistrate and judge of the Juvenile Court in and for the province of Alberta, and to represent the women of Canada by virtue of her connection with various women's societies . . . your petitioners pray that the said Mrs. Murphy will be appointed to the said Senate, in order that the said Senate might be better qualified to consider matters concerning the interest of the women and children of Canada."

So persistent did the campaign become that a number of legal opinions were expressed by government solicitors, all of them agreeing that women could not be considered persons. One of these legal opinions stated that women were a "totally new and preciously legally incapable class of voters".

To which, writing to Mrs. Scott, Emily retorted, "What a sentence! How inapt the adjectives! How unprofessional and unworthy! And what man before has ever defined us as 'preciously legally incapable'? . . . It seems to me as if someone is anxious to erect a barrier for us where none exists in order that the 'preciously incapable' ones may either turn back in alarm, or break their preciously incapable necks in trying to 'take it'.

"Madame how do you ride, and what about the girths?"

III

In February, 1922, one of the Senators from Edmonton died and there were many appeals to Ottawa to appoint Emily Murphy to the vacancy. Mr. King replied courteously that he would be very pleased to have a woman appointed to the Senate and would take steps to see that an amendment was made to the

Act. Moreover, in the "Orders of the Day" for June 25th, 1923, Senator McCoig of Chatham gave notice of motion in regard to the amendment of the Act so as to include women. However, the day passed, and Senator McCoig never rose to his feet. When it was checked a month later, Mr. Fred McGregor, private secretary to Mr. King, explained, in Mr. King's absence, that the resolution on the Order paper of the Senate "was one of a number of resolutions for which there was no opportunity. Mr. King had asked Senator McCoig to take in hand re-introduction of the subject." There the matter rested as far as the Government was concerned, for five years.

Not so, however, for Emily's friends; for public interest; or for press comment.

Hundreds of prominent persons of both sexes, including the Mayor and all the Aldermen of Edmonton, and organizations representing a membership of over 2,000,000 persons, asked for her appointment. Among these was the Women's Christian Temperance Union of the Province of Quebec.

Over 2,000 women of that province signed this petition. As far as was known, this was the first time the W.C.T.U. had joined with the French-Canadian women of Canada in asking for the appointment of a woman to such an office; or for that matter, that Eastern women had asked for a Western woman.

Contemporary opinion of Emily is indicated in a few excerpts from the hundreds of letters written on her behalf.

Nellie McClung, one of the five women eventually to appeal to the Privy Council, worked hard for Emily's appointment from the start, believing firmly that it would be for the good of Canada. In May, 1921, she wrote to Senator W. H. Sharpe:

"The only objection that any person can have to Mrs. Murphy for the Senate is that she is a woman. She can qualify in a dozen different ways, each one of them far beyond the qualifications of the average Senator. She is a writer, a lecturer, a public-minded citizen, a leader among women, a woman of open mind and generous heart, who has done much to bring about better conditions in Canada. She is recognized as an authority in matters of law, and above all, she is our choice at this time. Men and women all over Canada, east, west, north and south, are asking for her appointment."

Over the years, Emily had the editorial approval of the press throughout Canada. A few typical comments will illustrate the way newspaper editors felt about her proposed appointment.

"Mrs. Murphy has, in almost every sphere of activity she ever entered, become of nation-wide repute. Although she is very much of the West, she is first and last, of Canada" (*Canadian Morning Chronicle*, Halifax, 1921).

"Janey Canuck's interest in knowing what makes the wheels go round, has caused her to delve far under the surface of Things as They Appear, in the building of national life, and this is why her discoveries have been regarded as worth while. She is about the only Canadian woman who has been mentioned in many quarters for the Canadian Senate" (*London Advertiser*, 1922).

"The woman born for such a position, who would

fill the position better than any other woman in Canada, is Janey Canuck. She is the one woman who would get the best from the others with whom she came in contact" (*Woman's Century*, 1922).

"With Mrs. Murphy in the Senate, the good comradeship of Canada would be well represented in the Upper House" (*Fort William Times Journal*, 1922).

"Nobody who knows her, was the least bit surprised that she was boomed for the last Alberta Senatorial vacancy . . . The Senate does not know what it missed. Perhaps it never will, but everybody who knows the Judge knows it has missed a treat. In the Senate where humour is so dry as to have been withered before it gets by the Black Rod, they would much enjoy the Lady from Edmonton, but not half so much as the lady would enjoy the Senate" (*Toronto Star*, 1924).

So it went, until 1927, with revivals of interest throughout Canada as each senatorial vacancy occurred in Alberta.

IV

In all this, her brothers, as brilliant lawyers and devoted admirers of Emily, were keenly interested. Family history recalls that it was brother William who first called Emily's attention to Section 60 of the Supreme Court Act. This section permitted interested persons, appealing as a unit, to ask for the interpretation of a constitutional point raised under the British North America Act. If the Department of Justice agreed that the question was of sufficient public importance, it would be referred by the Governor-General-in-Council, to the Supreme Court.

Emily glowed with delight when she had read it,

and went again to her desk to find a scrap of paper on which, some time before, she had noted the way three tailors of London had presented a petition to the House of Commons, beginning, "We, the people of England . . ."

Did the word "persons" include women? What a question to put to the Supreme Court for final decision; what an opportunity the section gave to citizens with an insatiable curiosity!

Whom would she gather around her on such a programme? Names were written and re-written, checked and crossed off, in the following days, as Emily wrote post-haste to her brothers asking them if they felt it a wise undertaking for her.

Nellie McClung must be one of the appellants, of course. She was one of Emily's staunchest friends, a keen worker for women's franchise, and an imaginative thinker. Mrs. McClung was also former Member of the Legislative Assembly in Edmonton.

Irene Parlby from the little town of Alix, was a natural choice, too. She was the only woman member of the Alberta Cabinet, a clear thinker on all matters relating to women's franchise.

There was strength to be found in an association with resolute Louise McKinney of Claresholm, who, also, had been a member in the Provincial House.

With these three, Emily finally selected Henrietta Muir Edwards of MacLeod, whom she knew well through her work as Convenor of Laws for the National Council of Women.

Five women in search of an answer; the idea appealed to Emily immensely. Here was an opportunity for clear-cut action. "Yo-ho! and ho-ho!" sang Emily in her heart. "Away we go!"

Her brothers agreed that it was a good plan; the four women to whom she wrote asking for their association with her as the five appellants, agreed quickly, and Emily questioned Ottawa on the proper procedure.

This invoking of a hitherto untouched section of an Act which was the constitutional basis for the Dominion, meant many new problems for Emily, but she overcame them with her customary gusto, and wrote directly to those in authority for information.

First the interpretation of Section 60 was checked with the Department of Justice. Yes, the Minister agreed, the question submitted by Emily was considered by his Department to be one of sufficient national importance to be presented to the Supreme Court.

Yes, said a later letter, Emily could name her own counsel for the five appellants; and finally, yes, Mrs. Murphy was correct in her interpretation of the Act's meaning in regard to Section 60—the Department of Justice would pay all "reasonable fees" arising from the case, on behalf of the appellants.

Good! Emily felt her lines were clear now, and organized her little group of women. Scattered as they were through the immense areas of Alberta, she decided that the most orderly manner to sign all letters and petitions would be in alphabetical sequence.

Thus on all the documents pertaining to the case, the signatures were appended in this order:

Henrietta Muir Edwards
Nellie McClung
Louise C. McKinney
Emily F. Murphy
Irene Parlby

The case became *"the appeal of Henrietta Muir Edwards et al"*; and so the names are listed today on the memorial tablet in the Lobby of the Red Senate Chamber.

That same year in Edmonton, Emily had met the noted Toronto lawyer, N. W. Rowell, when he came to speak on the League of Nations, and she circularized her co-petitioners for their approval in briefing him. They agreed.

The petition was mailed to them from the Department of Justice for signature. Duly signed in order, it was returned to Emily. Nellie McClung signed her name with a flourish and wrote to Emily, "I have just sent the petition on with my blessing wrapping it around. God Bless our Cause, and confound our enemies."

Thus it was that P.C. 2034 was certified to be a true copy of a Minute of a meeting of the Committee of the Privy Council approved by His Excellency the Governor-General-in-Council on October 19th, 1927:

"The Committee of the Privy Council have had before them a Report dated 18th October, 1927, from the Minister of Justice, submitting that he has under consideration a petition to your Excellency in Council, dated the 27th day of August, 1927, signed by Henrietta Muir Edwards, Nellie L. McClung, Louise C. McKinney, Emily F. Murphy and Irene Parlby, as persons interested in the admission of women to the Senate of Canada, whereby Your Excellency in Council is requested to refer to the Supreme Court of Canada, for hearing and consideration, certain questions touching the power of the Governor-General to summon female persons to the Senate of Canada.

"The Minister observes that by Section 24 of the British North America Act, 1867, it is provided that

> The Governor-General shall from time to time in the Queen's name, by Instrument under the Great Seal of Canada, summon qualified persons to the Senate; and subject to the provisions of this act, every person so summoned shall become and be a member of the Senate, and a Senator.

"In the opinion of the Minister, the question whether the word 'persons' as in said Section 24, included female persons is one of great national importance.

"The Minister states that the law officers of the Crown who have considered the question on more than one occasion have expressed the view that male persons only may be summoned to the Senate, under the provisions of the British North America Act in that behalf.

"The Minister, however, while not disposed to question that view considers that it would be an act of justice to the women of Canada to obtain the opinion of the Supreme Court of Canada upon the point.

"The Committee therefore on the recommendation of the Minister of Justice, advise that Your Excellency may be pleased to refer to the Supreme Court of Canada, for hearing and consideration, the following question:

"Does the word Persons in Section 24 of the British North America Act in 1867, include female persons?"

Preliminaries were over; the argument was on.

CHAPTER II

Argument

It is truly encouraging—and we may take the assurance to our hearts, that no extension of the franchise has ever been defeated since John, the King of England, signed Magna Charta at Runnymede.

EMILY MURPHY,
(In a letter to the five Appellants in the Person's Appeal).

I

ARE WOMEN "PERSONS"?
  First asked in the dingy courtroom of a pioneer city in Canada, the question was to be finally answered at Number One, Downing Street, in England.

Tirelessly pursuing what she felt to be a truth, Emily set in motion a symbolic pattern of democracy.

Anyone, man or woman, may question the King on what his Parliament means; and the legislation of a nation may be based on the answer received.

This is the pattern which Emily found and followed.

The Dominion of Canada was given form by the British North America Act.

The Act was drawn up by the Imperial Parliament in London, and was formally approved by the representatives of the old Canadian provinces. These men, the Fathers of Confederation, discussed the Act in a beautifully proportioned old building in Charlottetown, Prince Edward Island, the smallest of the provinces. The great oak table around which they sat, in 1867, is still in the self-same room, not roped-off in austerity, but circled with its chairs, and in use, occasionally, for meetings on the Island's affairs.

It was in this B.N.A. Act, that Emily found Section 24 which she was to make the basis of Canada's most famous appeal to the Privy Council of England, a section empowering the Governor-General of Canada to summon "qualified persons" to the Senate.

The British North America Act established the Supreme Court, and it is Section 60 of the Supreme Court Act that gives the right to "interested persons" to ask for an interpretation of any ruling in the British North America Act.

The Department of Justice in Ottawa, as we have seen, might request the Governor-General to refer the matter to the Supreme Court.

Each province would be notified of the Reference to the Supreme Court, since the provinces were treaty partners in the B.N.A. Act, and, so, vitally concerned with the official interpretation of any section of it. They were offered the opportunity of sending Counsel to argue on either side of the question. The Attorney-General of Canada, representing the Crown, argued, in this particular case, against the Appellants, as the Government had given the decision that women could not be considered "persons", within the meaning of the Act, and that it would have to be amended before they could be summoned to the Senate.

It was also provided that if the Appellants were not satisfied with the judgment of the Supreme Court of

Canada, they could request the Department of Justice
to ask the Governor-General to refer the matter direct
to His Majesty, the King-in-Council, by appealing to
the Privy Council in London, as final authority.

In all this, the Department of Finance was empowered to pay all reasonable costs for the Appellants.

Convinced of ultimate victory, Emily looked, always,
beyond the immediate, to the next step. She saw the
question, too, in its proper perspective, not only as it
affected Canada's status in the British Empire, but as
it fitted into the sweep and rhythm of history.

Was not Canada empowered by the Imperial
Parliament to adjudicate on its own legislative inter-
pretations? Was she not mistress in her own domain
while looking to the Mother of Parliaments for the
initial constitutional basis?

As for history,—she envisioned it clearly in a letter
to the Honourable N. W. Rowell, K.C., on June 9th,
1929:

"Would it be that in Great Britain, their common
law has grown up without a written constitution, and
that in this Dominion, ours is growing from out of, or
alongside, a constitution?

"Surely the modern usages and the overwhelming
considerations of public good have the same right to
take their natural course in Canada even as in Great
Britain—and this without any expensive or contentious
reference to the Imperial Parliament.

"It is not even thinkable that the Imperial Parliament
intended that such should not be the case, especially
as it relates to the good of at least a half of the populace
under their national charter. In every age, and in

every civilized country, this has been the unwritten
rule—as soon as the hour had arrived and the tide
was in."

II

"What an absurd thing to say—of course women
are persons!"

"A woman in the Senate? Why, it's ridiculous!
Senator is a purely masculine term!"

As soon as it became public knowledge that the
question had been referred to the Supreme Court, the
country began to argue. While actually purely
academic, the problem was general enough in its
application to become part of the social chit-chat.

Individuals and groups discussed it. Editorial writers
had a hey-day pillorying the Government, the Senate
and the law-makers in general. The law-makers themselves argued endlessly on the fine points involved.

From the general public came generalizations.

If Senator were only a masculine term, people
argued—what about chairman, alderman, pedagogue,
president, journalist, doctor, dentist, lawyer? Weren't
these originally masculine terms now frequently applied to a woman? Then why not Senator?

Why was it, too, that a woman sat in the House of
Commons, where laws were made, but none were
allowed to sit in the Senate where these laws were
ratified?

Lawyers pointed out that the presence of Miss Agnes
MacPhail in the Commons had been made possible by
an amendment to the Dominion Election Act, some
years before. But, they added, if the Government had
the power to amend an Act so that a woman might

sit in the one House—why not the other? The grant
of legislative power as respecting membership in both
the Lower and Upper House was exactly the same.

One newspaper (*The Standard*, Strathmore, Alberta,
May 9th, 1928) summed up this point of view:

"To say a thing is right in one place and wrong in
another, when both are branches of the same government and separated by a hundred yards of corridor,
or a thousand miles of sea, is to make right or wrong
dependant upon geography or location.

"Both Houses have similar functions; each is an arm
of the administration of the country's affairs."

If the Government's stand in this connection were
right, and the British North America Act had to be
amended, then Miss MacPhail's position in the Commons would be illegal, some lawyers claimed. So
would many positions held by women throughout
Canada. Emily's appointment to the Bench, and those
of scores of other women, given responsibilities allocat-
ed in the Acts to "persons" were all illegal.

Lawyers made much of the matter of Intent—
arguing that the answer must depend on the *intention*
in the mind of the Imperial Parliament and the Fathers
of Confederation when the B.N.A. Act was passed.
Did they expect women would be appointed to the
Senate?

Emily discussed the matter in a long letter to Mrs.
John Scott:

"In spite of the arguments concerning Intent, when
you come to think it over, you'll find that sex, in itself,
is no longer a disqualification. All things being equal,
a woman is eligible for any office—with the unimport-

ant exception of being the father of a family. She
may be a queen, a cabinet minister, speaker of the
house, premier, pound-keeper, or any other old thing,
except—oh, presumption ineffable!—a senator."

While the discussion was going on among those who
were interested, Emily was working hard at assembling
data which she felt would be of value to Mr. Rowell.
There are many packets of letters outlining her thinking, and she forwarded a great deal of material for
his consideration.

Emily kept careful watch, too, on the public
development of the case, cautioning the women who
were associated with her as Appellants, to be very
discreet in any comment they made. One reason she
had selected this particular group was because she
believed that each one was capable of giving an account
of the principles that actuated her, should they be
called upon to do so. But, while the matter was before
the Courts, the less said the better. So, through the
long months, there was no acrimonious statement made
by any of the Five; instead, they were content, as
Emily pointed out, patiently to persuade the Government and the people, believing that, ultimately, a
common-sense focus would be taken of the matter. It
was also on record that in every province, except
Quebec, when the matter of fuller enfranchisement of
women was voted upon, no party had ever gone into
opposition.

At the same time that she held the vision of a new
charter of liberty for the women of Canada, she could,
on occasion, remind those who had forgotten that this
particular struggle for freedom was one launched and
developed by herself. Writing to Anne Anderson Perry

who was preparing an article on the campaign, she said:

"I am quite conscious that in forwarding you this data, my name appears a good deal—but this is inevitable in that it has been my movement first, last, and all the time. Others have surged in from time to time, giving right excellent advice and assistance but, by degrees, they have all surged out again and lost courage.

"On the contrary, I have become neither weary nor discouraged, and intend to persist to the very end."

One Sunday afternoon, Emily and Arthur were at tea with the Honourable Mr. Justice Ford and Mrs. Ford. Talk drifted to the status of women as "persons". Emily, all eagerness and driving conviction, outlined her thinking on the legal interpretation of the sixty-year-old Act, in the light of current conditions in Canada. The Judge listened intently and then turned to his bookshelf. He could, he told Emily, put his finger on a section from the Interpretation Act which expressed exactly what she was saying.

"The law shall be considered as always speaking, and whenever any matter or thing is expressed in the present tense, the same shall be applied to the circumstances as they arise, so that the effect may be given to each act, and every part thereof, according to its spirit, true intent and meaning."

It is a matter of record, that this key-noted the final decision.

III

In the small and musty building which had housed

Canada's Supreme Court for so many years, the question was debated by the Counsel for the Five Appellants, versus the Crown. The case opened at ten o'clock on the morning of March 14th, 1928, and, contrary to expectations, lasted all day. Mr. Rowell told Emily that he had been amused to learn that the counsel in the next case had been notified that they should be in readiness, as the "persons" case would be over within the hour—there being so little which could be said in the matter.

Only two provinces had been interested enough to appoint counsel to argue the case. Alberta had requested Mr. Rowell to represent its Government also, as supporting the Appellants; and Quebec had appointed counsel to argue in the negative, since it was then still twelve years before that province gave the vote to its women.

The court was full, with a number of women present, as Mr. Rowell presented his Factum, and argued throughout the day with Opposing Counsel. He had condensed his main argument into six very brief statements with only a sentence or so in each.

Speaking broadly, Mr. Rowell argued that there was nothing in the word "persons" to suggest that it should be limited to males. In its natural meaning, the word was equally applicable to women. The only limitation to the word "persons", as used in Section 24, was the adjective "qualified". A study of the qualifications of a Senator as outlined in the previous section, showed them to be very clear and simple. The person summoned to the Senate, must be thirty years of age, a British subject, and the possessor of four thousand dollars.

It was true that throughout the section dealing with

these qualifications, the words "he" and "him" were used. But the Interpretation Act, on which all clarification of the B.N.A. Act was based, stated expressly that all masculine words should be considered as including the feminine, and all singular, the plural,— unless the contrary was stated. Since there was nothing in the B.N.A. Act to state that "persons" should mean males only—it should logically be considered as also including females.

Throughout the Act, there were sections, referring to "persons", which obviously included women; why then should a special exclusion be deduced in this one section?

There seemed no reason for thinking that the Imperial Parliament had restricted the Governor-General from summoning women as well as men, since the Senate itself had been given full authority for deciding on the qualifications of any Senator, should they arouse any controversy. If, as a matter of argument, a woman were summoned, and the Senate decided that her qualifications were satisfactory, her position could not be challenged.

Opposing Counsel based their thinking on a number of English, Irish and Scottish cases, in which judgment had been given on the basis that, at the time of the B.N.A. enactment, women could not hold public office under the Common Law of England, therefore the Intent could not possibly have been to include women.

Mr. Rowell contended, however, that this was based on a view of public policy of one hundred years ago. This policy had been followed, because of an alleged inferiority, a lack of suitable education, or training, as well as the unseemliness of women taking part in public life. Times had changed this conception in every way, and women should not now be disqualified from the Senate because of this ancient bias.

Judgment was reserved. For five weeks, Emily held her patience, going on steadfastly with her daily routine. She already had made preparations, in case the verdict should be against them, and wrote to Mr. Rowell: "Whatever the outcome, we recognize that we are winning support for our cause, and ultimate success must await our efforts."

So it was that she squared her chin at the old indomitable angle when she received Mr. Rowell's telegram of April 24th, 1928:

"Regret Supreme Court have answered question submitted to them in the negative."

IV

Why did the Supreme Court consider women were not "persons" within the meaning of the Act?

Chief Justice Anglin read the judgment which based its conclusions on the main principle that the meaning of the B.N.A. Act must be interpreted in the light of conditions existing in 1867. The various provisions of the Act must bear today, thought the Court, the same construction which the courts would have given to them when first enacted. If the phrase "qualified persons" included women today—it had so included them since 1867.

Two important facts had a direct bearing on the judgment. The office of Senator was a new one, first created by the B.N.A. Act; and women were legally incapable of holding public office at the time the Act was passed.

DR. GOWAN FERGUSON, BROTHER
OF EMILY

ANNIE JESSAMINE FERGUSON-BURKE,
SISTER OF EMILY

THOMAS ROBERTS FERGUSON, K. C.,
BROTHER OF EMILY

HON. MR. JUSTICE WILLIAM NASSAU
FERGUSON, BROTHER OF EMILY

HARCOURT FERGUSON, K. C.,
BROTHER OF EMILY

EMILY (OVAL)

One of the most wise and learned judges of England,
Mr. Justice Willes, had ruled in 1868, the year after
the British North America Act became law, "That in
this country, in modern times, chiefly out of respect to
women, and a sense of decorum, and not from any
want of intellect or their being, for any other such
reason, unfit to take part in the government of the
country, they have been excused from taking any share
in public affairs."

While in the opinion of the Supreme Court judges,
the rights and privileges of women had been much
discussed in the intervening sixty years, it was significant that never had any woman sat in the Senate—nor,
until now, had any question of woman's eligibility for
appointment to the Upper House been made publicly.

The main question was this: had the Imperial Parliament made clear its intent to make such a striking
departure from the Common Law as the five Appellants
contended?

Had it considered women as eligible for the Senate,
at a time when they were neither qualified to sit in
the House of Commons, nor to vote for any candidates
for membership in that House?

Such an extraordinary privilege was not conferred
furtively, nor could the purpose to grant it, be gathered
from the remote conjectures based on a skilful piecing
together of the various expressions in a statute.

"There can be no doubt about it," Mr. Justice Anglin
concluded, "that the word 'persons' when standing
alone, includes women. It connotes human beings—
the criminal and the insane, equally with the good and
wise citizen; the minor as well as the adult. Hence the
propriety of the restrictions placed on its use in this

section which speaks of 'fit and qualified' persons. The terms in which the qualifications of members of the Senate are specified in Section 23 . . . import that only men are eligible for appointment." (This section, in noting property and citizenship qualifications, used the masculine pronoun throughout.)

The very day this negative decision was read in Ottawa, the Honourable Ernest Lapointe, Minister of Justice, arose in the Federal House and, in answer to a question put by Agnes MacPhail, announced that the Government would immediately set steps in motion for the amendment of the B.N.A. Act to include women in the Senate.

Emily realized that this was not as simple as it sounded. Since the Act was a treaty between all the provinces, no amendment could be made until all the provinces agreed. There would, she felt, be no end of argument before the question could be settled.

Because she had in mind, even before the case went to the Supreme Court, the possibility of an appeal to the Privy Council in England, she was not deeply disturbed at the disappointing verdict, and her only public comment was the statement that she believed the Supreme Court had given its judgment in all sincerity.

Mary Ellen Smith, however, who had been a member of the British Columbia legislature, spoke for thousands of women when she said, on learning of the verdict: "The iron dropped into the souls of women in Canada, when we heard that it took a man to decree that his mother was not a person."

Within a week of the verdict another "round robin" letter was circulating to the five women in Alberta,

suggesting an Appeal to the Privy Council in England.
Said Emily:

"Be it understood that this appeal must not be con-
strued as in any way expressing a lack of confidence in
the determination of the Honourable the Minister of
Justice and his colleagues of the Cabinet, to devise
means whereby the B.N.A. Act may be amended to
permit of women sitting in the Senate of Canada, but
only that we, as petitioners, can have no certainty that
the exigencies of politics, or the dissent of one, or more,
of the provinces, may not preclude the possibility of
such amendment . . .

"It seems to me, that we, as the petitioners, in requesting a reference in the first place to the Supreme
Court, decided that, for the time being, it was both a
wise and friendly procedure to lift the question from
the realm of politics and place it upon the highest
grounds.

"While we regret that the decision of the Supreme
Court of Canada was not favourable to our cause, I
am sure that we are agreed that their decision was a
sincere one, and should not be adversely criticized by
any of us.

"Of the ultimate results I have not the slightest
doubt. Nothing can prevent our winning . . . It is also
truly encouraging, and we may take the assurance to
our hearts, that no extension of the franchise has ever
been defeated, since John, the King of England, signed
the Magna Charta at Runnymede."

As always, however, Emily saw the broad outline
of what she was doing. On May 12th, a week or so
after the negative judgment had been given, she told
Mr. Rowell that she did not intend to forward her

petition for an appeal, or even let it be known that the "Five" were planning another petition, until after Parliament prorogued in Ottawa. "This will give the Government, if so disposed, the opportunity for stating the means they are devising, to amend the constitution. They have not in any way taken us into their confidence in the matter, apparently expecting that we consider these means to be invincible, as against any opposition or obstacles that may lie in the way. I sincerely hope that this may be the case in respect to the means, so that we may have the happiness and satisfaction of withdrawing the petition . . . If we lose in the Privy Council, we are still as far ahead in achieving our ends, in that the Federal Government has pledged itself to these."

The House prorogued, however, and nothing further had been done to implement the Government's promise of action. Emily forwarded the plea and was happy to learn that the Government approved of the appeal, and would not contest it. Accordingly, another Order-in-Council was shortly passed, referring the matter to His Majesty the King, as represented by the Privy Council.

To Emily's great delight, Premier Louis A. Taschereau finally withdrew his objection; thus the province of Quebec did not contest the matter before the Privy Council.

He did so, however, somewhat reluctantly. Writing to Emily on June 15th, 1929, he said:

"Although I believe that the great majority of the women of Quebec do not want the franchise, nor the right to sit in parliament, it was only fair that we should leave the determination of the legal aspect of the matter to the Privy Council without interfering. It is the decision to which we have arrived."

The next mail carried Emily's reply. "Miss Canada has now grown up . . . and has taken her place as partner at the hearth of the nations!"

This was an auspicious development, and Emily held high hopes for a favourable decision from London. She planned, for a time, to make a second visit to England, so that she might hear the case argued, and there was considerable pressure brought to bear on her by suffragist groups in England, who wished to pay her honour.

But the years had taught Emily wisdom. She explained her thinking in a letter which went to the Five:

"I had thought of attending this appeal in London—indeed, had intended to—but upon maturer consideration thought it would only prejudice our cause.

"To speak at such a gathering as that proposed by the 'Six Point Group', or to be entertained as suggested would, in my mind, be identifying ourselves with a group which, while non-partisan in character, is yet making strenuous efforts for the admission of peeresses in their own right to the House of Lords.

"While heart and soul in sympathy with their fight, I feel it would not be good policy to confuse the legal, political or public minds of Great Britain concerning our particular contention. While our ultimate aims are similar, our cases do not rest upon the same basis and we would not be well advised in drawing upon our cause any hostility that may have arisen against theirs. Indeed, I cannot think of anything that would more thoroughly kill our case.

"If we accepted this gracious and well-meant invitation, the newspapers in England would discuss the
matter and 'take sides' upon it, probably making
numerous mistakes about it, either wilfully or innocently. Besides we, as appellants, must properly feel
that public discussions are stopped. Others may discuss
it with propriety; but not any of us . . . If we lose our
appeal we will then be in a position to avail ourselves
of the most valuable assistance of the 'Six Point Group',
and we may probably need it. Maybe we will all want
to go to England then; educating the Canadian public
en route."

Mr. Rowell, K.C., with his assisting Counsel Mr.
Frank Cahan, went to England to argue the case on
behalf of the five women of Alberta. Since the Dominion of Canada was upholding the Supreme Court's
negative decision, the Attorney-General was represented by Mr. Eugene LaFleur, K.C., and assisting counsel.
The Hon. J. F. Lymburn, K.C. Attorney-General for
Alberta, appeared in support of the Appellants.

Emily stayed home and went steadily on with her
work. But in spite of her optimism, she was prepared
for another disappointing verdict, and wrote to Mr.
Rowell just before he left for England, outlining what
she felt should be the next step in such a contingency:

"I note that the Prime Minister goes to England
presently, to a conference on Imperial Affairs. As his
government, through the Minister of Justice, has
promised to 'devise means' whereby women may serve
in the Senate, it has occurred to me that in the event
of our Appeal not being successful, the aforementioned
'means' might be devised at this conference—that is to

say, the Canadian status might be made entirely clear in this, and in other matters, generally."

Thus to her lawyer. To her friend, Mrs. Scott, she dashed off a postscript to a long letter:

"Going to win, Dear? You bet!"

We have an eye-witness account of the hearing of the case before the Privy Council, given on July 22, 1929, by Lukin Johnston of the Canadian Press.

"In a quiet room at Number One, Downing Street, five great judges, with the Lord Chancellor of England at their head, and a battery of bewigged lawyers from Canada and from England, are wrestling with a question, propounded on behalf of their sex, by five Alberta women.

"The roar of London penetrates only as a distant murmur. Room thirty feet high. Walls lined with shelves filled with leather-backed volumes. Judges sit at a semi-circular table. They wear no robes, no wigs. Just ordinary, everyday business suits.

"Lord Chancellor Sankey, grim of countenance, and of few words, sits in the middle. On his right is Lord Darling whose eyes twinkle and whose lips twitch, as every now and again he cracks an irrepressive joke. Next to him is Lord Tomlin. On the Lord Chancellor's left is Lord Merrivale, famous as President of the Divorce Court, and next him, is Sir Lancelot Sanderson.

"On the table before them, are voluminous documents, and legal papers, brought to them ever and anon by watchful attendants. Each of them has a glass of cold water beside him. The only ornaments on the table are three large silver ink-stands. In front of them, below the low barrier, are arrayed the counsel, in wigs and gowns . . . "Rowell stands at the little rostrum in the middle, and propounds his arguments. A few members of the public, including half a dozen women, two or three bored-looking reporters, and a couple of ushers, make up most of those present.

"It is all very orderly and dignified. Everyone is very polite. Mr. Rowell makes a statement, or reads long extracts from the B.N.A. Act. Lord Merrivale, ponderous and very wise-looking, asks a question, and Mr. Rowell replies in many words.

"Deep and intricate questions of constitutional law are debated back and forth. The exact shade of meaning to be placed on certain words is argued to the finest point.

"And so it goes on, and probably will continue to go on for several days. At the end of all these endless speeches, lessons on Canadian history, and questions by five great judges of England, it will be decided, if one may hazard a guess, that women undoubtedly are Persons. Which one may say, without exaggeration, most of us know already!"

VI

Judgment was reserved. Then, on October 18th, 1929, before a crowded Court, the Lord Chancellor of Great Britain, Lord Sankey, read a scholarly and vividly human analysis of women's changing status through the years, in pronouncing the Privy Council's verdict.

Women were to be considered as "persons" within the meaning of the British North America Act; and so were eligible for the Senate.

While the judgment did not refer to it directly, Emily found that its principles were based on the section she had read at Mr. Justice Ford's that Sunday afternoon. *"The law . . . shall be applied to the circumstances as they arise . . ."*

For the following were the main principles on which the affirmative judgment was given:

The exclusion of women from all public office, was a relic of more barbarous days; but the necessity of the times have often forced on man, customs which, in later years, have not been necessary.

Originally, the exclusion of women from public office was probably due to the fact that when early tribes assembled for deliberations, they did so, under arms, for protection. Because of the likelihood of attack from other tribes, women did not attend.

This exclusion of women found its way into the opinion of Roman Jurists, and as the barbarian tribes who settled in the Roman Empire were exposed to constant dangers, they naturally preserved and continued the tradition.

However, conditions change, and what may be opinion grounded on experience under certain circumstances, may change under different circumstances.

In the course of centuries there may be found cases of exceptional women, but in England, too, chiefly owing to up-bringing and education, women were not deemed capable of holding public office. Their Lordships, however, did not feel it was right to apply rigidly to the Canada of today, the decisions and the reasoning which had been applied to different circumstances and different centuries. The appeal to Roman law, and to early English decisions, was not, of itself, a secure foundation on which to build an interpretation of the B.N.A. Act of 1867.

The communities within the Britannic system include countries in every stage of social and economic development, all of which are undergoing a continuous process of evolution. His Majesty the King-in-Council, is the final court of appeal from all those communities, and their Lordships felt they should take great care not to interpret legislation, meant to apply to one community, to a rigid adherence to the customs and traditions of another. Canada had its difficulties, both at home, and with the Mother Country; but it soon discovered that union was strength.

The British North America Act planted in Canada a living tree capable of growth and expansion within its natural limits. The object of the Act was to grant a constitution to Canada . . . and like all written constitutions it has been subject to development through usage and convention.

Customs were apt to develop into traditions which were stronger than law, and which remain unchallenged long after the reason for them has disappeared.

Examining Section 24 in the light of this principle, their Lordships felt that in its original meaning the word "persons," undoubtedly included women. But if used in an Act of several centuries ago, as well as in the B.N.A. Act, it would have to be understood that the word applied only to males, not because the word "person" did not include women, but because at Common Law, woman was incapable of serving in a public office.

Custom alone had prevented the claim being made or the point contested in regard to women's entrance to the Senate.

Their Lordships did not wish to cut down the

provisions of the Act by a narrow and technical construction, but rather to give it a large and liberal
interpretation, so that the Dominion, to a great extent,
but within certain limits, might be mistress in her own
house, as the provinces, to a great extent, but within
certain limits, are mistresses in theirs.

Examining the technical details in regard to the
argument, their Lordships felt that the Act should be
interpreted in the light of present-day custom. They
were not deciding any question as to the rights of
women, but only as to their eligibility for a particular
position.

As a matter of fact, no one, either male or female,
had a *right* to be summoned to the Senate. The real
point at issue was whether the Governor-General had
a right to summon *women* to the Senate.

Examining the separate headings under which the
B.N.A. Act is set up, there were many instances in
which the word "persons" might include persons of
both sexes. And to those who ask why the word should
include women—the obvious answer is—why not?

The burden was upon those who denied that it did,
to make out their case.

On every count their Lordships felt that the word
should include women, since there were so many
examples of the use of the word where it did include
them. For instance, in one section, there is a proviso
stating that every male British subject, in contra-
distinction to "persons" shall have a vote. Again, in
Section 133, it is provided that either the English or
French language may be used by "any person", or in
any pleadings in any court in Canada. The word
"person" here must surely include women, as it could

hardly be supposed that a man might use either French or English, but a woman might not.

If Parliament had intended to limit the word "persons" in Section 24 to males, it would surely have manifested such an intention by an express limitation as it had done in other sections.

After an exhaustive analysis of technical points raised by the Counsel, the judgment ended with this paragraph:

"Their Lordships have come to the conclusions that the Question propounded by the Governor-General, must be answered in the affirmative, and that women are eligible to be summoned, and become members of the Senate of Canada, and they will humbly advise His Majesty accordingly."

*   *   *

Electric waves trembled over an ocean, and over a continent. At three o'clock that morning, in her Edmonton home, Evelyn Murphy was awakened by the joyous calling of her mother. Judge Murphy in a white flannelette nightgown, her hair tousled, her cheeks flushed, was dancing with delight in the doorway.

"We've won! We've won!"

CHAPTER III

Defeat in Victory

Right can afford to lose.

JANEY CANUCK.

I

W E'VE WON!

It was a fundamental cry of triumph that was to find many an echo in the succeeding days. Nothing spoiled this, one of the highest moments in Emily's life. Heretofore, her victories had been in the local or provincial field. Now she had a world stage for her setting. Congratulations poured into the house. Moreover, her associates were generous in attributing all the responsibility for the victory to her.

Told of the judgment, Nellie McClung gave a press statement which was widely quoted:

"I am particularly glad for Mrs. Murphy's sake . . . It was she who wrote all the letters and arranged every detail in the controversy, assuming much of the expense and labour involved. Her handling of the whole matter has been a masterpiece of diplomacy and to her the victory belongs."

Louise McKinney, writing to Emily, expressed the feeling of all the Appellants:

"I am proud that Alberta saw this thing through, but

all through the litigation I have felt somewhat of a humbug, for I realized that you were the one who deserved all the credit, and the rest of us were getting all the publicity . . . I was pleased to be one of the Five, but have repeatedly said that you had conceived the plan and done all the hard work in connection with it."

Emily, glowing with happiness over the unanimous approval and backing of her associates, scribbled a truth which women have not yet learned:

"The appointment of women to the Senate depends entirely on women's own strength. They have the ballot, and can abolish the Senate, and elect a government favourably. In the end, the women must succeed. Their interests lead that way. This insures unity among them."

She noted her delight at the way things were going in a letter to her friend Bailey Price in Calgary:

"After all, dear girl, our successes do not mean much to us unless our friends approve—unless they pat us on the back and say we did well . . . I have been amazed by the interest which the decision has aroused and am being laden down with wires, letters and cables from people and organizations I did not know of.

"Wasn't Mrs. McClung a big soul to come out and say what she did? She need not have, either, because it was a wonderful thing for those four women to have left their names and reputations in my hands, not knowing what I was going to do or say. It was a matter of implicit trust on their part, and is one of the most beautiful things which has happened to me."

Her own public statement to the press was in line with her attitude throughout the long struggle: "It should be made clear that we, and the women of Canada whom we had the high honour to represent, are not considering the pronouncement of the Privy Council as standing for a sex victory, but, rather, as one which will now permit our saying 'we' instead of 'you' in affairs of State."

Friends, everywhere, were jubilant.

"We are unspeakably proud of you," wrote one of them, "and I greatly rejoice that the other women on the committee have been big enough not to detract in any way from the glory of the occasion for you by claiming any of the credit . . . Is it not splendid that this has come when you are here, and well, and young, and can go on to something else, rather than having wreaths and cenotaphs? . . . I just wanted to hug the cut of you in the paper, the one with your turban and fur collar, and roguish gleam in your eye . . . We are all standing by if there is anything you have in mind you would like us to do at this juncture."

From the scores of letters in similar vein, I pick another:

"It was a famous victory and you will go down in history. Now we are praying that you will be made the first woman Senator. How proud we would be to see our 'little general' there, taking her seat. How you would wake up that dull assemblage!"

Women's groups held appropriate celebrations throughout the country. The Montreal Women's Club planned a gala luncheon and invited all five women to attend; but none could take the time from their busy lives to travel so far. Emily, however, lingered with pleasure over the thought of such a colourful affair. It would have been nice to celebrate the judgment with the group who had, literally, started the whole affair. There would be fine dramatics, too, in the pilgrimage of the five heroines from the New West, to Old Quebec—still holding out against women's suffrage. The English "Six Point Group" too, urged Emily to come to England for a mammoth celebration, but she felt that she could not spare the time.

Again she had brought fame to her city, and, with its full Western enthusiasms, it lost no opportunity of expressing gratitude. Once again there were hearty congratulations as she walked to or from the office. The shrilling of the telephone meant probably some warm-hearted enthusiast, assuring Emily that she was a super-woman. In the court-house, or as she trod Jasper Avenue, she heard again and again: "Well, you've done it again, Mrs. Murphy! You showed 'em!"

A number of people approached Mr. Mackenzie King in the matter of her immediate appointment to the Senate. Word came back, as Emily had expected, that no appointment could be made from Alberta, until one of the half-dozen Senators allowed the province, died. That was fine. There was time enough. It was good to savour deeply the rich-flowing endorsation of her fellow-citizens. Writing to Mrs. John Scott, on October 30, 1930, about a year after the judgment, she said:

"There is a lot in that dictum which says, 'Having done all—*stand*.' We lose so much, both in private and public life, by receding from the ground we have won, either from indolence or some other cause . . ."

Emily was in fine fettle. When an American woman, speaking of her expected appointment said, "But, ma'am, won't you be afraid of sixty-two men?" Emily twinkled cheerily:

"Afraid, ma'am? Why should I be? I am used to co-operating with them. You see, my father was a man. I have four brothers, and I married a man. Indeed, and I've been obliged to send scores of men to jail!"

II

In the first flush of victory, when the press asked Emily what qualifications a woman should have for the Senate, she harked back to her favourite example —Article 29 of the Constitution for the Irish Free State, which provided that the Senate should be composed of citizens who have done honour to the nation by reason of useful public service, or who, because of special qualifications or attainments, represented important aspects of the national life. Did not the description fit her precisely?

Subconsciously, too, her thinking is evidenced in an article she wrote for *Chatelaine* a few hours after the judgment was announced:

"If women can do nothing else in their new sphere," she wrote, "they can render service by interpreting the Senate to the public. Hitherto, it has been only reported . . . Women in the Senate could also serve the public by their work on the Divorce Committee, so long as this Committee continues to last . . . Women should at least be judged by one of their own sex who ought to possess an intimate understanding of domestic and marital difficulties."

At sixty-two, it is a matter of record that Emily had always won what she set out to attain. Looking back over the years, she had every justification for a serene confidence. Her life had been spent, in the main, in a pioneer country, with little of the political intrigue about it. Feuds were direct and open. Enemies were acknowledged and attacked. One stated which side of the argument appealed the most; and then debated with every ounce of energy one had.

It had been Emily's great good fortune to fight, most of her life, in a fair field. Given a true basis for the fight as a start, she had found that the best man was likely to win, if only one had courage enough, vision enough, plus a capacity for downright hard work.

She had won a victory in her earliest days in Edmonton, over the Hospital affair. Her first bout with provincial legislation had brought what she desired in the passing of the Dower Act. The five years' struggle she had known, back-stage, for the full establishment of her court, had won for it the proper prestige. Now the greatest and longest struggle of them all had brought further triumphs.

Because she had fought without discouragement, women were the peers of men in the last male legislative stronghold.

Coming as it did, on top of years of agitation for her appointment, Emily was confident that the victory would mean that, in due time, she would be made the first woman Senator in Canada. How could it be otherwise? Not only did she feel that she had the esteem of the Prime Minister, but never before, she was certain, had there been such a public demand for the appointment of any individual to the Senate. Practically every newspaper had published editorials endorsing her. The thousands of resolutions and letters from influential men and women throughout Canada must have made an imprint on the minds in Ottawa.

Unconsciously, the broad principle of women's equal opportunity with men, for which she had fought so steadfastly, became more and more a personal dream. Perhaps if her friends had not been so insistent, the absorption of her daily work, and the demands of the unsolved problems it presented each day to her imagination, might, in time, have eliminated the idea from her mind. But, day after day, she opened letters urging her on toward the final achievement; the recognition of her "right" to be the first woman Senator.

"I want you to be Canada's first choice," said one writer, and her letter is typical of those which Emily received. "Not because I like you. (A woman's usual reason.) Not because you're a success. Not because you're a "Who's Who" lady—but because I know you are honest in purpose, level of head, and because you're big enough to do for East and West. Heavens! Think what you can do for Canada!"

Wrote another: "You'll have to work with sleeves up, to hold this Senatorship for the West. Mind you, it's NOT for Janey Canuck that you're working, but for the big, awkward, silent West. Get that through your mind. The West!"

It seemed a natural and inevitable culmination to her life, and she assured those who begged her to take more action, that the Government would not, surely, by-pass the five women of Alberta in making first choice.

Then, toward the end of 1930, just a year after the Privy Council judgment, the Government announced the appointment to the Senate of Cairine Wilson, a Liberal worker of note.

III

It was a definite disappointment; but Emily kept it to herself. She made no public statement of any kind, and letters to indignant women were full of reassurance. But her hurt was glimpsed in a letter she wrote to Howard Ferguson, Prime Minister for Ontario, and an old friend of the family:

"A good deal of chagrin was felt over the appointment of the Honourable Cairine Wilson, and I received many letters to this effect. In reply, I made no unfavourable comment, but still found myself too ruffled in spirit to forward any congratulations to Ottawa. I hope it is true; after all, as the Persian proverb has it, that 'God rights those who keep silence'. Nearly all the women, whether Conservatives, Liberals, or Progressives, felt that Mr. King would be taking high ground in making the first appointment on a non-partisan basis, but apparently they thought otherwise."

With characteristic good sportsmanship she readjusted her thinking. To her friends she indicated that they should rejoice that at last a woman sat in the Senate of Canada.

History moved on. Within a month or so, the King Government was defeated in the general elections and Mr. R. B. Bennett was called upon to form a govern-

ment. Emily could not help but feel this was an
auspicious development. Mr. Bennett had been the
young lawyer who first sponsored her Dower Act bill
in the Alberta House. Coming from Alberta with his
constituency in Calgary, he would surely have a special
interest in seeing one of the Five in the Senate. Emily
recalled the fact that since the first formation of the
first parliament in Canada a century ago, there had
always been a Ferguson or a Gowan in the Legislature
or the Senate; sometimes in both. All in all, her friends
assured her, the appointment must come!

In January, 1931, the Honourable E. P. Lessard,
Senator for Edmonton, died. Here was another vacancy
in Emily's home town.

The Montreal Women's Club held a special session
to forward the matter of Emily's appointment to Mr.
Bennett. Mrs. John Scott wrote to Emily: "Well, dear,
the issue is on the knees, not of the gods, alas, but of
the men, which is worse and more of it, I take it!"

In mid-April, the Edmonton Press Club wired to
Mr. Bennett, and asked the other Press Clubs throughout Canada to do the same, urging Emily's appointment because "this organization feels strongly that no
woman in Canada has given so freely of herself in the
public service of her country, and no woman is more
worthy."

Mr. Bennett wrote back promptly, and Emily copied
the letter that she might study its implications:

"The difficulty in the way of the appoinment of Mrs.
Murphy is one that cannot be overcome," he said.
"There are certain customs that have grown by practice
that now have almost the sanction of law. One is that

recognition must be given to the Roman Catholic minority. The late Senator was a member of that minority, and the new Senator will have to be, as the sole representative of the Catholic minority in our province. You must also bear in mind that practically forty per cent of the population of Canada are of the Roman Catholic faith."

Emily's mind fled back down the years to the excuses and evasions she had met; to the protestations made; to the assurances given that the Government would welcome women in the Senate—if only there were constitutional means for admitting them. Now, with the last hurdle passed—here was still another obstacle to be tackled.

She sharpened her pencil and drafted a reply:

"Much perturbed by your letter Edmonton Press Club saying that Alberta Senatorship 'belongs' Roman Catholics. The provisions of the B.N.A. governing appointment to Senate, take no cognisance whatsoever of creed or sex or custom or understanding. British nationality is the stipulated qualification."

On May 26th, 1931, a telegram went from Emily to a member of her family, devastating in its brevity:

"Vacancy goes Catholic."

Following that wire I can find no reference to the Senate anywhere. The hundreds of letters she had received about her appointment, the boxes upon boxes of notes and references, were stowed away. Buried in them was the letter written to her from Montreal in 1921, to which she pinned the note "How it all started."

IV

Some years after Emily's death, Lotta Dempsey, who had been Women's Editor of *The Edmonton Bulletin* for many of these years, was discussing the matter with one of the Senators from Edmonton.

"I wonder why they never did appoint Emily Murphy?" she asked.

The Honourable Senator spoke quickly, with deep conviction:

"Oh, we never could have had Mrs. Murphy in the Senate!" he said. "She would have caused too much trouble!"

PART V

CHAPTER I

"*Tubbie*"

One's best talents are required for the home.
                                    JANEY CANUCK.

I

IN ALL THIS, Emily was a "Who's Who" lady, as
her friend named her. But to her family, more often
than not, she was "Tubbie", and it is as Tubbie that
some of her most endearing character traits are revealed. Fundamentally, her attitude was no different
in her private life, to that of her public life. Indeed,
her charm lay in the fact that she translated much of
the same point of view into the ordinarily humdrum
matters of daily living, as she did into her court work.

To begin with, she was equally intelligent in both
spheres—a rare accomplishment for "career" women.
To every relationship, whether that of husband,
daughters, or maids, she brought the same frank ap-
praisal, the same sense of camaraderie, the same direct
approach. As a matter of fact, she went even further
than intelligence. Once she wrote: "Every home should
have a blarney-stone—and keep it bright with lip-
service," and liked to practise this graceful thought.

Just as she saw the wider horizons of community

responsibility behind each individual tragedy paraded
before her in the courts, so she envisioned almost a
mystical unity in her family associations. Each home
celebration was an "occasion" for her, and about it,
she wove a ritualistic appreciation. Perhaps this instinct
had been nurtured in the days when her mother
taught her the symbolic meaning for every design on
the banners used by the Loyal Orange Lodges in the
"Walks", which, to the uninitiated, were drab affairs.
Certainly her years of writing about day-by-day affairs
taught her to invest them with an importance others
did not—or could not—recognize. Whatever successes
she knew, or whatever problems dragged her spirit into
the depths, it was always as Mrs. Murphy, wife of
Arthur Murphy, that she entered her home. For one
thing, it had become a habit with her during the
twenty years before she entered public life; so that
Arthur was always the Master of the House to her. His
own work kept him absorbed, whether it was in the
high adventure of real estate in a boom period, or the
equally uncertain adventure of saving souls. In particular, when he returned to his first love, the Ministry,
his mind was withdrawn considerably into the progress
of his sermons, his congregation, or his theological
reading.

But he was always there when Emily needed him,
to listen in quiet concentration while she told of her
experiences. She liked to sound off her tempestuous
thinking against the steadfast balance of reason which
he maintained. She went her own way, followed her
own judgment, fought her own battles; but she alone
knew how much her thinking was influenced by the
serene wisdom of her husband. In one of her books

which she gave to him, she wrote: "To the dear Padre, with always the first, best love of Janey Canuck"; and meant it.

There was no competitive sense between them. He was very proud of his wife, seeing her always as his "Dear Old Girl". Each developed a sincere respect for the other's mind, and enjoyed still the good comradeship engendered in the Sunday drives to the churches round about Arthur's Ontario parishes.

To her girls she brought more of a sister-to-sister attitude than that of a conventional mother. When they were first going to school at St. Albans in England, and she was travelling with Arthur, Emily's letters to her daughters were so gay and newsy, that, small as they were, the girls kept them and have them to this day. In the years when the family was touring Ontario with Arthur on his Mission work, she never missed an opportunity for taking them through one of the factories in the bustling little towns. This was a form of education she felt valuable if the girls were going to have any real knowledge of what lay behind things as they seemed. Always, she encouraged them to read any books they wished. In her reviewing work she followed the publisher's lists closely, asking for the books she would particularly like to have. None of them was *verboten* to her daughters.

II

As has happened repeatedly in this study of Emily Murphy's life, she herself leaves an answer to our most pertinent questions. No study of her role as mother could have a better interpretation than that

she herself noted in a fragment on "Mothership" which
was never published:

"Although barely twenty years of age when I became
a mother," she wrote one evening, "I can see, in looking
back across the years, that the finest joys of life came
with my children: so close they are to one's heart,
these younglings, and so dear.

"In the outside world, argue as you may concerning
the proper placing of titular decorations, in the home,
the habit of wearing the heart on one's sleeve is unquestionably correct as well as deeply wise.

"Looking back, 1 can see also that the so-called
'hardships' of rearing children are largely imaginative.
For this reason I find it difficult to sympathize with
those persons who are ever wont to dilate upon the
'tears' and 'sacrifices' of motherhood. I even find it
hard to become enraptured over Mother's Day, in
that the strain running through most of the editorials
is one of pity and commiseration for the apparently sad
and serious woman who has reared a family . . . There
are the florist's advertisements too. *Don't forget the
mode. Pink carnation if she's alive; white if she's dead.*

"In art, the mother with a grown-up family is usually
portrayed with folded hands, a resigned-to-the-inevit-
able air, and in a gown that is drearily suggestive of a
shroud. If you wish to see this down-daunted type in
its full perfection, pray study that widely known, but
objectionable picture entitled "Whistler's Mother".

"It is my opinion and I hope that you will agree with
me, that there is no reason for burning incense to a
woman simply because she has fulfilled the natural

functions of her sex—because she has been no skulker of her maternal responsibility.

"This type of down-daunted mother is rapidly passing out, for we are coming to see that a mother who lets herself subside into a kind of burnt-sacrifice upon what is called the 'family altar' is not really a good mother, nor a good citizen.

" 'In weariness and painfulness'?—Yes! 'In watchings often'?—Yes, very often. But the recompense is ever infinitely greater than the sacrifice. Indeed, I have never been able to sacrifice myself for my children. The compensation has been a full hundredfold, and this is really quite a good rate of interest.

" 'In watchings often'? Yes—watchings such as the singing of rocking hymns and little sleep songs; the lulling of one's babies. Who calls this a sacrifice?

"No compensation in the love we get from our children?—Let the mothers answer!

". . . Now about my own children. Other folk may have thought them ordinary infants—purblind and inconsequential folk—but to me they were quite as wonderful as those plump little angel-children who, in olden pictures, sit at the feet of the Virgin and strum upon strings.

"As they grew up they were duty-full children, although we never had rules worth mentioning. As far as possible children ought to get their own gait. Why resist the course of a star in its natural orbit?

"Be this as it may, our house was a republic where all had rules of conduct explained and the necessity therefor. If they broke the rules, the self-imposed penalty was also explained. Our case rested there. There is no need to enforce commandments once the children understand that love is the fulfilling of the law. This is quite a good way, too, especially when one realizes that each child is a brand-new combination and reacts to life in its own way. After all, 'badness' is only mis-directed goodness.

"Pray do not think, however, that in our lessons, household duties, out-door sports and all the various etceteras of family life that I ever lost ascendance— that is to say, the children in my Maternal Relations Court understood that while the judge was lenient and fairly reasonable, she was never sitting blindfolded. Perhaps he was right, the fellow who declared that people are really governed by laws which never find their way into copy-books. Perhaps it is also true that one's best talents are required in the home, and that in life our finest parts are always played to small audiences. Indeed, I feel quite sure of this.

". . . But about the present and how it has all turned out for me. This is not a difficult matter to figure out, for now I am the youngling myself, my daughters having the care and control of me, and I know enough to get the principle at stake.

"Believe me, what I say is a fact, for at this very moment an anxious but withal persistent voice comes from a bedroom down the hallway, this being its third and last time of calling: 'Now, Mother, you go to bed right away. It's half-past one, and you know you'll not be ready for work in the morning. *Now, Mother, go right to bed!*'

"All this being so true, permit me, Sirs and Madams, to bid you a very good-night, and ask if it is not well that, after all the years, there is someone who cares so much?"

III

Emily was always deeply concerned with her home and its happiness, but knew how to adjust its mechanics to the right proportions. "I should like you to mention," she wrote to a journalist planning an article on her, "that I am interested in my home like that female Solomon tells about who looketh well to the ways of her household." Having spent twenty years setting an outline for the ways of her household she could devote most of her imaginative thinking to her public service. The creative work at home was accomplished.

The Murphy house was comfortably furnished, with the friendly ease of deep chairs about a fireplace, and bookshelves that reached to the ceiling. Her walls were heavy with photographs of family and friends. Proper respect was always given to certain treasures brought from the old homes—the spinning-wheel used by Arthur's grandmother; the walnut table about which sat Sir John A. Macdonald and Sir Charles Tupper, on that long-ago evening when she had recited "The Burial of Sir John Moore".

Emily was an inveterate collector and every home soon overflowed with her treasures. Early in her marriage she had gathered Indian relics and had spent many holidays digging for them in Western Ontario. One of the Curators at the British Museum had given her pieces of an old Mosaic Roman road, which she fingered with the same degree of awe, every time they were shown to visitors. Early in her marriage she had paid fifty-five dollars for a Breeches Bible, published in 1578, so-called, because it refers to the clothing of Adam and Eve as "breeches". She saved a potato that looked like a mummy; a shark's egg; and at one time had a notable collection of butterflies. Her treasures were tucked away in corner cupboards or open shelves, to be brought out for inspection whenever a guest showed interest.

The mechanics of home life went smoothly, in that, for one thing, Emily was always able to keep her maids. On more than one instance in her later life they were girls she had rescued in her court-work, girls who became deeply grateful to her. But whoever her maid was, Emily was wont to remind her that "she only is an underling who has the mind of one". She never nagged them about their work, being content if the house ran smoothly and things were kept in order. She would slip into the kitchen often to listen to love-tangled problems and liked to give advice on the way of men-folk.

She maintained her household with the same generosity that she brought to all her work. The only thing that really irritated her about her servants, was when they allowed supplies to run short. "Order groceries as if you were fifty miles in the bush," she urged them. "Buy as if you were only able to get supplies once a week!"

She was not fond of cooking herself, and it is doubtful if she ever baked a cake in her life. Yet she liked to star on special occasions by preparing a steak; she enjoyed making crocks and crocks of pickles.

On regular Sundays, Kathleen and her husband Cleave came to dinner. Emily made of this ordinarily routine meal, a significant feast. A gargantuan roast, whatever the temperature, was carved by Emily, and served with several vegetables, accompanied by soup,

EMILY, WITH HER YOUNGEST
DAUGHTER, DORIS BALDWIN
MURPHY

EVELYN GOWAN MURPHY,
DAUGHTER OF EMILY

EMILY DORIS CLEAVE KENWOOD,
GRAND-DAUGHTER OF EMILY

KATHLEEN FERGUSON KENWOOD,
DAUGHTER OF EMILY

dessert, cheese, and fruit. If her guests did not have a third helping Emily worried that the food was not as good as it should have been. She liked to open bottles from her well-filled fruit cellar, and spread what Cleave called "every kind of gadget" in the way of pickles and relishes.

She loved tea-parties, and most Saturdays were lively times at the Murphy house, when friends came to meet a visiting celebrity. What usually started as a small tea was likely to become a large affair, since, in her walks about town, Emily would invite groups of men and women, as she met them. Thus it was that, through sheer necessity, eighty cups and saucers were on her pantry shelves.

Before the tea, Emily would go into the kitchen to cut stacks of sandwiches—enough for a Sunday School picnic. As a result, the Murphy's often lived on toasted sandwiches for several days thereafter. But she was a warm-hearted hostess, pressing the family hospitality on everyone present; able with a passing word and a quick glance to make each one present feel a particularly honoured and wanted guest.

Emily ran her home with imagination, tenderness and a proper appreciation for certain essentials. She was always able to arrange her work so that she could be home in time of sickness or special need. Since Kathleen had married in the year of her appointment to the Police Court, there was only Evelyn at home, and as she described in her article on "Mothership", Evelyn became the one to shoo her off to bed at two o'clock in the morning. It was Evelyn who typed her manuscripts or letters for her in the evenings; who listened with mounting indignation to some of Emily's tempestuous local storms. Arthur and the maids became familiar with the oft-heard call from Evelyn: "Come on, Tubbie! Get your hat and let's go!" Or the protesting "Now lookit, Tubbie! You can't do that!"

She enjoyed the riches of her home life. She liked to make a "moment" of every little occasion. Never were the first spring strawberries placed before her, but she would declaim: "Doubtless God could have made a better berry than the strawberry, but doubtless never did."

No birthday passed without her quoting as if she had discovered it for the first time: "We can rejoice that she was born, and wish her born once more."

As Tubbie, she enjoyed being bossed by Evelyn, grinned at by Arthur, spoiled by her maids. She liked to be the Home-Mother for Kathleen and her family when they came dining. She welcomed the stimulation which entertaining always gave her.

These were the human associations in her home. There too, she gathered her treasures and fingered them lovingly. But it was in her own room that she spent most of her time. Many evenings after an hour or so with her family in the sitting-room, she would go up to her bedroom which overlooked the trim garden, and settle down happily before her over-crowded desk, topped by bulging shelves of papers and manuscripts. Whether she was noting the points she had made in some legal argument, writing to friends, revising a manuscript or annotating her court cases, she was withdrawn into her own world of paper and pen. This was her inner sanctuary, set within the encircling enchantment of her home.

IV

Throughout her life, Emily had a clear skin, and hazel eyes, bright with interest or amusement. She bobbed her very thick and heavy hair in 1926 and made the news columns as the "bobbed-haired magistrate". There is a photograph of her at this time, looking very severe and formidable, in a dress she had designed for herself. It was a much be-braided affair, faintly reminiscent, in its collar-line, of the Salvation Army.

She paid little attention to her clothes but liked well-tailored dresses for her court work. She never, however, wore a tailored suit, preferring, always, the softer fashion of dress and coat; and it was not long before the severe hair-cut had been replaced with the satisfaction of a good permanent. She liked to set a wide hat a-tilt on her short hair, and swing a vivid necklace about her throat. She was fond of tortoise-shell combs, and, when at home, had a weakness for high-heeled shoes, which her family feared would pitch her head-first downstairs. Beaded bags, brilliant parasols, peacock-tinted necklaces, she collected with a jackdaw fervour, seldom to wear, as she gave them away. There is an early Edmonton photograph in which, as Skip of the Women's Curling Club, Emily centres a group of Western matrons. No hat in the picture is more garlanded with birds of paradise plumes; no feather boa more enveloping.

Whenever she visited her family in the East, sister Annie took her shopping, and with many a shocked, "Now, Muddie, you can't buy that!" sent her home with a smoother silhouette. Emily submitted to this disciplining with her twinkling good grace, but, within a few days, another coloured necklace would be contrasting with her new, tailored neckline.

If there were any excuse for it, Emily "dressed up". She entered several competitions at masquerades in the early light-hearted days of Edmonton's blooming. Later, the annual dinners of the Women's Press Club gave her opportunities for masquerading which she seldom missed. On one such occasion, in a black dinner suit, white tie, slicked-back hair, and a silk hat she was a merry Tom Moore. Many friends remember her at one of the Horse Shows, as an Early Saxon. Enter Mrs. Murphy into the ring on her chestnut horse Major, one of sixty entrants, in a scarlet under-dress draped with the pelt of a timber wolf. Atop her head was a golden helmet with black wings; about her throat and wrists barbaric, jewelled ornaments—and she carried a heavy club. Exit Mrs. Arthur Murphy with first prize, and an air of triumph that harked back directly to the little Emily Ferguson posing before the Cookstown mirror, practising her recitations and preparing to be an actress.

She spent a little while many evenings with Solitaire. Ever since she had learned it when on a tour with Emmeline Pankhurst, it had become a relaxation for her. Gradually, as the burdens of magisterial work became heavier, it became the chief diversion that could slide her from the turmoil of the day into the introspective peace she knew in her own room. Often she reserved judgment in some case whose truth she could not clearly see. Night after night she would reach for the twin pack of cards, and spread them out before her on the sitting-room table. Her plump little figure intense in its concentration, she played out the game, enjoying the rhythmic flapping of cards, its soothing repetitions. Nor was she above slipping a black Queen on a black King to avoid delay, however shocked Evelyn's protestations: "Tubbie! You can't do that!" But Tubbie could and did, with a bland insouciance, while she weighed out apparent truth as set against equally apparent truth, in the legal nuances of her court argument.

Neighbours became familiar with the old Irish jigs Emily often slipped onto the Victrola when she was feeling light-hearted,—or, on the contrary, as she termed it, "down-jaunted". If Kathleen and Cleave were there, up came the sitting-room rug, while the four of them danced, and Arthur sat watching. Sometimes she danced by herself, her arms folded, moving with an instinctive sense of folk-music, to the ancient rhythms. Sometimes she played the piano, her small hands flying over the keys in the bumpy beats of the old songs. She liked anything with a strong romantic flavour to it, or the swing of marching men. "I'm Captain Jinks of the Horse Marines", "Jock o' Hazeldeen", "I'm Gonna Dance Wid de Guy What Brung Me"—the spirited old tunes released her pent-up tension, night after night.

On occasion she donned an old flowered flannel dressing-gown, and went on a painting spree. Either, she felt, the basement steps or the kitchen linoleum needed painting, preferably an intense royal blue or a barn red. "Something bright and cheerful!" She disliked leaving any paint to waste in the can, and so, splotched with colour, wandered through the house and garden looking for "spots to touch up". In short order the rails of the garden steps, the pipe under the kitchen sink, the chair in the bathroom, would glow in blue or scarlet. There was something she found particularly satisfying in the slap-slap sounds of the paint and the emerging, quivering colour.

V

Emily's mother died in 1911, but, throughout the years, a very close relationship was maintained between the brothers and sisters. Annie had been widowed in the year following her marriage. After the death of her husband, William Robert Burke, she lived with her bachelor brothers, William and Harcourt. The three of them created a home in Toronto which became noted for its hospitality in the Ferguson tradition. Emily frequently visited them, and, on occasion, her surgeon brother Gowan, who had lived for so long in Great Falls, Montana. Always, like a shuttle weaving still closer the strands of family affection, came and went the letters between William, Annie, Harcourt, T. R., Gowan and Emily.

Tragedy struck at the closely-knit family when three brothers died within five years. T. R. was the first to go in mid-June, 1923; Harcourt, the youngest, died in 1927, and, a year later, in the fall of 1928, William was dead. To the telegram announcing T. R.'s death while pleading before the Supreme Court of Ontario, Emily attached a note: "Died at his post like the gallant gentleman he was."

It was not possible, this time, for her to travel east to the funeral, but her letter is a poignant illustration of her approach to the bereavement. In it is reflected the almost mystical love which she had for her family.

Once she had written on the fly-leaf of William's copy of *Seeds of Pine*, a paragraph from its pages:

"And when those who are my own people feel their hearts to be of a sudden rifled of love, that someone has brushed their cheek, or that a head is resting on their shoulder, then do they know that the exile has come back, for I have told them it will be thus."

It was with the full-bodied longing of an exile for her "own people" that Emily wrote this letter on June 20th, 1923:

"My dear William, Annie and Harcourt:

"It had to come soon. A group of brothers and sisters that has held itself together for sixty years must prepare for inevitable dissolution. Yet now that the first rent has been made, I feel all the sadness of eternity in my heart. If there is any lesson to us, it means that the rest of us must line up closer than ever so that we may not, for a moment, lose the touch that binds.

"It is strange that he should have predicted, last Autumn, the very manner of his death. You remember we walked across the park from church, you and Annie ahead, and he and I behind. He said to me: 'I felt a wonderful happiness this morning that all four of us should have been in church and sat together.' Then he told me of his having such high blood-pressure and that some day he expected it would likely 'take him' in court.

"I tried to cheer him and to divert his mind from this idea. Maybe he thought me indifferent; but I wasn't. In spite of his words he enjoyed the sunshine that morning; we tossed the fallen leaves with our feet, and death seemed far away indeed.

"This morning, Arthur came up and told me the news. Because of the shock, I could only sob, and sob, and sob, but having spent the past few hours looking at his photographs, I feel calmer.

". . . When he went over my manuscript for *The Black Candle* and wrote me his criticism and correction I was amazed because of his judgment in literary matters, his keen sense of values. Personally, I know of no *literateur* in Canada who could have helped me as he did . . .

"Perhaps you, Harcourt, will miss him more than any of us. You were together, always, and shared each other's innermost confidence. The old office won't seem the same again, and you will have a sickening sense of loss that none will realize but yourself. Dear Hark, I give you special love, and my especial sympathy.

"Then there will be the Sunday dinners. I can see now that these were more than dinners. They were a kind of family communion and not without a degree of sanctification . . . I cannot close this letter without referring to the comparative happiness of the latter years of Brother. He seemed wanting in nothing that made for his material or mental well-being. What he lacked from the domestic standpoint was made up to him in the added affection which he received from his brothers and sisters. It must always be a great satisfaction for us to know this—that never for a moment did he slip from our ken or care.

"And also, 'the Darlin', wherever he's gone, is not unhappy. The grief is ours only. He is 'asleep' or 'gathered to his fathers' with all the quiet and dignity these words suggest. We can only hope that each of us may find as serene an ending to our particular DAY and may leave a record as honourable and as exemplary."

VI

While Emily entered public life only when her family was grown, she had always had personal interests, and had devoted a great deal of time to her writing. She believed that a profession of her own, or some vitally personal creative task, was essential to the well-being of any woman—married or no.

She was always a champion of women's ability to work in any capacity. Back in the early days when she was a bride, and the question of women's right to serve on church vestries was being mooted, she wrote two letters to the *London Free Press* which aroused a good deal of comment among the clergy. Of course, women could contribute much to this administrative body of the church, she argued. One of the Canons of the church, feeling very indignant about Emily's point of view, told her that he would resign from his office, if women were so privileged. "Sir, you present us with a terrible alternative," smiled the twenty-four-year-old Mrs. Murphy. "I have no doubt, however, that we should become reconciled to your loss in time!"

Throughout her marriage, she found that with intelligent handling, her own interests need not interfere with her home life. Most of her writing, as we know, was accomplished, in the early years, during evening hours when Arthur was deep in his reading and the girls in bed. By the time Kathleen was married and Evelyn was editing a department on *The Edmonton Journal*, Emily could attend meetings without being missed too greatly at home. Moreover, she usually concentrated on one major interest at a time, until she achieved results, so that demands on her time were not too heavy.

In regard to the question, discussed so often in the twenties and early thirties, as to whether married women should have their own work, she believed that, primarily, women are human beings of the mother-sex, just as men are human beings of the father-sex, with all the duties of human beings, applying these to the special duties of parenthood as the occasion might warrant.

"The very best of business men," she wrote in *The Canadian Home Journal* in April, 1932, "make the family garden, tend the furnace, paint the kitchen floor, turn the washer, hang pictures, and even care for the children. Because they do both, it does not necessarily follow that either their homes or their business is neglected. And even so, marriage and motherhood need not be a hindrance but rather an inspiration to industrial or professional work—this, presuming the woman has the physical ability.

"Women who learn to manage a business, observing its hours, routine, necessity for promptness, restraint, efficiency and economy, are bound to bring these qualifications to the better management of their homes. Besides the qualifications she has she inevitably improves her home by bringing to it the riches of mind which should always come from experience and a broadened outlook."

Emily closed the article with a statement which, in its implications, may indicate the fundamental reason for her whole well-balanced life:

"The only truly contented women," she said, "are those who have both a home and a profession!"

CHAPTER II

Mrs. Murphy

That's what we need. Women who will lead
the followers and not follow the leaders!

EMILY MURPHY,
(In an address to a woman's club.)

I

EMILY MURPHY, more than any other woman,
glimpsed the vision of what women might attain
through their united efforts—if they but cared enough.

Born in the first year of Confederation, living much
of her life in a far northern out-post, she was prophetess
of woman's power for good from the turn of the century, crying to her sisters, cajoling, scolding, inspiring
them to a greater awareness of all that they might
accomplish for their country.

As Janey Canuck, she sang the song of Canada; as
Emily Murphy she chanted the saga of Canada's
womanhood, holding up, always, the dream of what
might be achieved. Dominating this dream was the
hope of what women's organizations could mean in the
education of a swiftly-growing country.

Perhaps she expected too much of them. Perhaps
she was too great a visionary. In her lifetime, she did
not see women reach the goal she outlined for them;
no, nor even approach it. But she saw women learning

to work together, to think together, and she never lost faith in their ultimate victory over themselves.

The line-upon-line of her *Who's Who* summary, is but the abstraction of her efforts. The names of organizations make up the skeleton which she clothed with a living force; a framework on which she built her hopes for an enlightened womanhood in a new country. For a true comprehension of her life, one must read it carefully, remembering her own comment. In 1929, she sent it to her friend Isabella Scott, with a note:

"Here's my new 'Who's Who'. It only needs the office of Senator! At any rate, I can claim to having done some work for 'folks' generally—especially women."

She had said early in her life in the West: "It is good to live in these first days . . . to be able to place a stone or carry the mortar to set it good and true." It was with the same spirit that she approached her work with women's associations. She built for Canada, at the same time she built for women's enfranchisement and unity.

It was characteristic of her, as we know, to see always the Godhead within, or the symbol encircling the commonplace. So it was she approached her work with Canadian national organizations. She swung through the years with them, when East and West were learning to work together; when conflicts and sectional bitterness were lusty. She swept the great questions of the day before them, believing it was woman's first duty, as feminine members of church and state, to study the problems of the day and tackle them with vigour.

Away back in 1913, before Canadian women had the vote, she stated her credo to her fellow-members of the Canadian Women's Press Club, at the Triennial Convention in Edmonton. It was typical of Mrs. Murphy, national president of Canada's press women, that her address of welcome was no pretty-pretty inanity, but a declaration of faith which she was to try to implement the rest of her life:

"I believe in the future of our country," she said, tip-tilted a bit on her toes, hands clasped behind her back, as was her habit when excited.

"I believe there never was a country better adapted to produce a great race of women than this Canada of ours, nor a race of women better adapted to make a great country.

"I believe that the women of Canada carry its destiny in the folds of their garments. The men who, in the future, will people it, will be the fruit of their body and the fire of their spirit!"

II

These were glowing words to fire the imagination of women writers from every province. But Emily did more than set words rocketing across her audiences. She backed them up with years of hard work; with the best that her brain and heart could produce. She warned women's groups, always, that, in the same manner, their resolutions were little more than pious wishes, unless they, too, were implemented with work, courage and imagination.

She was a natural-born leader. She could speak well, and write her speech with words that burned or sang, as she wished. She had the Irish lilt to her voice and the smiling lines about her eyes that could beguile her audiences. Hers were the full resonant tones that measured out the emphasis she felt necessary. She had the knack of getting people to work with her, and, while she was fully conscious of their frailties, inspired them with the feeling that they could achieve all things.

Emily Murphy knew when to turn a blind, bland countenance on a person or event; when to tease away resentment; and when to speak with cutting irony. While she inspired respect among her fellow-workers with the amount of work and study she herself gave to the programmes sponsored by the various organizations, she knew, too, how to delegate authority and give others the joy of accomplishment. She was lavish with her praise; but sweeping in her condemnation when she felt it was warranted.

The very fact that she belonged to so many national groups in an executive capacity, meant that she was often travelling across Canada, with opportunities to speak in provinces east and west. She would make a habit, too, of dropping-off on intermediate points to meet with groups of women and impress her thinking on them. Any contemplated journey was always prefaced by a score or more of telegrams inviting her to speak, or to be guest of honour at luncheon or banquet. During most of the twenty years she worked with these groups, she was suffering from ill-health. Much of the time she was too tired and ill to undertake the journey, but she drove herself more often than was good for her, seeing always the need for further understanding. An English journalist who, in 1912, travelled many hundreds of miles, she said, to spend an afternoon

with Janey Canuck, described how she found the lady
—"the most charming I have met!"—on a couch recovering from a protracted illness. During the afternoon
word arrived that the final arrangements for the
Press-women's Convention had been cleared. The
journalist was astonished at Emily's enthusiasm. "We
must begin to plan immediately," she said, apparently
on the verge of getting off her couch that very moment,
"to give the girls the best time they've ever had!"

She knew anger often. Her work, in many instances,
lay with groups and officers experiencing, for the first
time, the task of planning in unison with East and
West. There were provincial jealousies. Women were,
as always, temperamental; individualists all. There
were many stormy sessions with some officers, and
many a woman echoed the old Edmonton cry, "For
heaven's sake—don't let Mrs. Murphy in on it!" But
Mrs. Murphy had a way with her, and Mrs. Murphy
usually managed to finish with the problem settled in
the way she had wanted.

Her letters to friends are peppered with explosives.
"They've just held a convention in Toronto. Wouldn't
you know this would result? I'm so mad, I'm blowing
fuses—one a minute!" Or again: "I'm so mad—I'm
going to put my head on ice!"

She knew disillusionment, too, and moments of
despair, for, from the outset, she worked with a full
realization of the weaknesses of her sex, as well as their
strengths.

One of her first major disappointments was in 1918,
when, in the English elections, Mrs. Pankhurst was
defeated in her riding. Emily wrote to the editor of the
Women's Century: "The cherished conviction of a

lifetime has turned out to be a silly illusion. The fact
that the first use the Englishwomen should make of
their franchise was to vote against the woman who
had secured it for them, shows that unless they change
their outlook, we are going to fail in all the big movements that are essentially women's."

Then, for a moment, Janey Canuck ousted Mrs.
Murphy, and the letter closed with this sentence: "If
it were not so very unlady-like, as well as illegal, I
could say some words which would just raise your
hat off, in spite of the fact that it is tied under your
chin with a veil!"

Ten years later, she was sympathizing with Isabella
Scott, in some of the troublesome experiences the
women of Quebec had known in trying to win the
provincial vote for their sex. The problem lay not only
in the attitude of men but in that of some women:

"I know just what you mean about the sycophants
among the women," Emily said, "The Zenana type . . .
who scuttle their principles, and knife other women,
just to gain a flattering word, or to secure some paltry
popularity. It doesn't make much difference about
them, however; they are just underlings, with the
minds of underlings.

"It doesn't pay to give them your advice or opinion.
The only thing you can do is to give them a strong
lead *and no explanation.* They are almost sure to follow. One wastes one's time and energy explaining
things or by telling one's plans. Besides, you incur the
risk—indeed, the absolute certainty—of their under-
mining your structure both for personal and party
ends."

She had her own philosophy in regard to enemies. For one thing, she thoroughly enjoyed a struggle of wits or of strategy, and often made friends of her erstwhile opponents, by the open-hearted attack she made on them and the seemingly ingenuous methods she used to outwit them:

"Enemies?" she scribbled on the backs of two blanks from a ledger. "Enemies?—The best way to destroy them is to make friends of them. If you get quite near to a person his blow loses its force. The same applies to the kick of a mule . . . Stand by, then, and stand close.

"The fellow does not like you. What about it? It often happens that you do not like yourself. If he knew your reasons for self-aversion, he would like you even less. Just remember this, my son, and be glad. He had sense and competence, that writer, who told his generation how the truly wise man would recognize no one as an enemy . . . We repeat it. Stand by, please, and stand close."

But all her moments of depression were submerged in her hopes of what might be. She worked with noble women throughout Canada, who were building up the great organizations of today; working to bring their sisters the benefits of the franchise, and to show them how to use it for the betterment of their own position, for the growth of their country and the promotion of individual, social and moral welfare.

One such important service Emily rendered was as the first National President of the Federated Women's Institutes. Created in Canada, this movement uniting rural women, spread into England and the

United States. At the outset, it was an ambitious union of provincial rural groups throughout Canada under one constitution. Emily's election as the president was a notable one, as it was the first time such an important office had been held by a woman from the prairies. To it, Emily brought all her imagination, energy and interest. As she had done in the early days in Edmonton, she persuaded the right women to help develop the project. She won approval from her Federal Board to ask the Duchess of Devonshire, wife of the Governor-General, to be the Honorary President; wrote to the wife of the Premier of Canada, the Leader of the Opposition, and the wives of all provincial premiers, asking them, also, to assume honorary positions in the Institutes. All of them accepted. She spent much time in the first year helping to write the constitution for the new organization which came into existence with a membership of one hundred thousand women. In her term of office she saw the Canadian Federation united with the English and American Associations. Her only disappointment was the fact that, try as she might, she could not get a grant from the Federal Government for the work of the Institutes.

Her best-loved Association was undoubtedly that of "her girls" of the Canadian Women's Press Club. Because of the Great War, and the fact that one of the Triennials, at which elections were held, did not take place, she was National President for seven years, from 1913 to 1920.

She reigned as queen over a group of prima donnas who were working hard to establish standards for their craft under many difficulties. Artists, poets, authors, newspaper women on city dailies, or isolated rural

weeklies—each member had a point of view all her
own. Emily's association with them was full of maternal
encouragement, jollity and camaraderie. She enjoyed
the relaxation she knew in meeting with her press
sisters, and believed, also, that they had an important
place in developing unity and understanding between
the various provinces. She preached that good citizenship was based on patriotism and, with Colonel George
Ham, Publicity Director for the Canadian Pacific Railway, who was one of the founders of the Press Club,
worked hard to increase the members' knowledge of
Canada. Every three years the press women met, with
railway passes enabling them all to attend. Emily
believed the ensuing discussions, and the articles which
the press women wrote on their return to their own
work, to be valuable.

Her "Who's Who" shows a discerning balance of
effort on the national as well as provincial scale. She it
was who inaugurated the system of public playgrounds, developed the plan for medical inspection
in the Alberta Schools, and helped to work out the
system for municipal hospitals. Too, she found time
to be the patroness for the Edmonton Branch of the
Army and Navy Veterans, and of the District Hospital
at Peace River.

But in any study of the *Who's Who* tabulation, one
comes back, inevitably, to the fact that the details of
the organizations are unimportant in a study of her
life—except as they proved a sounding-board for her
ideas; for the vision she upheld before them; for the
scope of work she believed possible. Undoubtedly,
she had the most imposing and long-winded list of
organization affiliations of any woman in Canada. In

all her work with them, large or small, civic or national, she stressed certain fundamental principles which are as true today as they were when she illumined them. The credo she had outlined to "her girls" in 1913, was one she strove always to implement. In doing so, she postulated some ideas which all women's groups could study with advantage today; and tomorrow.

III

For one thing, while she passed through an era when women had to fight vehemently for their rights, Emily always decried a militant approach.

"I do not like the word 'feminist'," she once said to an audience, during the suffrage campaign. "It is a poor and paltry word when applied to a movement which today dominates all other questions that involve the social, individual and moral freedom of the entire world. This is a 'humanist' movement.

"There is a marvellous quality in our bodies. We have two hands, two lungs, two eyes, two feet, and numerous other qualities, with two lobes of the brain to control them. If men or women persist in using only one eye, they not only restrict their range of vision but see things out of focus.

"Now hitherto, our social and national life has been largely one-eyed. For generations the men, our brothers, have idealized us without allowing us to realize those ideals of justice and the other great virtues which have been portrayed on canvas and cut in stone, as female figures."

Similarly, when it was the custom of leaders among women to criticize bitterly the "man-handling" men gave to public affairs, and to claim that women could do much better, Emily was never afraid to insist that it was not a question of sex, but one of capacity. "When Woman is fit to marshal the world's millions in the highest commercial spheres, no Exchange, or Board of Control will hinder her. When she is fit to preach, neither pope nor potentate will hinder her. Heart and brain will overflow every barrier that is put up.

"A woman has a right to do anything she can do, provided she does nothing which will prevent her from the procreation of healthy children . . . and this applies equally to men!

"A woman's attitude, then, does not require to be a militant one. Her incapacity alone will hinder her, in the long run, from occupying any position she may select."

With this as a basis for thinking, Mrs. Murphy, when asked to address public meetings, spoke often of the need for women in every walk and avocation of life. While they had shone in all fields of philanthropy she called on them to appear in positions as school-trustees; as principals of schools. "We want them in university chairs, and university senates. We want women to study the causes of unemployment, and to grapple with them . . . We want women statesmen who have wide vision and strong hands."

In the early days of women's organizations, since so many of them had been created in the period immediately following the granting of the Dominion franchise to them, there was great interest in politics. Many women urged the formation of a Woman's Party, and in 1918-1919, the movement gained a definite momentum. Emily spoke against the idea, at whatever opportunity presented itself. She made a number of women very indignant indeed; but the idea did not materialize.

There could be no future in a Woman's Party, she told women; what was needed was a Woman's Platform. If women were able to set out a clear-cut and comprehensive statement of what they believed essential they could then measure the claims of contending political parties against it.

It was at the Women's Institutes' first birthday celebration in Toronto, in 1919, that she set out her thinking on politics and women's organizations. She told her audience that it was a basic need on the part of women's groups, to take responsibility as feminine members of Church and State, and grapple with modern problems as they arose. "Does this mean," she asked "that the Federation will become a political force? It certainly does! But not in the partisan sense. Politics, in the ordinary sense of the term, would be a deplorable thing to get into such an organization. Indeed, it would be the beginning of the end.

"But politics in the broad sense of studying national problems must be taken up by these organizations if they are to keep abreast of the times—which is their hope in life. This is politics as it should be. After study and investigation, members can do their own choosing as to party."

While Mrs. Murphy stressed, throughout her association with women's organizations, these principles involving women's co-operation with men, their intensive study of all that affected the State, she made, too, a practice of arousing them from lethargy and driving them on to new conquests.

She liked to say to feminine audiences, as she said to women in her court: "Almost every experience is good for a woman that doesn't kill her!"

"Women too often lack initiative," she told the Calgary Business and Professional Women's Club. "They are afraid to launch out. The little experiment of Christopher Columbus cost $7,000. It was a good thing he had the nerve to try it ... Every new continent of achievement lies overseas. Many persons fear to undertake projects which they might easily perform, because they cannot see the end of them. They forget that at every point the question settles itself, when all the facts are considered.

"It is a great day in a girl's life when she begins to discover herself. The latent capacity in each one of us, is greater than we realize, and we may find it if we search diligently."

IV

The alliance Emily felt between her work in court, and that with public organizations was an inevitable one. Every time she faced a problem as Magistrate, arising out of human greed, ignorance, or perversity, she knew that, in the final analysis, the only solution lay in public education. She saw the opportunity there was for moulding public opinion in the great network of women's organizations which were springing up through the Dominion, chained together through their mutual interest.

So she urged on them all a study of welfare problems; told them of the heart-break and spawning ground for vice recruits which lay in bad housing conditions; insisted that women themselves should shoulder much of the responsibility for eliminating venereal disease; preached, always, the salvation for delinquent girls which lay in their hands. Roundly she condemned the "odious saints" who felt they had no responsibility in such unpleasant aspects of life:

"Go into the home of these women with love in your hearts and help in your hands. If you raise the fallen and cleanse the polluted, though these houses may be in the unfashionable area, still you will find that they have become a House of God and a Gate of Heaven."

Then would come the inevitable Murphy point of view:

"One recoils from the hot touch of vice and its hideous pollution . . . One becomes sick at heart. It is only when we see in them the divine spark . . . the image of the infinite . . . that we overcome our repugnance . . . And there is no greater reward for the worker than that of seeing a soul restored."

As Mrs. Murphy, key speaker for the evening, or guest of honour at the luncheon, she lost no opportunity for driving home the need of the average man and woman, linked in national groups, to see that all who lived in Canada became real Canadians. Her interest in immigrants had started that long-ago morning when she had climbed down into the steerage with Arthur, carrying oranges in her hand to give to the people there, after her husband had prayed with them. Throughout her life in the West, as we know, she made them her special concern. Now she took her knowledge of the strangers who came to Canada with her to the public platform, to urge that her audiences learn more about them. She liked to remind them that

"Canada's coat of arms may be one of many colours, but it must always be a seamless garment." Many remember her biting comment, too: "Yes, we sing O Canada—but we sing it as a dirge, and not as a march!"

Her thinking on new Canadians could well be studied by all groups, not only in relation to those already settled here, but to the new-comers who will surge in after this war, as they did after the last. Listen to her speaking, slowly and earnestly, from her heart, to an audience of men and women:

"This task of making real Canadians out of all who live in Canada, cannot be accomplished by coercive measures; nor by approaching these people in a superior, patronizing attitude, but by persuading them that Canada is their friend; that we desire to protect them against exploitations whether by their own people or by ours; that we are willing to guide and counsel them in their perplexity relating to laws, language and customs.

"Here in the West, we are beginning to learn that we have much to learn from these in-coming Canadians, which, hitherto, we have lost because of our presumed superiority. Many of these people come to this Dominion with a rich and varied handicraft; with a wealth of literary and artistic knowledge; a reverence for sacred things, for established order; with well-formed habits of thrift, and with a fine old-world courtesy. We would be well advised to benefit by their gifts and acquirements even as we would expect they would benefit by ours. What we have to teach them in citizenship, language and laws, can only be done by a sympathetic respect for their pride, and a wise patience."

Those who invited Mrs. Murphy to speak, were never quite sure just what she would say; but audiences were always enthralled with her, lifted momentarily from the work-a-day world into a realm where everything was possible for those who really believed its achievement could be made a reality, and who were inspired enough to work for it. It might be that, as on the occasion when she addressed a group of visiting musicians in Edmonton, a magic mood would be upon her:

"Some day a Northerner will compose a piece of music that will have in it the theme of the pines which I think Schumann tried to hold in his *D Minor Sonata*. This music will hold down the whisper of the Aurora Borealis that is like the whirr of swords or the slur of stealthy footsteps. What else?—Oh yes! The tang of prairie smoke; the weird quaver and hideous dissonance of the wolf howl; great arpeggios and chords such as the wind makes when it utilizes the tall poplars and spruce trees, as its many-manualled, needle-noted keyboard . . . the strong winds that are born two thousand miles to the North in the screaming ice-fields of the niggard Arctic, or away in the bitter glooms that lie beyond the world.

"There will be other things in it, that only a Northerner will understand; but whatever they are, the world will recognize in the whole composition a virile tonic for outworn schools and vitiated themes."

It might be an unexpected demand on women, as in her address before the first meeting of the Women's Canadian Club of Edmonton:

"I tell you women, the danger to which we are most liable is not one that springs from the rude hordes which we must convert into Canadians. Not by any means.

"Our chiefest danger lies in the fact that we are liable to be smothered in chiffon. In these days of ease and rapidly growing wealth, there is a tendency that we shall become anaemic, hair-splitting, or flabby parasites on the body politic. So, as first president of this farthest north Canadian Club, my message to you is a ringing call to endurance, to work, to out-door days!"

Sometimes she spoke to an audience with ideas that were so far ahead of the times, that only history justified the antagonisms she aroused. For instance, when it was the popular thing to applaud the League of Nations, Emily Murphy was probing its weaknesses and revealing them to unbelieving and resentful groups. On one such occasion she said—and it is only today that we can appreciate her wisdom:

"Just now the League of Nations is writing a new Bible . . . but it is altogether too mushy—that is to say, it has neither fibre nor flavour.

"You see, the League of Nations—fifty-five of them— decided that they could keep the peace of the world without any batting instrument of their own, and that all the world would assume a lamb-like attitude, because the League of Nations was there. These infinitely elevated representatives of the League, like the eastern sages, sat contemplating Brahmin and saying 'Om' to themselves in a manner that was highly mystic and impressive . . . Well, perhaps we exaggerate a little, for they did send out some sacred screeds to the world

at large, screeds which took the form of the ten commandments but which had no *Yawah* behind to enforce
them . . . no angel with a flaming sword to enforce
the law . . . there were no bobbies around with
sawed-off guns and batons to haul in the fellows that
broke the commandments.

"Being perfect gentlemen themselves they do not
seem to have grasped the idea that all laws must be
enforced . . . Really, when you come to think of it, we
might have been better to put the matter into the
hands of police officials and said: 'Here—you know the
game! The world will supply you with the instruments
of office, whether men or guns . . . and no one but
your men are allowed to have guns. It's your duty to
keep order. Like all police officers you will have the
authority to call on private citizens to assist you in the
performance of your duty . . . The chief sin shall be
the same as that of the Criminal Code—the crime of
impeding or assaulting an officer in the performance
of your duty!

"The world will never disarm until some such arrangement takes place."

But whatever the point was which she made, Mrs.
Murphy was always the visionary. When she scolded,
it was in order to "sting awake" as she called it, her
audiences, as she tried to arouse the prisoners arraigned
before her, in whom she glimpsed the divine spark.
When she voiced Canada's greatness, it was to lift
those who heard her to new heights of awareness.
When she scoffed, it was to clarify their thinking. When
she laboured late into the night writing letters; when
she travelled weary miles to attend conventions; when
she strove to disentangle confused and embittered

personalities, she did it all with one driving purpose—
to hold before Canadian women the need for their
united head-work and heart-interest in the growth of
their nation.

Her press sisters felt her greatness one night at the
Chateau Frontenac. The Triennial meeting assembled
in Montreal, had travelled to Quebec City for a special
banquet. The evening rollicked with laughter. Speak-
ers rose, one by one, out-doing each other in the
nonsensical mood of the moment.

It came Mrs. Murphy's turn. She stood up, smiled
at "her girls" and waited for some seconds until the
room quietened. She waited with as much tensed
aplomb as an orchestra leader stands, his baton poised
until his frozen anticipation of the music to come has
hushed every rustle and cough in the hall. Merry eyes
focused on her, standing straight and sturdy beneath
the portraits of Montcalm, Wolfe, and Frontenac.

Then, very quietly, working with a sensitized awareness of the modulation of their mood, she reminded the
press women of the history back of the place in which
they sat, and its flowering in the hearts of Canadians.
She talked of the kingdom of wider slopes, higher
mountains, and greater rivers that lay beyond this
cradle of the Dominion. In the depths of what she said
were mirrored the alien races who have trekked their
way across the land in long and lustful lines, gold-
hungry, grain-hungry, and just plain hungry. She spoke
of the task of fitting together the nine provincial blocks
into the one picture called Canada; of its need for
essential unity. "We march to Fate abreast!"

Afterwards, as the press women moved into the

foyer, Marshall Saunders, author of *Beautiful Joe*, said to a group near her:

"There is something about Emily Murphy just a little above the rest of us; something about her that takes us along with her, and pulls us up to her."

Might not that casual comment stand alongside her own:

"At any rate I can claim to having done some work for 'folks'—especially women."

CHAPTER III

"Dear Emily"

She loves all things both great and small. Love
is a prayer and prayer is labour.

JANEY CANUCK.

I

THROUGHOUT her life, Emily spent recklessly of
her time and energies on letters to friends, ac-
qaintances, strangers. There were, as we know, over
seven hundred letters alone in the file on the "Persons"
Appeal; and it was but a fragment of her correspondence. In one of her unfinished articles, she wrote, "I
have ten thousand friends . . . who are always passing
through town." That may have been the exaggeration
born of a depressing moment; but it was probably
close to an estimate of the number of letters she wrote
and received, in her threescore years.

There were many who mourned that her labour was
thus deflected from her literary work. There is no doubt
that the onslaught of her Court work in 1916 is
significantly associated with the fact that her last book
of literary sketches was published in that self-same
year. In the succeeding decade, she moved away from
a contemplative and interpretative role toward the
actualities of life, and so became immersed in an attempt to solve some of its complexities.

EMILY IN ENGLAND, 1899

EMILY AT SEVEN YEARS

EMILY WITH HAIR UP FOR FIRST
TIME, AGED 18 YEARS

EMILY AT EDMONTON

In so doing, she was lavish in her giving of herself; of her critical ability; her optimism. She made friends easily and kept those she valued for a lifetime. Her faculty for what she once described as a "rapturous contemplation of all things new and strange", made every new human being she met a potential comrade, worthy of the best she had to give. She was good company in person or on paper, and her letters to friends, professional confreres and to her family, all bear the mark of her personality. To her, there were no strangers in the world; only fellow adventurers stumbling along the same paths; eager, all of them, for a friendly word of encouragement. When she walked about the streets of Edmonton she nodded or spoke to nearly everyone she met, with an especial pause, always, for her good friend, the cop on duty. Every few moments, she must stop some man, woman, or child, to enquire after the progress made by a far-away member of the family; the latest word from the children. She never met with rebuffs, and never expected them. With an interest that was obviously very real, she studied the lives of her friends, frankly concerned with their welfare.

She watched the newspapers for word of any success in the lives of those she knew. On endless occasions, when she liked articles by "her girls" of the Press Club, she wrote to them, or to their editors. Her boxes filled with replies from young writers, palpitating with delight that Janey Canuck herself had noticed their effort, and had taken the trouble to read it.

But, gradually, there grew to be a number of them who looked to her to revive their low spirits. Without a doubt her generosity was abused, but it was not until late in life, that, through ill-health, she did not respond to such pleas as these:

"Mrs. H----- evidently doesn't think I write good stuff, and is too conscientious to pretend that she sees good work in it. But it made me long for you, Honey, with your beautiful faith in my work and me!"

Or again:

"When I am so worried, I just longed to tell you all about it and feel your understanding and sympathy. But as your shoulder wasn't there to be wept upon . . . I just wrote and spilled the beans and felt better for having confided in you . . . bless you!"

From a man, this one:

"Now, Janey, you mustn't spoil me with all this blarney, of course I like it, but principally because it comes from you, and you know better than anyone, except a few close friends, what I am about. Some of them are puzzled . . . some just think I am crazy . . . but you *know,* have seen right into me, and have understood precisely what I am trying to do."

To all of them Emily turned the benign blessing of her encouragement. She gave this spiritual aid, moreover, with no complaint to the family of the demands it made upon her. A heavy morning's mail with calls for help, or requests for counsel, lay in her consciousness all day, luring her back to her desk in the evening hours. Small wonder that her literary output dwindled.

Many of her close friends were indignant, feeling that she gave too much of herself. Typical of this point of view, is an outburst from a well-known Canadian writer, condemning Emily—and yet asking more for herself.

"Your letter tells me what I know damn well . . . you're right and I'm wrong, I'm jealous, that's all, but you can't make me think you're not wasting a lot of valuable time trying to help a lot of no-goods that God himself couldn't make anything but fish-fins out of! . . . You get out and work with your equals, and get out now!!

"But, God bless you, Janey Canuck. Your notes (and I know how little time you have to give away) keep me alive. Otherwise the worms are eating my courage away.

"But, believe me, that's your one weakness. You lose time with damn tripe! Never mind, I love you, always, ever and after . . ."

To all appearances Emily's giving of herself in her answers to the hundreds of people who wrote her, was effortless. On one of her scraps of paper is a note, written with much the same impulse that a flutist follows in rippling a brief snatch of melody. "She loves all things both great and small. Love is a prayer; and prayer is labour."

II

Her interests were catholic. She wrote with the same zest to industrial leaders, politicians, soldiers and journalists, as she did to the girls she rescued in her court work; to the mothers she committed to the Mental Hospitals; to her own family.

It might be a case like that of Rosa Ginsberg. Emily noticed, in the morning newspaper, some time in 1929, a few lines of type at the bottom of a column commenting on the fact that Rosa Ginsberg, first woman lawyer in Palestine, was struggling to win the right to practise her profession. Beginning in 1922, she had made three unsuccessful attempts to be called to the Bar.

Emily clipped out the item. At the moment, the "Person's" Case was before the Law Lords of the Privy Council. She put the clipping on her desk and bided her time.

On an evening in November, 1929, she wrote to Miss Ginsberg in the care of the Law Association in Jerusalem:

"Some time ago I read in one of our Canadian papers of your struggle to practise law in the Palestine Courts. I hope that you are meeting with success. Keep right on whatever happens. Ultimately you are bound to win.

"I am herewith sending you an account of our victorious fight for the right to be considered "persons" under the British North America Act—our national charter. It took me thirteen years and nearly broke my heart—but it was worth the fight. This is just a short word to cheer you and let you know we are with you."

Some weeks later there appeared in the Canadian papers an interview with Miss Ginsberg on her final success, and her admission to the Bar of Palestine. She said to a reporter in Jerusalem:

"Mrs. Murphy's letter was very important to me. I

was fighting with my back to the wall when I received this letter from a woman far away—one who was a complete stranger to me. I was touched. One expects sympathy from one's own people, but to have encouragement from a Canadian woman, thousands of miles away, was splendidly encouraging. I thought that if it took the Canadian women thirteen years to win their battle, I shouldn't complain with only seven years of effort."

Rosa Ginsberg described how, with this fresh incentive, she applied again to the courts, pleading her own case, and hinging her arguments on the official interpretation of the term "persons" in the Canadian appeal.

In much the same way, Emily noticed in June, 1927, that Magistrate Hugh Macdonald of Winnipeg, seventy-seven-year-old son of Sir John A. Macdonald, had lost his leg in an accident. The tenor of her letter to him may be judged by his reply:

"Your letter conveying your sympathy with me on the loss of my right leg was duly received and very much prized. The cheerful strain in which you wrote did me a lot of good, and I often quote to myself your remark *'What's a leg, anyway?'*"

Journalist Mike Jay Svenceski, a young Russian-Jew, found himself in Edmonton, with no job and no money. Somehow his path crossed that of Emily's. She was instantly interested and listened to his adventures for an hour. She advised him to apply for a job she believed was vacant on one of the Calgary papers, advanced him his railway fare, and enough to live on for a week or so. She wished him God-speed with that cheery confidence in his ability which characterized her attitude towards all youth. He got the job in Calgary and wrote to Emily for many years thereafter, from all parts of the world. He, it was, by the way, who told the story of Emily's visit to the cabin of the northern settler, mentioned in Chapter Seven, *Open Trails*.

She reached out to this lad, gave him a practical suggestion and financial aid, and maintained an interest in his ensuing adventures with the same personal enjoyment she showed, one morning, in the court-house elevator. A nervous-looking woman, the only other occupant, asked Emily on which floor was the Women's Court. Emily told her and then, inevitably, her interest bloomed. "Are you concerned about a case?" The woman nodded apprehensively. "Yes. I'm from the States and want to give evidence for a friend. I understand the Judge is a woman—and I don't like the idea one little bit!"

Emily grinned. "Cheer up," she said, lifting a red rose from her dress and pinning it on the stranger's lapel. "Here, take this! Perhaps it will give you good luck!"

She was dignity itself, ten minutes later, as the court stood for her entrance; but she missed not a flicker on the woman's astonished face.

III

Emily nourished her friendships over many years, tending them with a devotional responsibility. "Ever your old Pal" swung hundreds of letters to a close. Nellie McClung was one of her staunchest comrades throughout her life in the West. This popular author, famous suffragette, and Member of the Provincial Legislature for many years, worked with Emily on questions of community welfare for over twenty years. She had met Emily in the first week after she arrived in Edmonton. The two women, much of an age, each with the same intent interest in women's progress, had an enduring admiration for each other.

There was never any room in Emily's mind for jealousy nor a competitive spirit with her friends—nor with anyone, for that matter. Her enthusiasm for Mrs. McClung's writing, as well as her public activity, was wholeheartedly sincere. The two women spent much time together discussing family, people, and problems. Theirs was a true and vigorous partnership in all forward-thinking movements in the West.

Mrs. McClung's letter, written on leaving Alberta for British Columbia, was brief and very sincere:

"I do not want to leave Alberta without bidding you an affectionate farewell. You welcomed me most heartily when I came, and you have been a very sincere and altogether delightful friend to me in the eighteen years I have spent in the province. So I leave you, dear Janey, with sincere regret and a great thankfulness that we have met, and known, and loved each other."

It was thus only logical that Nellie McClung who, for a score of years, played Jonathon to Emily Murphy's David, should write the introduction to this biography.

In a different vein, altogether, was Emily's friendship with Mrs. John Scott, for many years President of the Montreal Women's Club. Although they met not more than half a dozen times, they wrote voluminously to each other from 1921, when first the Montreal Women's Club asked Emily to be their appointee for the Senate, until Emily's death.

The two women could not have been more dramatically contrasted. Emily gave an impression of magnificence in spite of her short stature; Mrs. Scott, of exquisite, bird-like fragility. Emily's handwriting flowed in its large rhythms; Isabella Scott's was feather-fine and tiny. Mrs. Scott, because of her environs in a province which obstinately refused to permit any freedom of the franchise or professional advantage to women, was the more militantly aggressive in her attitude. She was fond of berating the men in power, and found little for commendation in their method of running affairs.

Emily was more "sweetly militant", as someone said of her. She preferred the use of a rapier-like keenness and wit. She liked to parry and persuade; to ridicule, perhaps, but with a hint of laughter to it. Some of the closest friendships of her life were those with men. She liked them, and worked well with them, usually winning any battle, because she understood thoroughly the male point of view, and appreciated why the men felt in the right. She believed, always, in working with men, while using her own inimitable method to achieve her goal. As she wrote in an article discussing the right of married women to work outside the home, in *Canadian Home Journal*: "Thinking the whole matter over, without any personal bias, one can easily see that there is neither room nor occasion for sex animosity. One can see that we, men and women, must just go on loving and helping each other in the same

old way." Good words—backed by Emily's capacity
to pitch in and fight when she saw the need for it!

Throughout the thirteen years until her death in
1933, Emily followed the progress of feminism in
Quebec with a steadfast interest, and gave it all the
support she could. She clipped scores of newspaper
items which she felt might be of use for Mrs. Scott
and her confrères. She followed the campaigns of such
leaders as Idola St. Jean, Thérèse Casgrain of Montreal,
and Madame Marchand of Ottawa, learning of ad-
vances or retreats from Mrs. Scott.

These two, the one from a tradition-bound, old-
world province, the other from the eager West, developed a rare and intimate association of soul and
mind in their hundreds of letters to each other. Pages
and pages of current politics, on public figures, on
women's strengths and weaknesses, on their work and
ambitions, on family matters, passed between them.

Emily's letters were often emotional fragments,
limned on the instant. For example, this, written on
June 14th, 1930:

"My Dear Old Dear:

"This is just a line to congratulate you on your article
in *Saturday Night* . . . I am off to Fort Saskatchewan
in a few moments to try two Gents for 'contributing
to the delinquency of juveniles'. (What polite names
we apply to hideous crimes!) I have just been trying
to identify a young half-breed girl at the undertaker's
who died in a store here from hemorrhage . . . A pretty
little girl, almost white, who wore 'whoopee' trousers,
a gay cap, silk underwear and lovely slippers . . . all
of these soaked with her life's blood. She had been

round the city, I believe, serving the taxis, and here she is at the end of the road, and no one knows her name. She had a heart—a lovely crimson heart—and some roses tattooed on her arm. Poor child! 'Only a half-breed.' I'd like to tell the world some of the things I know about 'superior men'—but I've just got to keep the heart-break of it all to myself."

Her friendships with men were as many and as varied as those she knew with women; her letters to them are glittering in their contrasts. She became the confidante of young men in the tumult of living. Older men turned to her for a gaiety and an impersonal comradeship that lightened the dullness of daily routine.

Some of her friendships, like that with the young Canadian writer and literary critic, William Arthur Deacon, endured until her death. Some, like that of J. M. Dent, senior, of London, England, continued over the years, with only one week in her home as its basis. There were others, like that of Don Munday, the young soldier, which brought her first-hand stories of experiences in the War.

Again she knew a light-hearted, but none-the-less devoted comradeship with men like Colonel George Ham. From the outset, he called her "Lady Jane". She liked to tell of the brief conversation they had one morning between trains, he eastward-bound, she westward. They were teasing each other about how well they were looking. "Mark my words, Lady Jane," said Colonel Ham, "I'm going to live so long that I'll be franking your body through to Cookstown!" "On the contrary," smiled Emily, "I'll write your epitaph." With sadness of heart, she did.

Emily was deeply concerned at the tragedy that befell a lad of eighteen, living on a poverty-sparse farm near Edmonton. The boy had been sent to one of the hospitals in Edmonton for an operation. It was his first visit to the city. His nurse was young, with shining eyes and hair; it was inevitable that he should fall in love with her.

It was inevitable, also, that when he returned, inarticulate but worshipping, to the meagre world he had known, the two embittered, scrawny women who inhabited it with him, his mother and sister, should discover his secret—and think it very funny. What started in a spirit of rough-and-ready fun, became unbearable taunts to his brooding misery.

One day, the momentum of their jeers swept up to the moment when, his head full of dreams, his body filthy from his work, the boy came up from the barn. The two women lolled in the doorway of the squalid cabin and howled with laughter at the very idea that a nurse could ever love such a creature. Black with hatred, their derision a whiplash to his despair, he pulled a gun from the wall and killed them both.

The jury was unanimous in its verdict; the boy was sentenced to be hanged.

Emily could do nothing for him, but the humanity of the story haunted her. Years after her death, the means she took to help him, became known. Each week she searched her mind, her books, her notes, for a "thought" to send the condemned prisoner; something for him to think about, she told him, until another one came next Sunday. An officer of the Salvation

Army, his spiritual advisor, went down to the jail to visit the boy each week and took the messages for Emily. He told his wife about the incident, and showed her the weekly message—just a sentence, written on a piece of paper, with no comment or amplification. She was so impressed that, one by one, she copied them—and nearly ten years after Emily's death, came across them in an attic trunk.

Emily never saw the boy; but from the riches of her mind she gathered courage for him. Her assortment, as usual, was infinitely contrasted; there were texts from the Bible; thoughts from Cervantes, Guyon, William Osler, Burdette, Seneca, and some of her own —twenty in all.

Among them were these:

> "Calmness is power; say unto your heart, 'Peace be still'.
> "Every hour is a last hour because we cannot live it again.
> "He who repents having sinned is almost innocent.
> "No suffering need be only suffering.
> "I shall waste no time in whining, and my heart shall know no fear.
> "Death is a release from, and end of all pain. It restores us to the peaceful rest in which we lay before we were born."

V

There is an overwhelming amount of human interest in the letters written and received by Emily. In every chapter dealing with her life in the West, I have had to make some reference to her correspondence. Without this reiteration, I could not have hoped to mirror its dominating place in her life. She believed, as we saw in her early days in Edmonton, that whichever side of the street she walked on, might be fraught with adventure. The same impulse, albeit subconsciously, lay in many of her letters.

She set in motion a rare adventure, as she studied a photograph from England in the morning newspaper. It portrayed a group of men in traditional robes, who were members of The Most Noble Order of Crusaders. They were joined together, she saw, to fight in the Tenth Crusade. The Great War, they felt, had been the Ninth, and the Order was established to perpetuate its spirit of comradeship. The occasion for the photograph was an impressive ceremony in Westminster Abbey in 1923, when, because the ideals of the Order were those for which the Unknown Soldier died, he was made the perpetual Grand Master. A great sword, forged in Canada, was carried at the head of the procession through the Abbey.

All day, the thought of a modern crusade against the powers of evil, a crusade based on good comradeship, lay in Emily's mind. That night she wrote to General Sir Edward Bethune, K.C.B., in London, England, mentioned in the caption as leader, to ask for information.

She learned that, by a strange coincidence, early in 1921, two groups of men met in London, England, and in Hamilton, Ontario, within a few weeks of each other, to found an Order with exactly the same purposes, principles and name. The Most Noble Order of Crusaders had shortly joined forces, and now was organized in South Africa, India, Australia, Canada.

Writing to her from Hamilton, the leader for Canada told Emily that Alberta had not yet founded a Chapter, that it would be a "unique and highly gratifying thing" if a lady were to be the medium whereby it were brought into being there. Up to the present, he said, there had been no thought of inaugurating a ladies' branch.

The more Emily studied the Objects of the Tenth Crusade, the more interested she became. The booklets are marked with her insatiable pencil, particularly such paragraphs as this one, stating the purpose of the Order:

"To give service to brother Crusaders, to women, to the poor and weak, to the rich and strong. To fan the flame which will lead men in every part of the world, in every walk of life, to consecrate themselves on the altar of service, so far as lies within their power, to their fellow-men, without hope of material gain, without consideration of self. For selfless service alone is the true wealth of life."

And, again:

"Can you now not hear above the machinery's constant drone, the clarion call of the Silver bugle?"

As always, she set to work to implement her interest with action. "To my mind", she wrote to one of the Crusaders, "the movement is fraught with immense potentiality, and is one which at this particular period in our history is more needed than ever before . . . Naturally my interest is that of an outsider, but still it is a great satisfaction for me to watch, and if possible, foster, The Most Noble Order of Crusaders."

Foster it she did, and, through her efforts, the Alberta Order was founded. She interested bishops, generals, railway-superintendents, chiefs of the Royal Canadian Mounted Police, overseas officers, as well as business and professional men. She wrote many letters to English and Canadian leaders of the movement, discussing the programme with them, suggesting matters which should be given first attention, and names of notable men who might be interested. Among the most important, she considered, were the dangers to Canada's unity. With the polyglot population pouring into the West, some strong focal point was needed which would serve by fostering Canada's growing awareness of itself as a nation.

In 1925, the Provincial Order for Alberta was formed, and the following year, the Provincial Master wrote to Emily: "I have been studying the file for the Province. To me, the remarkable association of your name with the movement is evidence of the refreshing discovery of one who could not possibly hope to be even a member of the Order, and yet sufficiently recognized its boundless promise of doing good in the world, that she did all within her power to promote its establishment among us."

Emily swept The Most Noble Order of Crusaders into the cycle of her interest, seeing, as always, the potentiality behind the mundane reality. She gave them suggestions for special activities, pointed out opportunities for service. She enjoyed arranging for the ceremonial robes and utensils; wrote with pleasure when she was able to find silver trumpets, rather than ordinary bugles.

When the Grand Conclave of the Order met in

Edmonton in August, 1927, to consecrate the Alberta
Chapter, they brought with them the first Decoration
of Merit the Crusaders had ever presented anywhere
in the British Empire. The Decoration had been made
in England, to a special design. From the Badge of the
Order, set in gold and enamel, hung the Cross of St.
George on a ribbon of Arctic White.

It had been designed for presentation to Mrs.
Arthur Murphy, "For Merit". It was not only the first
decoration awarded by the Order, but the only one
ever presented to a woman.

She sat, a small figure in black, amidst the fluid
colour of pageantry. Centuries were swept away as
heraldic symbols and traditional costumes took form
once more. Individuals were lost in the pomp and
panoply of chivalry. About her moved knights from a
legendary vision; men of the ages, who, like herself,
were ever lovers of lost causes. The accident of time
and personality was swept away, for all the Crusaders
were in the long-flowing robes with cowls falling on
their backs. Colours were rich as stained-glass windows. Companions of the Order were in church-
window blues and scarlet, banded in silver and old
gold. Each Crusader himself, wore over his long tunic
a surcoat in green, brown, or grey, according to rank.
Whatever the colour of his robe, each Cruader bore
on his breast the flaming Cross of History.

Emily watched the scene with the same rapt ecstacy
that she had known in the Ruthenian church; the same
spirit with which she approached all such ceremonials.
Remember? "I look into the faces of the men and
women and I can hear what their eyes are saying.
What odds about low foreheads, thick lips and necks

like the brown earth, when each has the god within?"

So these were not the men from Alberta, from beyond the mountains, or across the Great Lakes. Here were men of all time, dreamers of the centuries titled as once they had been: the Custodian and Scribe; the Keeper of the Records and the Keeper of the Chest; Marshal and Seneschal; looking as men looked when they served under the battle-cry which rang across the fields of Palestine: "It is the Will of God." She saw them, not as a group of business men striving to implant in the practical and tradition-less West an ideal from another culture and another era; but as men without time and without identity, who, under the modest guise of modern life, still knew an adventurous enthusiasm and patient endurance.

Here was, in verity, the Brotherhood of Chivalry; the comradeship of man.

Emily Murphy rose at the Companion's bidding, and heard, through the mists of time, his voice:

"Please receive this symbol of the affection and regard in which you are held by all true crusaders." He pinned the decoration to her shoulder. "Although no woman has been admitted to the Order we shall call on you by the name of Brother Murphy, and we love you as one loves a member of his family to whom he is united by ties of blood."

Brother Murphy stood quietly for a moment; and then spoke in full-rounded, resonant tones:

"I shall always strive to wear the Cross worthily, and in the manner enjoined by Pope Urban II, in his instructions to the First Crusaders . . . 'You are Soldiers of the Cross. Bear then on your hearts, and on your shoulders, the blood-red Cross of Him who died for

the salvation of your souls!' . . . The men of the Ninth
Crusade died elate for this radiant land of Canada.
Their bodies broken, their blood out-poured . . . must
ever prove to be the elements in the sacrament of
Empire."

Brother Murphy they named her, and she was, in
very truth, brother to all who would have her. In her
mind was a vision; in her soul a prayer . . . the prayer
she knew as labour. The gift of her spirit was for all
who asked, be they condemned criminals, hopeless
misfits, far-famed men and women, or the little folk of
life. Hers was the magic of an unselfconscious generosity of mind; and hers the knowledge of an unending
toil behind the gift, stretching through hours, days,
years.

"Dear Emily . . ." those who invoked her friendship
were invoking humanity itself. For it was Brother
Murphy who replied.

CHAPTER IV

Janey Canuck

And even so, my Canada, should I forget thee,
may my pen fingers become sapless and like to
poplar twigs that are blasted by fire. And may
it happen in like manner to any of thy breed
who are drawn away from love of thee.

JANEY CANUCK in *Open Trails*.

I

TUBBIE, the wife and mother; "Dear Emily", the
comrade; Mrs. Murphy, the jurist and club-woman;
these three aspects must be set firmly in any character
study of Emily the woman. But assuredly, the inner
core of her consciousness, the motivating force of her
life, is revealed most fully as Janey Canuck the writer.

Read her four books of sketches and you will find
reflected in them a buoyant spirit, full of delicious
whimsy; a perpetual interest and sympathy with men
and women; a pioneer lustiness of heart. Because she
enjoys everything so much, one is caught along on
her tide of enthusiasm. Because she is so sensitized to
the revelation of truth and beauty in the homely
things of life, one moves with her, newly aware of their
manifestations.

Through these past years, I have studied her notes
and journals, her letters and books, setting her attitude

319

towards life as shown there, beside the evidence of her actions wherever she might be. In all of it, this spirit of Janey Canuck is the common denominator for all she thought, and wrote, and tried to do.

It matters not whether we watch her moving sanely through the fantasy of the asylums; or in the police court, sympathetically questioning Betty, the coke-fiend. It does not alter one iota whether we read her most personal letters, or hear her addressing any audience anywhere. This attitude of mind, shown throughout her writing, is at the root of her fierce crusading for the down-beaten ones of the world. It is the lodestone which drew people to her. As I have worked on page after page of her life story, lo, Janey Canuck is there before me—reacting with directness to whatever befalls her. Nothing has been out of focus.

As Janey Canuck the writer, she captured the elusive spirit of the West, and set it down on paper. She found her vein from the beginning; hers was the exulting challenge of all the great explorers of history.

It was in this spirit of exultation that she found every morning a new and entrancing day. Her faculty for sensing the charm of the commonplace, for seeing the periphery of the whole truth in any minute revelation of it, was a potent factor in every phase of her life. It is a power which genius usually turns to symbolism, for things are not seen for themselves alone. Janey was touched with this genius. William Arthur Deacon, writing of her work in *National Life* in 1922, said:

"There is more genuine adventure in Janey Canuck reading the Bible in bed on a wet morning, than most people get out of disobeying its injunctions."

Her books were the direct result of experience. She

strove not for style, but wrote as she spoke, and spoke
as she thought. Thus she developed a unique style of
her own, embodied in what are really a series of descriptive essays—"diarizing of a high order", Deacon
called them. Unhampered, she caught the bursting
energy of her country in the first twenty years of this
century. Her books are the epitome of Canadian life
in the pioneer tradition; of the grandeur inherent in
open country and the hardihood of the men and women it produces.

Her pages glow with her tales of Western Canada,
its questing immigrants, its lonely forests. She writes
of adventures at the end of steel; of journeys to the
Peace River district; of the men who made lumbering,
mining, engineering, an historic contribution to Canada's development. No other writer has mirrored these
times and settings with more penetrating truthfulness.
Yet all of it was in such an irresistible mood. "It is good
to ride on a long trail and laugh aloud with sheer joy!"
And again:

"There are songs to sing at times like these, and I
would set them down for you, only they are lightsome
words, with a hey! and a ho! a laugh and a lilt, and a
secret word for your lover."

II

Janey reverenced the multitudinous life of nature
and the mystery of the great mechanical forces of life.
Those who respond to it with her, find this deep-rooted
love throughout her books; endless repetitions of such
a sympathetic mind as in: "Oh, but this is a hot day,
and every leaf seems a green tongue thrust out with
thirst."

Many an unpublished fragment in her desk, too, reflects her delight in such imagery. Turn the back of a mimeographed report and read the song she set down one evening:

"Spring has a baton of wizard green. He is the concert master who halts the feathered migrants on their way from wintry skies. With a gentle stroke he loosens the wing of the homing dove so that she rests on the air and waits to preen her feathers. Watch how he sends the keen-winged hawk loud-whistling through the air, like an up-shot arrow. See the dip and dart of the martins; have an ear to the barking crows and the clip of their wings.

"You'd think to watch these blackbirds step sedately across the ploughlands, they were Daniels come to Judgment. See the black-blue of their throats, and how they primp about to show their scarlet epaulettes. Roving bachelors every one—but hesitating, hesitating!

"Lilt of Meadow Thrush, honk of geese, call of prairie pullet;—and hark you to the mellow song of the robin. He wasn't killed at all. It is very demurely spoken that the fly who saw him die was bonused by the lark. He is the uniformed scout of spring, this swashbuckling fellow, with his scarlet surcoat, and would make belike to be lordlier than his fellows.

"Spring on the prairie, with soft grass for the early weanlings; spring on the prairie and the herbage quivers into flowers. Some day a young-hearted boy who has been playing among the stars will come anear and fill a book about the plains. It will be a large, large book, there is so much to write about.

"Maybe he will see the prairie as sleepy and satisfied;

maybe he will notice the roll of the land that seems to be activity in immobility; maybe it will be a parchment that God has unrolled to his reading. But mind you, Boy, to tell the homely things; how the prairie is lonely for the boughs of trees, and for the sound of falling waters; how he draws sap from the primal soil as the willows draw sap from slough mires; and how he is a guiltless pagan bowing to the moon and singing to the sun instead of Christ, Our Lord, who lives in the blue of the skies."

III

Alas, for those who love her in this mood, that Janey ever turned aside to wear the yoke of life's burdensome troubles. When she was asked to become a Magistrate she hesitated: "How can I keep court when I am trying to be a writer?" That was in 1916. Up to this time she had published *Janey Canuck Abroad, Janey Canuck in the West, Open Trails* and *Seeds of Pine.* What books she might have written in the fifteen ensuing years!

She knew the joy of finding an audience for her work. Over sixty thousand copies of *Open Trails* were sold, a very considerable figure for a Canadian book in those days. *Janey Canuck in the West,* and *Open Trails* were republished by J. M. Dent and Sons in the Wayfarer's Series, because of their popularity.

The Black Candle affected public thinking very definitely; and there was a slender volume published later on the life of Bishop Bompas for school study, and an American printing of her children's book *Our Little Canadian Cousin of the Great North-west.*

Critics around the world were enthusiastic about her books of Canadian sketches. One or two raised objections to her frequent quotations from other writers, finding it an annoying habit. It was a practice ingrained in her from childhood, beginning with the keen memory she had begun to develop at Bishop Strachan's school. There, on Sunday afternoons, the Lady Principal had enjoyed gathering her pupils around the fire for tea—and a test of her amazing memory. One of the girls, taking down a volume from the book-shelf, read aloud several pages. Miss Grier was able to repeat them almost verbatim. Emily fostered this art herself and throughout her early marriage worked with Arthur on searching out and memorizing quotations from the classics. A habit of marking her books, and underlining passages she wished to remember, lasted throughout her life, so that she was able to quote as effortlessly as she wrote. William Arthur Deacon, analysing her style, said that she showed "A tendency to gather and quote unusual bits of information gleaned from older writers. This seems to be chronic with all genuine essayists and in direct ratio to the homeliness of their respective styles. Thus, great 'natural' writers like Montaigne and Thoreau are forever bringing out, for our inspection and delight, weird things which they have brought down from the dusty attics of the world's libraries. Janey has a mind well-stored with the thoughts of master pen-men, which she used with a skill alone sufficient to distinguish her work from the great mass of ephemeral productions."

Emily's close association with books of other writers was very much a part of her life. She lived, always, with them about her, packed in open shelves. While she had assembled the usual conglomeration of volumes which is the lot of any book-reviewer, she had always studied publishers' lists, and asked for those which caught her interest. In her own collection of Canadiana were autographed books from the majority of Canadian writers, and from many English and American authors as well. Set aside, in special shelves, were the volumes she read throughout her life; such books as *Josephus, Lavengro,* and the *Romany Rye* of George Borrow; the Koran, Conan Doyle's *Through the Magic Door*; the Russian classics, the English poets.

She loved to read aloud, and was eager, always, to share a poem with her friends. Wherever she went, a book was tucked into her bag. She clipped verses from newspapers and magazines and pasted them into books of similar mood. One volume, "Heart-Throbs", bulges with scores of these added verses. Always, she possessed her books for her very own with pencilled comment. She was not, however, inevitably approving. At the end of one novel, culminating in a highly sentimentalized love scene, Emily has noted: "Here the door closes. And very properly too. It should be fumigated."

"Books were her life, and words her tools," she wrote once on a slip of paper. It might have been written for Janey Canuck.

IV

Emily's keen interest in quotations only intensified her own enjoyment in turning a phrase. There must be, literally, hundreds of them among her papers. For some time she published one every day in *The Edmonton Bulletin*, and "Janey Canuck's Motto" became a popular tidbit. She cannot be fully known unless one pauses, for a moment, to savour them. A number have been used as chapter headings in this book. Consider, also, these homely ideas:

"Love reverses the order of conjugal obedience. It makes the struggle an eagerness to serve and not to command.

"What is good enough for 'company' is not too good for your family, be it courtesy or the silver teapot.

"The heart, like the body, hungers for food, and finds it in the heroic deeds and noble traits of those who have gone before.

"The commonest and cheapest of all pleasures is conversation. It is the greatest past-time of life.

"Do not waste your powers by disclosing your plans to people of whose sympathies you are not certain. It will cripple your decisions.

"Avoid like the plague the company of despondent people; pessimism leads to weakness, as optimism leads to power.

"Lean on no one. Find your own centre and live in it, surrendering it to no person or thing.

"It is quite possible that a plate of soup may be a comfort to the soul."

V

Her association with editors and publishers was in the same mood as that in which she wrote and lived. In particular, she developed a lively correspondence with Henry Button during 1910-12 when, as manager for Cassell and Company, he published two of her books. There was the occasion, for instance, when Emily had questioned his firm's plans regarding serialization. Henry Button chided her gently:

"If you can arrange anything better, go ahead. This is your first 'kick', if one might like to term it as such. I hated to feel that you meant it, for it would worry me, in this case especially, as I thought you were pleased with what little we had done with Janey and the enthusiasm we displayed about it and your other ventures."

Back came Janey by next mail:

"Dear, oh dear! And he's mad mit Janey! He's sarcastic and says the awfullest things to her. But Janey is not in the least mad. Not even flustered, for I refuse to take you seriously when you get cross, so I just laughed and said 'Well, if he doesn't beat all!'

"If I have offended, will you overlook it this once? Dear man! I do appreciate more than I can tell you, your efforts on behalf of Janey and would not for a great deal hurt your feelings in any way. I wish I were down on Adelaide Street talking this over with you, instead of writing it. It doesn't sound the same at all, so please make allowances for the medium of pen, ink and paper."

Henry Button was equally gallant: "It was indeed a relief to get your letter," he wrote. "Your previous one was a surprise, I admit, but before I could get mad with you, I would throw myself into the Bay and have my soul charged up to your account . . ."

Here is an extract from an otherwise business letter,

written in protest to the subscription manager of a Canadian publishing house. She knew this man in relation to bulk subscriptions arranged for one of the National Women's organizations in which she was an officer. It so happened that a sister publication editorialized against the enfranchisement of women. Emily wrote formally, and then dashed into this postscript:

"Lest you should take this to be personal, it gives me pleasure to say that you are the squarest, most active and fairest subscription manager that I know. You can even stand up and take a beating with grace, which is a rarer quality than is generally supposed.

"There is nothing personal in this letter. I am sorry for you in that it has been shown how seriously handicapped in your work you are, by certain pawing, rearing palfries in your editorial stables, who, like some horses of scriptural lore, snort volumes of fire from their nostrils on the slightest provocation. Maybe they snort glanders too, this, I believe, being a disorder to which equines are alone disposed. I would respectfully suggest that the sorrowful gentleman who pays the bills of the Company, puts them on rations of straw and bran mash, putting a salt lick in their mangers.

"It was one of these same palfries who wrote the editorial the week before about the enormity of 'them wimmin' being federally enfranchised, in that they know no more about the tariff than about the methods of an eel who is love-making.

"I have been immensely excited by this editorial and must, with shame and confusion of face, acknowledge to be wholly uninstructed on a subject which is, apparently, one of common knowledge among males. Somehow or other, I had the hazy idea that eels made love in a kind of pleasant, interlacing manner, but I see that their amours may possibly be much more involved and difficult. I intend to look closely into this matter, at the earliest moment, and will shortly write a story about it for those unenlightened females who are troubling you."

VI

Thus the woman, enchanting in the variety of her mood; consistent in the basic point of view which motivated her.

Without audacity, Emily Ferguson Murphy had adopted the mother-name of Canada—Janey Canuck. No other woman has more right to bear it symbolically; in all probability no other woman ever will.

In her work she reflected the constructive thinking of the woman-mind faced with wanton destruction. In her writing she captured the bursting energy of her country, with a woman's appreciation for its full creative measure. In her life she evidenced, with inherent lightness of heart and simplicity of nature, that nobility which marks true heroines, be they historic, legendary, or national.

Yet, like the Gothic cathedrals, her pinnacles were unfinished. Her own writing was put aside, so that she might devote her energies to problems of social welfare. Many of the reforms she urged have not yet been adopted. Her vision of what an enlightened womanhood might achieve for Canada, has not yet been fulfilled.

But the very fact of this incompleteness enhances

Janey Canuck's challenge to her people. What she said will be as true tomorrow and tomorrow, as it is today. Her beckoning spirit will burgeon in each generation of Canadian women; for what Janey Canuck felt about Canada, how she worked for Canada, the dream she dreamed for Canada, must go marching down the years.

And yet—and yet, one lingers with the Janey Canuck of *Open Trails* who whispered of her secret dream:

". . . The small, small house in the woods, and the black and white cow, and of my churn that will go round and round and make little rolls of butter like to August corn in the ear . . . My four white hens that will plump out their feathers and scold at me, and a pontifically-mannered cockerel, like to flame colour. . .

". . . There will be a stream where I may fish for hours, and bathe on warm days. There will be no wires, or post office, or any church, but the Padre will say to me every day, 'The Lord be with you'; whereupon I shall bow to him and make reply, 'And with thy spirit.'

". . . We shall have books a-plenty, and a fireplace. My pans will hang on the ends of book-cases, so that when I cook cakes or mix other things that are good for us to eat, the Padre may read to me. I will halt him and say: 'Ho! Ho! Not so fast, sir! Just see what the brown book on the top shelf says about that.'

"How we will argue and laugh! Oh! we'll be great laughers, I can tell you. And of night the wind will make plaint in the trees and cry, so that we may be glad for the shelter and for the feel of the heat from the fire.

". . . I shall one day find it, for so it is written; and may it happen, my gentle friend, that you may find one too."

Rev. Arthur Murphy, M.A.

PART VI

CHAPTER I

Brief Moment

... I have lived so much, and been so happy.
JANEY CANUCK.

I

EMILY MURPHY remained on duty until she was sixty-three. Then in October, 1931, she wrote her letter of resignation to the Attorney-General of the Province.

"Having served fifteen years as stipendiary magistrate in and for the City of Edmonton, and having passed the age period for retiring, it is now my desire to resign from this position.

"If it meets with your approval, I still desire to remain a police magistrate and judge of the juvenile court in and for Alberta, my services being available for relief work, or for any special duties such as you might require, either in the courts or in institutional supervision.

"It is with deep regret that I feel obliged to take this step, having been deeply interested in my work and in its various phases and having always received the utmost consideration from yourself and your predecessors in office.

333

"It is my desire, however, to finish a very considerable amount of literary work which is only partially written, and also to give a more personal attention to my own business affairs."

She was giving herself exactly two years.

II

They were happy years. It was Emily's good fortune to know in them a period of time given to few. Hers was the fulfilment of a public career, and she felt its honours bright about her. Yet her imagination brimmed with eagerness for work yet to be done.

Body, mind and soul were at the apex. Her spirit knew the calm of a garden on a bright October morning, when jewel-bright flowers and grasses are luminous in the amber glow, and the world seems poised on the thin edge of perfection, before it curves into the shadowed months. So it was with Emily.

To witness the pressure of vice and degradation, applied, day by day, to an endless chain of broken men and women had been a heavy burden. Now, removed from actual combat, she could abstract the truths she had learned and use them to arouse the public to its responsibilities. Moreover, she had for her writing the fresh hours of the early mornings.

Outside the square of dawn which was her window, and beyond her neat and flower-fringed garden, radiated the city of Edmonton—not yet the dream city of that long-ago day when she and Arthur looked across the valley to Clover Bar, but well on its way to fulfilment. Wheeling out from Edmonton, stretched the majestic provinces of a vast country, young and strong, not yet conscious of its power, its full nationhood. She had been born to greet the first birthday of the Dominion. For sixty-three years she had paced with it, giving of her imagination, her vision, her strength. Now, out of contemplation of the struggle, she still had much to give.

Most mornings Emily spent in bed, writing steadily at a large bed-table of apple-green wicker. There were deep pockets at each side into which she could stuff her papers. Across the room were the wide shelves that reached from her crowded desk to the ceiling, jammed with notes for unfinished articles. "I've so many bones in my own backyard to dig up!"

She completed in these hours a sixty-thousand-word manuscript on Birth Control, titled "Pruning The Family Tree". In the early thirties few people dared to discuss the subject publicly. Emily felt that proper birth control information was essential if many of the social difficulties she had tried to solve were ever to be cleared away. Vehemently she poured out her insistence on a proper campaign of education, and had the satisfaction of seeing her work typed and ready for the publishers, before she died.

She wrote many articles on her work in prison and asylum; she outlined her religious experiences; prepared a series slashing at public apathy towards venereal disease; an appeal to women imploring them to help prostitutes rather than scorn them. Much of her work was published; many manuscripts lay unfinished on her shelves. With all the time there was—there still wasn't time enough.

She travelled to the Pacific coast, and back to Ontario again. She kept up many interests and found some new ones. The Canadian Authors' Foundation, for instance, which was a plan to aid distinguished authors in financial distress, concerned her deeply. She was made a Director and spent a good deal of time in helping to clarify its legal angles.

It was all, however, in a gentle mood. These months gave her time for family hours, for friendly cups of tea at her fireside, for long discussions with her companions in Edmonton, for reading, for listening, for thinking.

III

Emily knew the last full-rounded measure of morning sun and dark of night on October 26th, 1933.

The day was a typical fragment of her life; she kept the pattern to the end.

In the morning she went to the police-station, visiting her cronies and joking about many a past dilemma. The early afternoon found her in the public library, notes spread around her, hard at work upon an article denouncing the C.C.F. Its theories were barely emerging then, but Emily apprehended the impact they would make on the thinking of Westerners. She believed them fallacious, and was writing a fiery denunciation of them.

At four o'clock Evelyn came to drive her mother to Kathleen's. Her grand-daughter Emily Doris had given Emily much pleasure these past few years, and she loved to be with the child whenever opportunity occurred. At a nearby bakery she bought a large bag of raisin buns. Workmen were renovating Kathleen's house, and some buns would be nice for tea for them all.

Presently Emily sat with her daughters on the edge of the chaos wrought by an inner wall torn down, happily munching her raisin bun, and pleased that the men, too, were taking a momentary respite for tea. She was aglow with a fresh enthusiasm—the new mausoleum. After much discussion, and a visit there, Emily and Arthur had decided to buy crypts in it. They were breaking the tradition of "Going back to Cookstown", but surely, since they were so much a part of the West, they should lie under its wide skies, rather than taking the long journey back to the Ontario hillside.

Evelyn told of the evening hours in a letter to one of her mother's friends:

"Mother was as well as could be, and had spent most of the day down-town, trotting around the stores and down to see the old haunts in the police-court. She visited around the offices and at supper that night, we had such a jolly time, with Mother telling all the police-court doings and chuckling over some of the funny bits.

"Dad was going to a basket-ball game with his friend, Bishop Burgett and when he kissed Mother before he went out, Mother was joking with him about how young he was, going to a ball game, and they laughed about it. Then, in the evening, after reading the papers, she puttered around a bit, did a little writing, and went to bed about ten.

"I brought her up a hot drink, as I generally did, and sat on her bed and talked while she drank it. She had her face all cold-creamed up, and I laughed and called her a nice greasy little Eskimo . . . Tubbie said, 'Well, indeed, I'm not going to let myself get old and wrinkled!' I turned out her light for her, and a few minutes after I called in to her what the basketball score was. She was so pleased our girls were winning.

"She must have gone right off to sleep, as she was sleeping when Dad got home, and I told him not to go in and disturb her. I read in bed till about twelve and had just turned out the light, a very few minutes, when I heard just one short cry.

"It was so strange that my feet hit the floor, and I ran as fast as I could in my bare feet into her room, just next to mine. I switched on the light; but she had left us. The doctor who came immediately said she had never really waked—that the little cry I heard was just an involuntary gasp for air, and that the passing over had come in her sleep, as she'd have wanted it to. It was happy, and free from all foreboding or sickness."

IV

In her life she had recognized the Godhead in man; her love for people had been utterly natural and unafraid. So now, as she lay in the final dignity of death, they came to stand by her for a moment, with a complete lack of self-consciousness; sensing only that the loss was personal, and greater than each one knew.

Here were the people of the West, bereft of all individuality of rank or race. The great ones of the city passed by her bier, and those who crept from out of the dark places to look once more upon one whose authority they had recognized: Gentile, Jew, Catholic, Protestant, Polish, Ukrainian, Canadian, English, American. The representative of the King; judges and statesmen; artists and laymen; the suffering and the suffered; men, women and children; friends of a lifetime, and those who had never spoken a word to her—all these came.

They came by the hundreds to look once more upon that noble head. They lined the streets for blocks as her funeral cortège passed toward the church, where a guard-of-honour from the city police stood at salute. They jammed the great church to its doors, and the sound of their weeping followed her, when their prayers were said.

In those few hours when she was brought again to her own drawing-room, flowers from friends across Canada banked the walls to the very ceiling. Through the city, shimmering in an early snowfall, came those who loved her most, and with them those who wanted to say farewell in her own home. A group of nuns enfolded in prayer drifted by; a Captain from the Salvation Army; the cop from the nearby corner who whispered to Evelyn: "When I heard she was gone—I just couldn't go on with my beat." A woman on relief trudged many blocks, her child in her arms, to see her friend again. Two girls timidly unwrapped a rose from its protective newspaper, and placed it by Emily's hands. Looking at them, and knowing of their life, Kathleen left the token there. It was inevitable that a rose from prostitutes would go to the grave with Judge Murphy.

Thus detail crowded upon detail—until the final blankness of marble and a closed door. The sun sliding low in the sky glowed through purple and scarlet of stained glass, to the carpet of flowers about the crypt.

It illumined the little band of her own family who
had waited with her until the door was sealed; Arthur,
the lad she had met at fifteen, still over six foot, but
with snowy hair; Gowan, the only one of her four
brothers still alive—here from Montana to visit his
sister, too late; her two daughters and her son-in-law.

The light fades daily there on a few lines cast in
bronze:

"EMILY FERGUSON MURPHY ("JANEY CANUCK").
BELOVED WIFE OF REVEREND ARTHUR MURPHY,
    M.A.
DAUGHTER OF ISAAC AND EMILY FERGUSON.
BORN AT COOKSTOWN, ONTARIO, MARCH 14th, 1868.
DIED AT EDMONTON, ALBERTA, OCTOBER 26th, 1933.
DECORATED BY HIS MAJESTY KING GEORGE V,
    A LADY OF GRACE OF THE ORDER OF ST. JOHN
    OF JERUSALEM, IN 1914.
FIRST WOMAN IN THE BRITISH EMPIRE TO BE
    APPOINTED A POLICE MAGISTRATE.
BEING ALSO JUDGE OF THE JUVENILE COURT FOR
    THE PROVINCE OF ALBERTA.
ORIGINATOR AND LEADER OF MOVEMENT ADMIT-
    TING WOMEN TO THE SENATE.
AUTHOR, JURIST, CRUSADER IN SOCIAL REFORMS,
    GREAT CITIZEN."

"AS WHEN A STANDARD BEARER FAINTETH."
                                    Isaiah X, 18.

She Being Dead Yet Speaketh

The following letter, under this title, written ten months before her death, was found in Emily Murphy's safety deposit box.

Hello, Everybody! Hard to get rid of the "Old Girl"—isn't it? . . . Well, none of you ever wanted to, at least I don't think so; you hid it darned well if you did. And when I think of all those times you sat up and nursed me when I was crying and near to "pushing off"—Oh, you're a great family, all right!

I hope you'll like the contents of this lock-box and will make good use of its contents. It makes me happy as I write this, to know you are to have it. . .

I want you all to remember at this time, that I had a fairly long and fairly full life, and that I was happy most of the time—happier than I deserved. For this reason, now, don't any of "youse" cry. I'll be watching around to see if you do. Now don't offend "Aggie".

I expect Dad will miss my fussing about now and then (the Dear Thing) but if he just stops and throws me a kiss, I'll be sure to catch it! I'm too gay to be a ghost. There is a poem called "Emily" I pasted into "Heart-Throbs". It says:

> *"She bragged her stock was Puritan,*
> *Her usual mood was Cavalier."*

There is another poem pasted in called, "Daughters":

> *"I know I never did devise,*
> *Two tall girls with kind clear eyes,*
> *Tis more than life allows*
> *Two tall girls with candid brows."*

Tell Emily Doris, she is to take up my work and carry it on when she grows up. She's in training for it right now, only she must be better and stronger than me. She's my "baby" in a very special way.

Now I never had a son in the family till the Kenwood boy came, but he has been an adopted son in the very best sense of the words, not a son-in-law, but a son in verity. I want him to father you all now, and take the best care of the remaining family, and see that they do keep out of scraps. Goodbye, Johnny, and good luck!

Gracious, I'd like to go on gossiping, but if ever you want to hear my old tongue wag, just take down some of my books or articles and read them. Maybe, too, I'll have something to whisper about when you come to the cemetery. Like as not I will.

Anyway, all of you stand still right now, and take all the love and kisses you are receiving this very minute. Dad and Kathie and Evey and Cleave and Wee Emily. It is such a lot of love!! (I'm sending the same thoughts and the same kisses to dear old "Doc" in Montana, and to my ever-devoted Nancy Ann in Toronto.) .....

Dear me, I'd like to go home and have supper with you, and carve the roast—that's the worst of being dead. You can't hear the news or read the evening papers. I hope though, that my room is actually tidy at last, and that no one will take up my way of spilling ink on the counterpane. If ever you find such conditions you'll know that the ghostie was there of nights—I might even leave the lights turned on downstairs. You needn't blame it on Father.

  An infinite of Love
          From Old Mother

December 8th, 1932.

To a Great Woman

Paeons of praise they sing, because you stood
High in the world, and raised one steady hand
Against the wrongs that women suffer most,
And being leaderless, misunderstand.
And they shall call your name, because your pen
Was mighty as the sword, and followed swift
Upon long, deep injustice, and laid bare
The jagged danger of some hidden rift.

*   *   *   *

And we, who saw you far from lines of battle,
And knew the gentle tenor of your wit,
Who felt your quick response to all earth's beauty
And this great-heart that would be sharing it,
Who knew the quick forgiving of your spirit,
The tender sympathy for those who wait
Without the temple, and your quiet mercy—
Shall silent be, before one very great.

LOTTA C. DEMPSEY

This poem, which appeared in the *Edmonton Bulletin*, October 28,
1933, was written by Lotta C. Dempsey, as a tribute to Emily
Murphy, on the day following her death.

From Who's Who

Emily F. Murphy (Janey Canuck), Author

Born Cookstown, Ontario, daughter of Isaac and Emily
Gowan Ferguson.

Educated at Bishop Strachan School, Toronto.

Married Arthur Murphy, M.A.   Has two daughters.

Moved to Alberta in 1907.

Decorated by His Majesty King George, a Lady of Grace
of the Order of St. John of Jerusalem.

Author of *Janey Canuck in the West* (Cassell & Co. 1910)
(J. M. Dent & Sons, "Wayfarers Series" 1917).

Open Trails (Cassell & Co. 1912) (J. M. Dent & Sons
1920).

Seeds of Pine (Hodder & Stoughton 1914) (Musson Book
Co., Toronto, 1922).

The Black Candle (Thomas Allen 1922).

Our Little Canadian Cousin of the Great North West
(Page & Co., Boston, 1923).

Bishop Bompas (Ryerson Press, Toronto, 1929) Canadian
History Series.

Elected member of Board of Governors, Canadian Authors'
Foundation 1931.

Contributes to Canadian, English and American magazines.

Literary editor of *Canada Monthly*, 1902-4.

Literary editor of *Winnipeg Telegram*, 1904-12.

President, Canadian Women's Press Club 1913-1920;
Honorary President 1920-23; Historian 1926-29.

Honorary Secretary for Canada of the Society of Woman
Journalists of England 1913-25.

Member of the Imperial Press Conference, 1920.

Councillor of Canadian Authors' Association 1921-27.

Police Magistrate in and for the Province of Alberta,

1916-31, being the first woman in the Empire to be so appointed.

First President of the Federated Women's Institutes of Canada, 1919-21.

Vice-President of National Council of Women of Canada 1918-26.

Convenor of National Committee on Peace and Arbitration 1914-15.

Vice-President of Social Service Council of Canada 1920-31.

Vice-President of Canadian Association of Child Protection Officers 1921-25.

Vice-President of Canadian Social Hygiene Council 1921-31.

Member of General Committee, Canadian Society, League of Nations, 1923-25.

Director of Canadian Council of Child Welfare, 1923-27.

Member of Executive Committee, White Cross Association, United States 1922-31.

Member Board of Directors, Big Sisters' Association, Montreal 1928-31.

Member of the War Conference of Women held at the invitation of the War Committee of the Dominion Cabinet, 1918.

Appointed by Order of Lieut.-Governor-in-Council, Province of Alberta, to report on public institutions operated by the Government, 1926-31.

Appointed by the Government of Alberta to special committee to report on international property laws relating to women, 1926.

Patroness, Edmonton Branch Army and Navy Veterans, 1928-31.

Patroness, Edmonton Branch of Royal Life Saving Society of Canada, 1927.

First President of the Canadian Zenana Bible and Medical Society, 1903.

Member of American Archaelogical Society.

Member of "Westward Ho", the first chapter of Imperial

Order of Daughters of Empire, established in Alberta.

Vice-President of Alberta Association for Prevention of Tuberculosis, 1914-16.

Member of the Charter Committee of City of Edmonton, 1914.

Organizer of Women's Canadian Club of Edmonton and first President, 1911-13.

President of Board of Control, Swan River (Manitoba) Victorian Order Hospital, 1905-07.

Inaugurated movement for establishment Victorian Order of Nurses at Edmonton, 1910.

Inaugurated movement for establishment of Municipal Hospitals in Alberta, 1910, and was first woman member of Hospital Board of City of Edmonton.

Honorary President of District Hospital, Peace River, Alberta.

Inaugurated a movement for Medical Inspection of Schools in Alberta.

Organized in Alberta and Saskatchewan the first branches of the Canadian Committee of Mental Hygiene and was member of the National Board of Directors, 1918-25.

Inaugurated movement for public playgrounds at Edmonton, 1911.

Inaugurated movement for election of women as school trustees in Alberta, 1912.

Inaugurated movement for enactment of Dower Law in Alberta, 1910.

Arranged at Edmonton the Commission on Immigration, held under auspices of Child Welfare Association by Margaret Bondfield, Sec. of Labour, British Government, 1924.

Inaugurated a campaign against the importation and use of narcotic drugs in Canada.

Inaugurated and for thirteen years worked to establish the right of women to sit in the Canadian Senate under the provisions of the British North America

Act, winning by decision of His Majesty's Privy
Council in 1929.

For Imperial Service, was decorated by the Most Noble
Order of Crusaders, 1927.

Religion: Anglican.

Address: 11011, 88 Ave., Edmonton, Canada.

Office Address: The Police Court, Edmonton, Alberta,
Canada.

INDEX

349